# THE THINKER'S BOOK

## 101 VIGNETTES, THOUGHTS, IDEAS, AND CAPTIVATING TOPICS TO THINK ABOUT

Jerry Hirsch
Happy Reading!
2017

JERRY HIRSCH

Beach Road Press

# THE THINKER'S BOOK

## 101 VIGNETTES, THOUGHTS, IDEAS, AND CAPTIVATING TOPICS TO THINK ABOUT

JERRY HIRSCH

The Thinker's Book - 101 Vignettes, Thoughts, Ideas and Captivating Topics to Think About



Published Beach Road Press, Agassiz, B.C. Canada V0M 1A2

Cover design and interior design by Wendy Dewar Hughes
Edited by Wendy Dewar Hughes

ISBN: 978-1-927626-61-0
Digital ISBN: 978-1-927626-62-7

# CONTENTS

## Popcorn – The Good, the Bad, and the Ugly

I recently read an article by Jennifer Sygo in which she described popcorn as North America's favorite movie snack. This isn't big news. There has, however, been a massive amount of discussion about whether popcorn is good for us, and it turns out (like many other things) that the answer is yes, no, and maybe. And as they say in diet programs, portion control is also a big factor. Depending on how it is prepared and cooked, some consider it to be a health food while others caution against it for a variety of reasons.

Let's start with an explanation of why popcorn can be good for you. Plain popcorn is a low-calorie snack that contains barely 300 calories for a fully popped bag holding three or four servings. These servings also provide impressive levels of fiber and protein while being basically sugar-free and salt-free.

But (there's always a "but" when health and food issues are discussed) popcorn isn't a good source of other nutrients. Even the natural disease fighters, polyphenols, are at low levels in popcorn when compared to various fruits and vegetables.

And it gets worse.

Just plain air-popped popcorn is okay, even good for you, but plain popcorn is not what they serve at the movie theatre. A medium sized bag there can have almost 800 calories, and of course you will want tons of butter with that, adding about 250 more calories. Movie theaters have used coconut oil to pop the corn, and then topped it with butter so a medium-sized bag of buttered popcorn may contain as much fat as three Big Macs.

The specialty popcorns that you see at the mall or at an airport concourse have also been described as a nutritional landmine because of the high levels of calories, fat, sugar, and sodium. Even the innocent sounding kettle corn has high levels of sugar, as does caramel corn. So whether you're snacking in a movie theatre or snuggling at home, try to get the old plain variety, at least some of the time.

Popcorn is a type of corn that expands from the kernel and puffs up when heated. Corn is able to "pop" because its kernels have a hard moisture-sealed hull and a dense starchy interior. This allows pressure to build inside the kernel until an explosive "pop" results. Some strains of corn are now cultivated specifically as popping corns.

There are many techniques for popping corn. Commercial large-scale popcorn machines were invented in the late 19th century. Charles Cretors developed a machine that popped corn in a mixture of one-third clarified butter (milk fat rendered from butter to separate the milk solids and water from the butterfat), two-thirds lard, and salt. This mixture could withstand the 450 °F (232 °C) temperature needed to pop the corn.

Popping results are sensitive to the rate at which the kernels are heated. If heated too quickly, the steam in the outer layers of the kernel can reach high pressures and rupture the hull before the starch in the center of the kernel can fully gelatinize, leading to partially popped kernels with hard centers. Heating too slowly leads to entirely unpopped kernels where the tip of the kernel is not entirely moisture-proof, and when heated slowly the steam can leak out of the tip fast enough to keep the pressure from rising sufficiently to break the hull and cause the pop.

## Don't You Hate it When...?

Some *bon mots* encountered by experience or sighted while mining the Internet:

- You ask people, "How are you?" and they actually tell you their troubles rather than automatically saying, "Fine".
- You think of a clever response two hours too late.
- People brag about how easily they lost weight.
- You just started your shower and already the water is getting cold.
- A person walks out of the store washroom without washing their hands and then touches the stuff on the store shelf that you wanted to buy.
- Your friend asks you a question but somebody else butts in and answers for you.
- Your know-it-all friend knows it all.
- You accidentally start brushing your teeth with your Athlete's Foot ointment instead of your toothpaste.
- There's always a car tailgating when you're slowing down to find an address.
- The person behind you in the supermarket runs his cart into the back of your ankle.
- The elevator stops on every floor and nobody gets on.
- When people get up from their seats before the bus has stopped but then fall into your lap when the bus jerks to a halt.
- You leave a leaky pen in your shirt pocket when you put it in the wash machine
- There's a dog in the neighborhood that barks at everything.
- You can never put anything back in a box the way it came.
- You slice your tongue licking an envelope.
- You wash a garment with a tissue in the pocket and your entire laundry comes out covered with lint.

- The car behind you blasts its horn after you let a pedestrian finish crossing the street.
- A piece of foil candy wrapper makes electrical contact with your tooth filling.
- You set the alarm on your digital clock for 7:00 PM instead of 7:00 AM.
- Your friend brags about the great deal they got but you didn't.
- You rub on hand cream and can't turn the bathroom doorknob to get out.
- People behind you in a supermarket line dash ahead of you to a counter just opening up.
- Your glasses slide off your nose when you perspire.
- You can't look up the correct spelling of a word in the dictionary because you don't know how to spell it.
- You have to inform five different sales people in the same store that you're just browsing.
- You had that pen in your hand only a second ago, and now you can't find it.
- It rains on your first day off in three weeks.
- You reach under the table to pick something off the floor and smash your head on the way up.
- That fabulous sale that you were looking for ended yesterday.
- Your car has a major breakdown the month after the warranty expires.
- The quiet hotel room that you reserved has a loud party next door that goes until 3:00 AM.
- You are in a hundred-car lineup at the border and the other line moves so much faster.
- You are in a family restaurant and the guy at the table next to you licks the top of the ketchup bottle after smothering his fries.
- Someone who doesn't know what a breath mint is talks at length right in your face.

## Saddle Bronc Riding Should be an Olympic Sport

I find that watching the Olympic Games is both fascinating and enjoyable, but also frustrating sometimes. As they used to say in ABC's Wide World of Sports, we see the thrill of victory and the agony of defeat. Behind the scenes we see much more. The variety of sports in the summer games ranges from the track and field events to rowing, to volleyball, to swimming, to diving, to weight lifting. There is Greco-Roman wrestling, not the Hulk Hogan staged villain type. I prefer the events where there is a clear winner based on time or score. In some events the judges seem to play an inordinately important role, sometimes subjectively determining winners to the third decimal point.

Diving, synchronized swimming, and gymnastics seem to be difficult to judge, at least from a casual observer perspective, and it's interesting to hear the commentators point out supposed mistakes that we ordinary people don't usually see. There have been cases where judges simply were not honest in their assessment. Then there is something called rhythmic gymnastics which, from my untutored male perspective, seems to involve a lot of aimless twirling around but which devotee professionals breathlessly and excitedly provide commentary.

But I have a problem with the equestrian events. Horse jumping as an Olympic event? How does this fit? Is it because the rich and powerful in the early 1900s wanted to have an event they could enter without sweating (sorry, I should say "perspiring") too much? And then they also have, I think they call it, "dressage", but a common, unsophisticated person like me would call it horse dancing. Horse dancing!

If this can be an event for the elite wealthy, I think they should have saddle bronc riding for the common people, like cowboys. I know it takes talent and time to train a horse to dance or jump, and creativity to have them do this in time to music like "Pomp and Circumstance" or other high-brow music, but using this logic I suggest that NASCAR racing could be a new Olympic event since this takes a lot of time and also doesn't just depend on the individual.

If you go to a typical small town fair you may see mini-horse competitions; these could be the Olympic sport for ordinary people who can't afford big horses. I suppose that bull riding is too gauche for the mandarins on the International Olympic Committee (IOC), and bull fighting has pretty much lost its appeal, but saddle bronc riding would be great as an Olympic sport. There must also be other sports that could also reflect the supposed "Olympic Spirit" if this still exists and hasn't been surpassed by corruption, nationalism, and commercialism.

There still is some tension between "amateurs" as defined by the wealthy as recently as fifty or sixty years ago where "amateurs" could enjoy their sport for the pure joy of participation and achievement (see horse dancing) while "professionals" were looked down a upon because they needed to earn a living in their sport. Kayaking, gymnastics, and diving are sports that are still pretty much amateur even while they travel the world, but there are other sports where the best athletes become very wealthy.

There still are lots of questions as to why some sports are in the Olympics and others are not. Why has tennis been in the Olympics for a long time, but golf (at least at this writing) is just now being considered? Both sports are widely pursued by both professionals and everyday folks. It's interesting that soccer is in the Olympics; this is possibly the only sport in the world where the world championship (the World Cup of Soccer) has more prestige than the Olympic champion.

Softball and baseball seem to have been rejected as Olympic sports because they aren't popular in enough countries. But there are some rather unusual or less popular sports in the summer Olympics, as least as far as North Americans are concerned. Water polo, modern pentathlon, and European handball come to mind.

There are some interesting sports that are no longer included in the Olympic Games. Would you believe that croquet was once an

Olympic sport? Motor boating and tug-of-war were Olympic sports at one time. So was cricket, which is wildly popular in many countries but isn't considered worthy of Olympic status today, perhaps because some think that watching an all day cricket game is as exciting as watching paint dry.

I think that the IOC should consider adding some new sports to the summer games menu. I have already mentioned saddle bronc riding, but how about ballroom dancing? This requires as much athleticism as rhythmic gymnastics. I briefly watched a program called "Prime Time Sports" recently and they had two good suggestions. The first one was Synchronized Cannonball Diving.

To minimize the influence of judges, half of the marks would be for "water displacement" and the other 50% for artistry. Didn't ABC's Wide World of Sports broadcast the world belly flop championships some years ago? The other suggestion was distance diving. Why stop at a ten-metre platform? Even if they have to cut a hole in the roof of the pool, why not go as high as the bravest athletes want, with extra points for higher dives?

I almost never watch "American Gladiators", but there must be some sports in their repertoire (which includes games such as "Gauntlet", "Earthquake", and "Joust") that are of Olympic caliber. I saw another intriguing suggestion in the comic strip "Blondie" during the London 2012 Summer Olympics. Dagwood advocated a "sandwich building" event, and anyone who has seen his masterful sandwich creations would agree that this requires real creative talent. There are world championships for "Rock, Paper, Scissors" but I suppose the practitioners of this sport are too eclectic for the IOC.

Pierre de Coubertin, the initiator of the modern Olympic movement, said that the important thing is not to win, but to take part, so it would be great to have more people participate. I suspect that some sports now in the Olympics don't contribute very much to the Olympic Spirit whose objective is to build a peaceful and better world involving mutual understanding with a spirit of friendship, solidarity, and fair play. De Coubertin ideally wanted to inspire and motivate the youth of the world to be the best they can be through educational and entertaining interactive challenges, but money, as in $$$$ has mostly taken over.

One of my friends suggested that one sport that should be in the modern Olympics is "lying". The sport of lying gained popularity soon after creation in a small garden somewhere in the middle east, and it rapidly spread to Greece where they euphemistically called it philosophy. Individuals and teams could compete in three weight classes: Light (little white lies or fibbing); Medium (hyperbole, fable telling, spin-doctoring); Heavy (big whoppers, propaganda, terminological inexactitude).

Lawyers and politicians are often the primary experts, but in today's spirit of political correctness we have spin-doctors, or lobbyists, or market analysts, or in some cases, athletes. Probably every country is adept at the sport so it would meet the criteria of being widely practiced, plus that of being ancient. I suspect that no country would want to place last as this would tarnish their national pride.

We know that everyone has had some experience in this sport, and it wouldn't take expensive facilities or a lot of training because most participants have natural ability. However, there are several problems with including lying as an Olympic sport. Determining the winner would, of necessity, be subjectively decided by the judges, and since it is clearly possible that judges may actually be better liars than the contestants there always would be some uncertainty whether the identified winner was actually the best. And there may be some conflict with the Olympic motto of "higher, stronger, faster".

## Baseball and Bubble Gum

When my sweetie and I picked up our granddaughter from preschool one day, the little tyke kept singing a ditty, the first verse of which went something like this: "My Mom gave me a nickel / to buy a pickle / but I bought bubble gum / balloon, balloon, balloon, POP!"

The catchy tune and topic led me to reflect on the use of chewing gum, and bubble gum in particular.

First, we should dispense of the myth that if you swallow a wad of gum it stays in your stomach or gut for months. I don't know who looked in kids' stomachs but apparently this myth isn't true. Anyway, my sweetie seems to have taken a renewed interest in chewing gum, not necessarily bubble gum, but any kind of gum. I don't mind this, really, but my problem is that sometimes she chews gum with the vigor of a young teen-aged girl using two-thirds of the Rice Krispies® approach.

This means that there is a lot of snap and crackle (though not too much pop, since this isn't bubble gum) and vigorous jaw movement. I'm sure you will agree this can be a tad annoying after a while. Occasionally she offers me a piece. I normally refuse because, after a few minutes, I find that the gum has the flavor and consistency of the chewing gum you might pry off the bottom of a church bench or a movie theatre seat.

This, naturally, leads me to baseball, a game involving long periods of inactivity interspersed with short bursts of intense action. With the possible exception of semi-sedentary sports such as lawn bowling, baseball seems to be the only sport, at least as far as I'm aware, where most of the participants routinely and incessantly chew gum during the game. One baseball player was even videoed blowing a huge bubble milliseconds before swinging at a pitch.

If a hockey or a football player tried to chew gum the earthquake force of an opponent's assault would cause surely the player to swallow the gum wad.

My point, finally, is that baseball players and coaches seem to chew their gum for hours (that is, the length of a typical baseball game) with the same prolonged level of enjoyment. So my question is—does the flavor really last that long, and, if so, what brand of chewing gum are these guys chewing? It is possible that with their zillion dollar salaries they can buy some ultra-expensive special long lasting gum, but somehow I don't think that's the explanation.

Someone from the Fleer Chewing Gum Company discovered bubble gum in 1928, when they found that a new product stretched more easily and was less sticky than regular chewing gum. This highly successful new gum was first called Dubble Bubble and was pink because that was the only color available.

People had to be taught how to blow bubbles. (If they had used kids that probably wouldn't have taken long.) Natural rubber, such as chicle, may be used to make bubble gum today although synthetic gum-based materials are now widely used, supposedly because they provide better texture and longer-lasting flavor. (I haven't found the "longer lasting" part to be the case.)

Apparently, chewing bubble gum keeps the mouth occupied and moist, and the brain alert, which may be one reason why chewing gum is popular. The culture of baseball, and stress relief (not boredom relief?) is possibly the most common reason why most players chew something, whether it be gum, tobacco, or sunflower seeds. Baseball has a lot of " between" time…waiting to bat, waiting for the next pitch, waiting while the pitcher warms up, waiting for the national anthem, waiting during the rain delay, and so on.

Chewing tobacco became common in professional baseball's early years. Some players still chew tobacco as indicated by chew or dip placed between their lips and gums. In 1998, a Cleveland Indians player who used a smokeless-tobacco chew got throat cancer, and major league baseball subsequently barred teams from providing players with tobacco products. Players are still free to use their own tobacco, but common sense and health issues gradually reduced the use of tobacco chewing. Baseball players found that chewing bubble gum was almost as good, and was considered safe. Not as many players are dipping snuff on the field now and there is not as much spitting going on.

So, what kind of gum do baseball players chew? It seems that there is no specific kind of gum but a popular one is "Big League Chew" which has many flavors and is said to be "addicting". "Big League Chew" was introduced in 1980 by pitchers Rob Nelson and Jim Bouton, who came up with the idea of shredded bubble gum in a pouch as something different and fun. The basic "Double Bubble" brand of bubble gum is also often found in baseball dugouts. We know this because ground crew duties include sweeping the dugout to clear away gum wrappers and other mundane items, such as sunflower seed husks and paper cups.

Of course, commercial motives also played a role in the use of bubble gum by baseball players. Bubble gum companies, such as Topps, sold collectable baseball cards for every player starting in the 1950s. Cards in the '50s and '60s smelled like bubble gum and were often stained by the gum. But no one cared, since no one thought they were valuable, and kids loved the gum and their heroes. However, commercialism took over and most cards are now sold separately, mostly for collectors, not for kids.

## What's *Not* in the Queen's Purse?

As a loyal Canadian citizen I am periodically bombarded by media attention given to the Queen of England when she visits Canada as the titular "Head of State" or performs some royal function elsewhere. The Queen is always pictured wearing some fabulous hat worn by the rich and famous in the 1930s, plus a modest purse that prudently matches her outfit. While "ordinary" modern day women, even quite young ladies, seem to carry purses weighing seventeen kilograms, the Queen's purse doesn't seem to have room for much in it.

This isn't the sort of thing that normal people worry about, but I've started to wonder, "What's not in the Queen's purse?"

Not cash or credit cards. She didn't get to be one of the richest women in the world by spending her own money.

Not a lottery ticket, since she already won the lottery—she gets the English people to give her a huge allowance each year.

Not a Sudoku book or a pencil in case she has to wait for her doctor or a dental appointment. The Queen doesn't wait; she gets waited on.

Not a spare "green" grocery bag in case she needs to pick up some vegetables for dinner on her way home from work. First, the Queen doesn't *go* to work; her work comes to her. Second, she has people to do her shopping and cooking.

Not keys. The movie "The Queen" with Helen Mirren suggested that the Queen sometimes drove a Range Rover on her estate, but I don't think that she does this very often. And I don't know who locks the doors at Buckingham Palace, but I'm pretty sure that the Queen doesn't do it.

Not a little flask of sherry or something stronger. The Queen's mother was known for enjoying a bit of gin every day, perhaps more than once a day, but the Queen doesn't seem to need this type of pick-me-up.

Not a receipt for the little black dress she bought last week and plans to return after the party. The Queen would not be amused if anyone suggested that she would consider this sort of thing.

Not a camera. The Queen doesn't take pictures; everyone else takes pictures of her.

Not a cell phone or a smart phone or a tablet or even an address book. She has other people to take her calls and plan her schedule. Somehow I don't think that the Queen "tweets" and even if she could have a zillion Facebook friends I suspect that she would consider this as undignified.

Not a pack of cigarettes or an e-cigarette. While many modern women demonstrated their independence by smoking, (or at least they used to before the hazards became known), the Queen is much too sensible to engage is this sort of silly and dangerous behavior.

Not a comb or a tube of lipstick. She has worn the same hairdo for over sixty years, while looking quite dignified. And not a can of hair coloring, since she has gracefully become grey over the years.

Not a paperback book. Her various good will "walkabouts" or tours keep her much too busy, and when she's at home she reads official government dispatches.

Not a copy of "The Sunday Report" (a newspaper which has been described as practicing "yellow journalism") or other English tabloids, which sensationalize the activities and foibles of celebrities.

Not a ball of yarn and a crochet hook or knitting needles. Many grandmothers may have such items in their purse, but I've never thought of the Queen knitting a sweater for the grandkids or crocheting pot scrubbers.

Not a travel pill container with aspirins or heart medication. She has people who take medication for her.

Not a package of "Tide" Spot Remover in case someone spills something on her. She probably wears an outfit once and then gives it to a charity.

I'm sorry that I haven't been more helpful. We don't really know what is in her purse even if we're pretty sure what's not there! Perhaps it's just a tissue and a tiny mirror. Maybe a lipstick, too.

## NEARING HOME WITH HOPE

This is my attempt to summarize the 2011 book, "Nearing Home" written by Billy Graham. This book presents an engaging description of Dr. Graham's experiences in getting old and provides insights and advice for all of us.

Near the end of his life, Mickey Mantle, the iconic but free living New York Yankee baseball player said that he would have taken better care of himself if he had known that he would get that old. Billy Graham has no such regrets but he still said, "Getting old has been the greatest surprise of my life." He goes on to say that he had been taught during his life how to die as a Christian but not how to live in his later years. He said something else that most elderly people can relate to, namely that old age is not for sissies. At the same time, Billy Graham acknowledges that the Bible doesn't paint old age as a time to be despised or a burden to be endured.

When I turned seventy, I was very surprised (they say that behind every seventy year-old is a surprised thirty year-old wondering what happened), and Billy Graham relates to this when he writes that: "I am not sure exactly when it happened, but as the years passed, it gradually dawned on me that I was growing older."

Graham advises us not to retire from life, since work (and activity) is part of God's plan for our lives. Work is not something we do just to put food in the table; it is one of the major ways God has given to us to bring glory to Him. Plus, we shouldn't allow retirement to put us on the shelf. One of the important activities older people have is to pray for others as we support younger folks still carrying heavy loads. Even when retired we should look for God's leading to find ways to have a positive impact on those around us, and seek the Lord's purpose in every circumstance and person that we encounter. Many people use retirement to indulge themselves, but we will be blessed if we use it to make a positive impact on others.

Another specific thing that Billy Graham says is, "...having our house in order is one of the most important things parents can do for their children. Give them the peace of mind by letting them know that you have taken care of the business that has come about from your lifetime of labor. More than anything else, let them know where you stand with the Lord Jesus Christ, for this will be your lasting legacy".

Graham identifies the one word summarizing the changes that happen to us as we grow older: *Decline.* We lose physical strength over the years, our energy levels decrease, as do our mental capabilities. Watching family members and friends become weaker and older and then die is an inevitable feature of aging, and it is important that we work to maintain strong emotional and spiritual reactions during these experiences so we are not overwhelmed. We can overcome the perils that may steal our zest for life by letting the promises of God's word in the Bible uphold us each day. Graham encourages us to maintain a connection to other believers who can encourage and help us, plus he reaffirms the words of Romans, Chapter 8, where it says that nothing can separate us from the love of God that is in Christ Jesus our Lord.

Someone once said that we all live as though we are going to live forever, and that's a healthy approach to take, but at the same time we need to realize that someday our physical bodies will give out. Looking forward to eternal life in heaven is a healthy thing to do. Graham quotes John Newton who said that, "I am still in the land of the dying: I shall be in the land of the living soon". Ruth Graham asked that these words be on her tombstone: "End of Construction. Thank you for your patience". Billy Graham writes that we may retire from our careers, but we must never retire from being filled with the abundant gifts from God that bring hope and satisfaction.

Billy Graham also provides advice on how to cope with grief when loved ones die. This includes accepting that we will grieve, letting others help us in our grief, but then turning your heart and mind to the future and taking your burdens to God. We can also help others who grieve by telling—and showing—them we care, that we are praying for them, and staying in touch with the remaining family beyond the first few weeks after a death.

We know that death is not really the end since we know that although our bodies will die, our souls and spirits will live on eternally in heaven with God if we have become Christians by accepting Jesus as Lord and Savior.

Graham ends his book by telling us that God wants us to "finish well"—to have a forgiving spirit and a consistent prayer life in addition to being a positive example through our actions and attitudes. One of the best ways that we can do this is by passing on our values and faith to those who will follow us. He writes that the greatest legacy that we can pass on to our children and grandchildren is not our money or other material things but our character and faith. This is what they will remember about us when we are gone—our integrity (or lack of it) and our faith in God so that this encourages them to become men and women of compassion, honesty, responsibility, selflessness, loyalty, discipline, and sacrifice. Our hope should be that they will become men and women of faith, trusting Jesus Christ as their Savior and seeking to follow Him.

One positive note about getting old: Graham mentions a 104 year-old woman who said that the best thing about being 104 was that there was no peer pressure!

I encourage you to buy or borrow Billy Graham's book, "Nearing Home", and read it thoughtfully to encourage you as you grow older and to live now in a way that invites God's blessings!

## Interesting and Provocative Quotes

I collect quotes, perhaps because I have so few original thoughts of my own. I enjoy the wisdom others demonstrate. Here are some quotes that you may enjoy cogitating about. (Some may need to be taken with a pound of salt or a sense of humour.)

If you have a talent, that's God's gift to you. If you use that talent, that's your gift to God. Red Skelton

The trouble with the world is not that people know too little, but that they know so many things that ain't so. Mark Twain

The unexamined life is not worth living. Socrates

An ounce of prevention is worth a pound of cure. Henry DeBracton

A good name is more desirable than great riches; to be esteemed is better than silver or gold. Proverbs 22:1

Above all, guard your heart, for it is the wellspring of life. Proverbs 4:23

All men by nature desire to know. Aristotle

How can a young man keep his way pure? By living according to your Word. Psalm 119:9

Most people do not listen with the intent to understand; they listen with the intent to reply. Stephen Covey

Doubt is not the opposite of faith, nor is it the same as unbelief. Doubt is a state of mind in suspension between faith and unbelief so that it is neither of them wholly and it is each only partly. Os Guinness (I once read a book by Os Guinness and I didn't understand it either!)

On occasion my information-overloaded brain needs daydream breaks now more than ever. Yours probably does too, so take time on occasion to do nothing—in the presence of God and to the glory of God. Donald Witney

Every religious belief makes exclusivist claims. So why are only Christians perceived as arrogant? Is it just because they are perceived as a soft touch? Andy Bannister

All it takes for evil to prevail is for good men to do nothing. Edmund Burke

To have a Big Bang you need a Big Banger. Sean McDowell (speaking of Creation)

Any time we can do something, we are suddenly forced to ask whether we ought to do it. Paul Chamberlain

We are placing technological solutions to moral problems. John Patrick

Truth is not bigoted. People can surely be bigots...How we approach and communicate truth is what determines bigotry and narrow-mindedness. Chad Meister

Cynicism and doubts are corrosive acids that can corrode everything. Andy Bannister

Life is not about how to survive the storms; it's about how to dance in the rain. Anon

To teach is to learn again. Anon

A man convinced against his will is of the same opinion still. Anon

Never rent a vehicle in countries where they believe in reincarnation. Indian Proverb

As we have seen so often before, it's easier to bring down a dictator than to build a democracy. Jeffrey Kaufman in a 2012 CBC Radio documentary on Libya.

If at first you don't succeed, try doing it the way that your mother told you in the beginning. Anon

If you have an apple and I have an apple and we exchange them, then you and I will still each have one apple. But if you have an idea and I have an idea and we exchange these ideas, then each of us will have two ideas. George Bernard Shaw

If everything seems to be under control, you are not going fast enough. Mario Andretti (race car driver)

Things turn out best for the people who make the best of the way that things turn out. John Wooden

Horse sense is the thing a horse has that keeps it from betting on people. W.C. Fields

The simple words, “I love you,” said with glances or with murmuring lips, fill the soul with quiet rejoicing. Alexsandr Solzhenitsyn

I’m not afraid to die. I just don’t want to be there when it happens. Woody Allen

God may give us more than we can handle, but he never gives us more than he can handle. Sheila Schuller

To gaze into a person’s face is to do two things; to recognize their humanity and to assert your own. Lawrence Hill

It is to the man who rules over minds by the power of truth, not to those who enslave men by violence, it is to the man who understands the universe and not to those who disfigure it, that we owe our respect. Voltaire

The difference between perseverance and obstinacy is that perseverance means a strong will and obstinacy means a strong won’t. Lord Dundee

# I Believe in Santa Claus!

What? Really?

You probably already thought that I was weird by writing these "vignettes" that range from saintly to scientific to silly. But believing in Santa?

Well. Let me explain. Actually, I believe in St. Nicholas. I read a 2012 interview with Dr. Adam English in Christianity Today where he explained that St. Nicholas was an "ordinary" man of God who was a social activist, a politician, a businessman, a judge, and a protector who stood up for his faith and helped others. St. Nicholas lived at a time in church history where he witnessed and encouraged the transition from Christianity being persecuted to becoming accepted. He is said to have helped others, particularly the poor, often anonymously.

The transition from St. Nicholas to Santa Claus is somewhat murky but there have been people willing to fill in the blanks. The famous poem known as, "'Twas the Night Before Christmas", published in 1823 and usually attributed to Clement Clarke Moore has had a substantial impact on our modern perception of Santa Claus.

The ideas about St. Nicholas varied considerably before that time. Moore had done some shopping for gifts and also was inspired by a local Dutch handyman as well as the historical Saint Nicholas. His imagination added or borrowed the names of the eight reindeer as he filled in the story to write his poem. Moore portrayed a jolly Santa as bearing gifts on Christmas Eve which was intended to serve the purpose of shifting the focus of gift giving away from Christmas Day and allowing the religious significance of Christmas Day to be maintained.

The custom of children hanging stockings and eagerly anticipating gifts from Santa Claus also originated from St. Nicholas. Legend has it, St. Nicholas heard about a poor man who had three beautiful daughters but had no money to marry off his daughters so they would be taken care after his death. The good Saint knew that the old man wouldn't accept charity so he decided to secretly help by coming down the chimney at night and leaving a bag of gold for each girl in their stockings that were hung over the mantelpiece for drying. The girls were then able to get married and live happily ever after.

This eventually led to St. Nicholas being associated with giving gifts to children. I found it interesting that St. Nicholas also challenged those who did wrong which helps explain why those who had been too "naughty" found a piece of coal in their stocking on Christmas Eve.

Dr. English also proposed an approach that Christian parents may take in dealing with the concept of Santa Claus. He suggested that emphasizing the concepts of giving and loving our neighbour can be an antidote to the commercialization and greed that often characterizes the modern approach to Christmas. English believes that people want something more substantial than Santa Claus and can find this in the real St. Nicholas who exemplified goodness rather than greedily acquiring things resulting from commercialization. He indicates that it's helpful to look back at the traditions of St. Nicholas.

I suppose that Dr. English is correct, but I think that we need to go much further than that. I suggest that it is more important that we find the something "more substantial" in the Christmas story where Jesus Christ came to earth as a baby, lived a sinless life, and then died for our sins. The love that the triune Almighty God demonstrated by sending His Son to earth to pay for our sins is the ultimate demonstration of love and gift giving! Believing in Santa Claus, or at least in the good things that St. Nicholas did, is okay but let's go much further—let's believe in the Lord Jesus Christ!

# Moravians – The Oldest Protestant Denomination

Someone asked me recently about my earliest memories, and I immediately recalled going to a little Moravian Church a few miles from our home, which was on a farm just south-east of Edmonton, near a village called New Sarepta. I remember going to church on Christmas Eve night via a sleigh pulled by our two work horses; this would be about 1947.

There were four of us kids then and we were tucked in the straw with warm blankets as we trundled several miles to church. I also remember our family going to the "Festival", or "Fest" as it was known, in the summer time to the little white church with a high steeple. After the Sunday morning service there much eating and talking, and games for the kids. A bee once stung my younger sister while she was playing on the iron railing fence that surrounded the churchyard.

I hadn't thought about this Moravian church for years but I decided I should find out a bit more about my heritage. I understand that my Moravian heritage came from my Father's side since my Mom's family came from Lutheran Germany.

My ancestors migrated to Russia from Moravia and Germany because the Russian Czar wanted these hard-working people to farm the land. The Russian government made various promises, including grants of land and religious freedom, but eventually the immigrants encountered religious repression and the loss of promised incentives and exemptions from military service. In 1894, the Moravian colony in Volhynia, Russia, feared that things would get worse since it seemed that Russia would be taken over by a dictator and they would lose both their land and their religious freedom.

They had heard about the wonderful country called Canada, which offered them not only farm land at favorable terms to sustain their families, but freedom to establish Moravian churches and worship as they pleased.

The first group of Moravian families, which included my grandmother's parents, traveled over 500 miles by wagon, and then by train to a Baltic seaport, then on to England and Canada in 1894. My grandparents arrived in Canada with another group in 1902. The first Moravian settlements in Alberta were at Bruderfelt and Bruderheim, near Edmonton.

The Moravian Church is said to be the oldest Protestant denomination in the world, having its origins at least sixty years prior to when Martin Luther began the Protestant Reformation in Germany. The Moravian church traces its beginnings to the pre-reformation teachings of Jan Hus, a Czech reformer and professor at the University in Prague. Moravia is a region in Central Europe in the east of the Czech Republic; the largest city is Brno, its historical capital.

Moravia borders Poland in the north, Czech Silesia in the east, Slovakia in the southeast, Lower Austria in the south, and Bohemia in the west. Some Moravians also came from neighboring Bohemia. The name Moravian comes from the Morava River.

The historic Moravian church was born out of persecution and has a long history of mission and evangelical witness. The church believes that God has called people from varied backgrounds to live out their faith through service to those in need. Moravians are part of the Moravian Unity of the World Wide Moravian Church. Over the years, Moravians have developed a clear statement of faith, and a guide of the principles called "The Moravian Covenant for Christian Living" by which their members should live and bear witness. The Moravian Church had more than 750,000 members worldwide as of 2011. In Canada, there were congregations in Alberta, as well as in Ontario and Newfoundland/Labrador.

The ethnic origins of the Moravian Church in Canada has, perhaps inevitably, meant that many of the subsequent generations have been assimilated into other evangelical churches such as the Mennonites and Baptists, but those who continue in the Moravian churches generally continue a strong witness to the Christian faith, although modern day liberal pressures continue to be exerted. The Moravian Church website describes some of their practices and beliefs. The seal of the Moravian Church goes back to the 16th century. In the center is the Lamb of God, a favorite symbol of the early Christian church. A lamb is holding a staff, and from the staff waves a banner of victory. On the banner, a cross is clearly displayed. The inscription reads "Our Lamb has conquered, let us follow Him."

Small, lighted candles made from beeswax were distributed from the beginning to Moravians in America. Beeswax, considered the purest of all animal or vegetable waxes, suggested the purity of Christ. The candle, giving its life as it burned, suggested the sacrifice of the sinless Christ for sinful humanity, and also represented Christ, the Light of the world, and the light shed by the burning candle suggesting our Lord's command, "Let your light shine."

Moravian "stars" today decorate many homes and churches worldwide during Christmas, often appearing at the start of the Advent season and remaining until Epiphany in January. The star proclaims the hope of Advent and is supposed to remind us of God, who caused the light to shine out of darkness, and of the light of Christ. Moravians believe the reality of God's love offered in Christ is what our life of faith is all about. They say that individuals don't understand or experience Christ in exactly the same way, but that's not what is important. What is important is faith in Christ and commitment to live as his followers.

## Reflective Questions

It's interesting to think about life experiences and how we might react to various questions. I'll answer the following questions for myself but I hope that you will give some thought to them and reflect on your own responses.

**If you had a time machine and could go back to any year, what year would you choose?**

I would like to choose the years following 1500, which was when the Renaissance flourished and technological ingenuity was rewarded. This was the time of "unquenchable curiosity" when Leonardo da Vinci conceptualized new things like helicopters, solar power, calculators, as well as doing a bit of painting.

I could talk to Erasmus in Holland, who is generally credited with sparking the Reformation, plus he published an edition of the New Testament in Greek.

I could go to Germany and ask Martin Luther to tell me more about how he came to understand salvation by faith and grace, and to England to find out from Thomas Cranmer how he found the strength to repudiate false Catholic teachings. There were many individuals alive at this time demonstrating prodigious scientific and religious talents, so I would have a busy and productive time.

**What was the best vacation that you ever had?**

This is difficult to answer since we have had many great times including all sixteen members of our family at Palm Springs and Disneyland, and enjoyed some cruises. Perhaps the best vacation was the two-month odyssey that my sweetie and I took going across Canada in our motor home. We saw sights like Niagara Falls, the Parliament buildings in Ottawa, Peggy's Cove, Magnetic Hill, Confederation Hall, and the Confederation Bridge on Prince Edward Island, and many other memorable places. We truly have a great country!

**What is the most beautiful place you have ever seen?**

Some years ago I taught a laboratory quality assurance course in Port-of- Spain, Trinidad and Tobago. Before the course my sweetie and I visited various parts of Trinidad, and afterwards we took a twenty-minute flight to the other island in this picturesque country, Tobago. I think that Tobago is perhaps the most beautiful place in the world with its fabulous beaches and blue-green water. Estonia is probably the most interesting place I have visited. And from our front window in Abbotsford we can see the Sumas Prairie and Mt. Baker, so that's pretty special.

**What are some of your best life memories?**

I have had great times with my two daughters; going skiing, and seeing them do well in whatever they tackle. I also remember watching my son play hockey and win a city championship, and also playing catch with him. We have had great family times at home, and also when camping and sitting around a campfire beside our tent trailer. I remember my kids becoming Christians; I remember their wedding days, and I remember the births of my grandchildren.

And I remember the kiss my fiancé gave me when I came to see her the morning after we became engaged, plus more than a few after that.

**What is one thing that not many people know about you?**

I almost drowned when I was seventeen while playing "keep away" with some high school friends at a lake. When I went to retrieve the ball I stepped into a huge, water-filled hole and might have drowned if the teacher hadn't rescued me.

I took swimming lessons in my first year at university as part of the gym class for a few weeks, and I sort of learned to swim as my kids learned, but swimming is my least favorite ways of getting exercise.

**Have you ever been afraid for your life?**

No, but a couple of times I have had a "near miss". One evening while driving along a major city street at about sixty kilometers per hour, a car sped through a stop sign not more than twenty feet in front of us. If we had arrived at the intersection three seconds earlier we would likely have been killed or severely injured.

**How would your life be different if you knew that Jesus was/were returning later today?**

I heard this quote recently: "Plan like you are going to live forever; live like He's coming back today." Christ may return any day, so it's not as if this is a hypothetical question. I suppose that I would stop worrying about the little or even big frustrations of life and do more to help family, friends, and strangers have assurance of eternal life as well as have the daily necessities of life.

**If you could choose one job or career, other than then one you have or had what would you choose?**

I have sometimes thought that I would like to be an "Oxford Don", that is a Professor at Oxford University in England where I would hold tutorials with individual students or small groups and share and obtain wisdom. I visited Oxford a few years ago and was impressed with both the historical and modern approaches to learning.

**What would you hope that Jesus might say to you when you die and arrive at the "Pearly Gates"?**

"Hi, come on in; I've been expecting you, my good and faithful servant!" would be nice. Or, "I'm sorry that it took so long!" Or, "Thank you for your excellent work while on earth". Or, "I have some heroes of the faith I would like you to meet".

**If you could choose one person you have never met personally, with whom to have dinner with, who would you choose?**

I'm not one inclined to hero worship, but sitting down with our Prime Minister to talk about the nuts and bolts of how government works would be interesting. Since I asked the question, I'll give more than one answer. Having dinner with Christopher Columbus and picking his brain to see where he summoned the courage to venture into parts unknown would be fascinating. I could offer many other suggestions, but I'll stop at Nicholas Copernicus who revolutionized how Europeans thought of the world and God. (Copernicus was persecuted for his conclusion that the earth revolved around the sun.)

## Pets, PETA and People

I grew up on a small farm in Alberta where animals had a utilitarian purpose. Chickens provided eggs for meals and weekly income, plus regular chicken dinners. Our dairy cows provided milk, cream, and butter, and income from selling cream. Beef cattle provided more family income, plus pot roast and other beef dinners. Even the pets had jobs. The cats protected the stored grain by reducing the mouse population, and the two dogs helped herd the cows and controlled the gophers and mice that would otherwise harm the crops in the fields. When I was small my Dad still used horses to pull the farm implements to work the fields.

Although Disney has given us many hours of wholesome family entertainment, I think they have done society a huge disservice in many of their movies, TV programs, and books by giving people the false impression that animals are "friends" with each other.

Disney gives animals a wide range of anthropomorphic characteristics where we get the impression that these animals think and act like human beings. For example, kids' TV programs give the impression that a bear is best friends with a chicken. Even documentaries of wildlife in areas such as the Serengeti give us an unrealistic picture of how nature works. Survival of the fittest is not a theoretical concept. Nature is brutal and there is a real food chain. Animals prey on each other for food just to survive.

The vast majority of people now live in cities, and many of them have little or no understanding of how food gets to the grocery store, whether chicken legs, beef ribs, or turkey breasts—or even milk and butter.

Organizations such as PETA (People for the Ethical Treatment of Animals) propagate the belief that animals have the same moral value as humans. I support the proper treatment of animals and I believe they should not be abused, but I don't fully understand what "humane" treatment of animals really means.

Is a "free range" chicken happier than a chicken raised together with hundreds or thousands of other chickens? How would we measure this happiness or contentment? Aren't we attributing or transferring human values to chickens if we answer the question in the affirmative? Is a steer raised with nine other steers on a ten-hectare farm more content than a steer raised with a thousand others in a feedlot?

I heard recently about a chef who claimed to be able to tell the difference in taste between an unhappy cage chicken and a happy free-range chicken. That's what I call a discriminating palate. (He didn't identify the supposed new chemical that would explain the taste difference apparently only detectable to PETA activists.)

Then there's the ethical question. We can't feed everyone raising five cows or ten chickens at a time on a little acreage. While we're on the subject, how is it that plants get such a raw deal? Why is it that it's fine to kill and eat plants but wrong to kill and eat animals? Just asking.

People throughout history have kept some animals as pets but we have seen an explosion of this as our society becomes more affluent. Having a pet isn't a bad thing but sometimes our priorities become severely skewed. Many folks treat their pets better than some people treat their kids. In 2013, Americans spent more than 52 billion dollars on their pets, primarily on food and medicine, while Canadians spent about six billion dollars. It's easy to say that we could better spend this money on starving families in Somalia or Ethiopia, but as a generalization that may be unfair since many people also give to charities.

But when we show little or no consideration for the poor in our communities or in other countries, we need to start asking some questions.

There is another perspective about the value of people. There are some "ethicists" such as Peter Singer of Princeton University who said that those who are weak or disabled or old or handicapped in some way should be euthanized since they don't contribute sufficiently to society. One can see where this thinking comes from if you believe that a human has no more value than an animal.

## The Wall Goes Up and the Wall Comes Down

A subtitle could be, "Freedom is Precious and Tyranny is Terrible".

I watched a TV documentary describing the history of the Berlin Wall. After WWII ended, Germany was divided in 1949 into West Germany under the direction of Britain, France, and the United States. East Germany (ironically, it was officially called the German *Democratic* Republic) became controlled by Russia. However, the control of Berlin, deep inside East Germany, was a problem, since the western allies were not prepared to let Russia control the entire city. As a result, Berlin was also divided among the four powers, although the western allies worked closely together.

It didn't take long for the people of East Berlin to understand that communism was a failed and autocratic idea accompanied by a dramatic reduction in personal freedoms and a reduced standard of living. They soon began to flee to West Berlin and West Germany by the thousands. By 1961 more than 2.5 million had escaped from East Berlin. The East German leader, Walter Ulbricht, realized that this massive exodus of citizens would quickly lead to economic collapse if something drastic weren't done. Since he had announced that he would never build a wall, Ulbricht surreptitiously acquired barbed wire and other building materials and stored them in secret locations in East Berlin. But overnight a barbed wire fence was constructed, which was soon followed by a great concrete wall. Some apartment and office buildings right on the border between East and West Berlin had the back windows facing West Berlin while the front door opened in East Berlin.

Many East Berliners were separated from their families. One man happened to be working in West Berlin the day the fence went up but his wife and two children were in their home in East Berlin. After a couple of months he had constructed a tunnel under the wall and was able to bring his family to West Berlin. In the first few months many people escaped across the wall into West Berlin, some jumping from the building windows facing West Berlin. Before long these windows were all bricked in.

The East German authorities systematically increased surveillance to make escape more difficult while continuing to beef up the wall. First there was an eight foot barbed wire fence equipped to set off alarms, followed another smaller metal fence. Then a wide "death strip" was added and finally a twelve-foot high concrete fence with watchtowers manned by armed guards. Eventually, ninety-six miles of fence totally surrounded East Berlin. Almost no one successfully crossed this intimidating barrier though many were killed in the attempt. A few tunneled under and one enterprising attempt flew over the wall. East Germans recognized that their homes and their city were now a large prison.

The Stasi (secret police) kept files on "suspicious" individuals and everyone knew they were being watched. These files grew to include about one-third of the population. The police regularly sabotaged ordinary citizens, by means such as barring them from attending university. Many citizens were arrested and interrogated for hours or days.

By 1980 East Berlin had its own paranoid culture. Erich Honecker, the new leader, tried to convince East Berliners and East Germans their freedom and standard of living was the same as in West Germany. The people knew this wasn't true. Many commodities were in short supply; it could take seven years to purchase a car.

The East German communists unwittingly orchestrated their own downfall. They wanted to show that religion was dead so they allowed churches to open in the belief that the churches would dry up and disappear due to lack of interest. Instead, the churches began to flourish as people flocked there to pray for peace and freedom. This was particularly evident in the city of Leipzig where a peace movement soon began. The churches were protected and since the secret police wouldn't be caught dead in a church they didn't know what was happening.

Other cracks began to appear. East Germans realized that their country was one of the most polluted in the world due to poor industrial practices and an environmental movement began out of a feeling for self-preservation.

In 1985 the reform-minded Mikhail Gorbachev became head of the USSR. He realized that East Germany was one of the most repressive regimes in the world but their leaders resisted his reform suggestions. President Reagan went to Berlin to meet Gorbachev and told him that the Berlin Wall must be torn down; Germans saw this as a demand to reunify Germany.

The Stasi tried to enforce the ban on free speech but opposition grew bolder, and the first holes in the Iron Curtain were appearing across Eastern Europe. Poland pushed for democratic reforms, and changes in Hungary in 1989 enabled many East Germans to flee there. I guess they couldn't build a wall all around the GDR!

In October 1989 Gorbachev went to East Berlin for the 40$^{th}$ anniversary of the GDR. During the celebration thousands of youth chanted for freedom. In Leipzig, thousands went to church and more than 70,000 met in the streets of East Berlin. Erich Honecker warned the hospitals to prepare for many casualties. He was prepared to shoot demonstrators but the officials declined to order the police to fire. Suddenly, the GDR was different. Honecker was replaced as leader and the new government tried too little, too late to respond to demands.

The wall finally came down almost by accident. A local official announced a relaxation of travel restrictions and when asked when these would take effect he mistakenly said they would begin immediately. Guards opened a section of the wall and masses of East Berliners walked through. West Berlin and the American media promptly announced that the wall was coming down. The officials were overwhelmed while the police stood by, bringing to an end the ignominious history of the Berlin Wall.

Germans on both sides of the wall were jubilant but West German politicians led by Helmut Kohl were concerned about the process of stabilizing this "new country". East Germany was so poor and many had been brainwashed in the socialist bath. West Germans would need to make substantial sacrifices and changes to stabilize the united Germany. There were growing problems, but we now know that the Germans were successful in their reunification. Germany eventually became the strongest country in Europe.

The wall went up and the wall came down; Humpty Dumpty had a big fall and the Germans put their country back together again.

## Christ of the Klingons

A 2012 Vancouver Sun column by Ben Hirschler reported that English astronomers have suggested that there may be "billions of habitable planets" in the Milky Way—those that are potentially warm enough and wet enough to support life. They believe that "red dwarf stars" could theoretically support life. However, since they are cool compared to our sun, any planets with water would need to orbit much closer to the star than the earth is from our sun and therefore, these planets could be subjected to damaging x-rays and ultraviolet radiation. Still, the possibility of life elsewhere in the universe is intriguing.

The following is a summary of a December 2010 Christianity Today article entitled "Christ of the Klingons" by Trevor Persaud, which began this way: "We have learned a lot since God humbled Job by daring him to comprehend how Orion and the Pleiades held together. But some scientists and philosophers say our idea of the universe is still too small for the infinite mind of God." Persaud reported that scientists, and humans in general, have gone through stages since we first expanded our understanding of the cosmos from a single planet with an intriguing and sparkling sky overhead to a system of planets circling the sun, and then to a galaxy of stars. Now we know that our galaxy, comprising at least a hundred billion stars, is one part of a universe that includes immense superstructures containing thousands of galaxies, millions of light-years across.

Theoretical physicists proposed a super string theory called M-Theory to explain how the universe works. M theory is said to be the best chance scientists have for arriving at a complete picture of the universe and they suggest that our entire universe, including planets and stars, is just one of many more like it.

Some scientists, however, doubt that M-Theory is anything more than a collection of fascinating but fictional equations. Still, there may be an incredibly diverse array of possible universes with different sets of physical laws. We likely cannot ever reach them, and in any case, only a few would be hospitable to human life.

One of the most famous physicists, Stephen Hawking, suggests that the multi-universe eliminates the need for God since the theory predicts that a great many universes were created out of nothing. Others say that Hawking can't escape God that easily, since if the universe arose from the laws of physics, then who designed the laws of physics? And why does the multiverse work the way it does?

Science often tries to portray God as someone who can only fill in the gaps that science can't explain, but Christians perceive God as the primary source, and the laws of physics as secondary. The Bible, in Romans 1, says that creation manifests the eternal attributes of God and his eternal and infinite power. It follows that an infinitely creative being *could* create more than one universe.

C. S. Lewis' fictional *Chronicles of Narnia* include one of the classic depictions of a multiverse in western literature where the heroes of the story can enter not just Earth and Narnia but also countless places stretching off into the distance. They see an old "universe" destroyed and a new one created and they meet the one who is Lord over all of them.

Did an infinite God create life just on our earth, just for a few human beings? Some Christian scientists are intrigued by the possibility that Jesus the Messiah could take on other incarnational forms and redeem even living forms that look something like the Klingons of Star Wars fame. God the Son, being infinite, could take on the Klingon nature, that is a Klingon version of Jesus, when visiting some far off planet rather than a human form as he did on planet Earth. These scientists indicate that the Christian church should address the idea of life existing elsewhere besides earth (I assume in concert with scientists). It's interesting that the Catholic Church held a conference on the possibility of life elsewhere in the universe several years ago involving both theologians and scientists.

Christian scientists remind us that we serve a God who is easily capable of holding many universes in the palm of his hand. They say that the universe is structured for beauty and elegance. Showing the beauty and the order in the creative nature of God allows us to expect science to reveal physical truth to us and that the universe or the multi-universe does not "just happen" to exist.

## Strange But Common Expressions

Idioms are words, phrases, or expressions commonly used in everyday conversation. They are often metaphorical and make our conversation more colorful. We regularly use various archaic expressions, but since we use some of them almost every day everyone intuitively knows what we mean. The origins of some of the expressions are uncertain and the relevance of others is rather dubious since both language and life change over time. In any case here are some expressions that you probably used recently:

**"The writing is on the wall."**

This is an idiom for "imminent doom or misfortune" and for "something is predetermined; we know what's going to happen". The expression originates from the book of Daniel in the Bible. The handwriting that appeared on the wall was witnessed at a banquet hosted by King Belshazzar. After the king had profaned sacred vessels pillaged from the Jerusalem Temple, a disembodied hand suddenly appeared and wrote on the palace wall the following mysterious words, "Mene, Mene, Tekel, Parsin."

The prophet Daniel was summoned and interpreted this message as the imminent end for the Babylonian kingdom. That same night, Belshazzar was killed and the Persians sacked the capital city.

**"Face the music."**

This phrase means that one must accept the consequences of one's own actions. Years ago, soldiers who were dishonorably discharged from the army were forced to march slowly between ranks of their peers while drums and other instruments marked the somber occasion.

**"Don't let the cat out of the bag."**

We know this phrase means revealing a secret, but its origins are uncertain. One suggestion relates to the fraud of substituting a cat for a piglet at markets. If you "let the cat out of the bag" you disclosed the trick—and avoided "buying a pig in a poke"_ (bag).

This form of trickery was mentioned as early as 1530. Another theory is that the "cat" referred to is the cat o' nine tails, which was used to flog misbehaving sailors. The 'nine tails' part of the name derives from the three strands of cord that the rope lashes were made from and when unbraided the rope separated into nine strings. The 'cat' part alluded to the scratches that the knotted ends of the lash made on the victim's back, like those from a cat's claws.

**"He couldn't cut the mustard anymore."**

The origins of this term are about as clear as mustard. Some say that this expression comes from "cutting" or diluting mustard with vinegar, which makes it taste better. However, if someone was not as skilled in diluting the mustard, it was said, "he couldn't cut the mustard". Others believe that "mustard" might have been confused with the word "muster". The idiom "to pass muster" referred to assembling military troops for inspection, so that a soldier who had achieved excellent performance in some area was allowed to skip, or cut the formal muster or formation and go on liberty early.

**"That's like the pot calling the kettle black."**

We understand this idiom to mean that a person is guilty of the very thing of which they accuse someone else. The person accusing (the "pot") shares some quality with the target of their accusation (the "kettle"). The pot is mocking the kettle for a little soot when the pot itself is thoroughly covered with black soot since after being held over a fire.

**"He was sweating like a pig."**

Pigs don't sweat much, which is why they wallow in the mud to cool off their bodies. So how did this expression originate? It's actually a reference to pig iron—an intermediate product of smelting iron ore to obtain iron. The smelter heats the ore to extreme temperatures then moves the liquid metal into a mold. The traditional shape of the mold was a branching structure with many individual forms at right angles to a central channel. This configuration is similar in appearance to a litter of piglets suckling a sow. When the metal had cooled and hardened, the smaller ingots (the pigs) were simply broken from the main channel. How does the smelter know when the metal is cool enough to do this? When the pigs sweat! As the metal cools, the air around it reaches the dew point, causing droplets to form on the metal's surface.

**"Barking up the wrong tree."**

This is an idiomatic expression used to suggest a wrong assumption or to pursue the wrong course to obtain something. The phrase is an allusion to the mistake made by dogs when they believe that have chased a prey up a tree, but the target apparently escaped by leaping from one tree to another.

**"Shooting the breeze."**

This idiom originated in the early 20th century and comes from the imagery of the Wild West. Cowboys and others with nothing to do would find ways to kill time by, say, shooting into the air at nothing in particular, thereby "shooting the breeze". We still use this term to describe killing time by engaging in idle conversation.

**"Let sleeping dogs lie."**

An English major may know the origin of this phrase. Chaucer wrote this phrase in a slightly different way, basically saying that it wasn't wise to wake a sleeping dog. Charles Dickens, when writing David Copperfield, used this idiom in the way that we are familiar with today. It's still often not wise to create a disturbance or start an argument by arousing a person or bringing up a distasteful issue.

**"There's no free lunch."**

This phrase that communicates the idea that it's impossible to get something for nothing. References to this saying go back to the 1930s and 1940s. One possible origin relates to the nineteenth century temporary practice in American bars of offering a free lunch as a way to entice drinking (and paying) customers.

**"I made it by the skin of my teeth."**

The source of this saying is the Book of Job in the Bible even though this wasn't exactly what Job said. It's unclear what the "skin" of one's teeth might be but it may refer to the thin porcelain exterior of the tooth. Job may have been saying that the margin of his escape was very narrow. The phrase has been used ever since to mean a narrow or arduous escape.

**"It is as clear as a bell."**

When we say that something is "crystal clear" the meaning is obvious, but why do we say that it may be clear as a bell? In the "olden days" every village and city had churches with large, loud bells, which could be heard from great distances. Church bells sound a single, clear distinctive sound. Bells were therefore a valuable means of signaling people and alerting them of important events. The bottom line was, and is, that a message was clearly understood.

**"Burning the midnight oil."**

This phrase is still in everyday use, meaning to work late into the night. Originally this was by the light of an oil lamp or candle. However, I like this explanation: The phrase is actually said to have originated in the Catholic Church where oil was used for anointing the sick and to consecrate those who were being ordained as priests. Each year, the bishop blessed these oils for use for the coming liturgical year on Holy Thursday. Thus, on Wednesday, the night before, any remaining oils from the previous year were burned at midnight, in anticipation for the new oils at the Holy Thursday morning Mass.

**"It's raining cats and dogs."**

Apparently this expression isn't related to the antipathy between dogs and cats (fighting like cats and dogs is a different expression). Another suggested origin of no validity was that cats and dogs, in the Middle Ages, often slept on the thatched straw roofs of their masters' houses and sometimes when it rained they would fall off the slippery roof. A more likely origin is that, in the filthy streets of England in the 17$^{th}$ century, heavy rain would occasionally carry along dead animals and various kinds of debris. The animals didn't fall from the sky, but the sight of dead cats and dogs floating by seems to have caused the use of this colorful phrase.

**"You're fired!"**

One theory is that in days gone by, if a clan wanted an undesirable person or family to leave their community they would burn their house down. Today this expression is an exclamation used by an employer to inform employee of their dismissal for reasons perceived to be the fault of the employee. Another possible explanation of the origin of this expression is that miners in England were the ones to incorporate the metaphor of firing to losing a job. If any miners had stolen ore their fate was banishment, plus their tools and instruments were set on fire. A related expression, especially in North America is that of "getting one's walking papers". "Getting the boot," is said to have started in the 1800s as was "getting the sack", and "getting laid off" began to be used in America after the Civil War. We also have the expression of "Getting a pink slip". Legend has it that Henry Ford's idea was to evaluate his employees using a color scheme but it isn't clear why he picked pink to be the color of the slip that showed rejection of an employee's work.

**"Not by a long shot."**

This of course means something that is highly unlikely to happen. It seems that the most likely explanation for the origin of this expression relates to the inaccuracy of early firearms, which when shot over a distance rarely hit the target. Some say that this expression first arose in British racing circles in the 19th century when a bet was made at large odds. A less likely explanation is that the origin comes from the use of chalk for reckoning points in tavern games where beating an opponent by a long chalk indicated a substantial win. The British expression is, not by a long chalk.

**"Cup of Joe."**

Shortly after 1913, Josephus Daniels, as Secretary of the U.S. Navy, established the practice of allowing women into the service while also abolishing the officers' wine mess. From that time on the strongest drink aboard Navy ships was only coffee and over the years a cup of coffee became known as "a cup of Joe".

**"Henpecked husband."**

(Please note that I didn't ask my wife if I could write about this.) Henpecked is an adjective used to mean a husband is browbeaten, bullied, tormented, or intimidated by his wife by persistent nagging or intimidation. A hen is the female domestic chicken and the term is sometimes loosely applied to female Homo sapiens. A hen frigate was a ship where the captain's wife interfered with the performance of his duty. The term "henpecked" is from a hen's practice of plucking at the rooster.

## Famous Scientists

This little treatise might be considered Scientific History 101. I earned a BSc in Pharmacy and briefly went into drug research after obtaining a PhD in Pharmacology, but it didn't take me long to realize that I would be a bust as a researcher, perhaps because I had only ever had three or four original ideas in my whole life to that point. So I moved into analytical laboratory management and developed a reasonable career. My goal as a manager was to hire people smarter than I (which wasn't too difficult) and provide them with the tools and opportunities to do their jobs well. In spite of my limited scientific capabilities I have always admired brilliant people, including colleagues I encountered in my work or researchers I heard and read about. Even if you don't share my fascination with science, by reading this vignette I hope that you will gain some further appreciation of the ways in which brilliant scientists have improved our understanding of how the world works and how science has improved our lives.

**Isaac Newton**

Perhaps the most influential scientist in history—Einstein is generally regarded as second—Newton was an English physicist, mathematician, astronomer, natural philosopher, alchemist, and theologian. His Philosophiæ Naturalis Principia Mathematica, published in 1687, is considered to be the most influential book in the history of science. In this work, Newton described the law of gravity (the story is that he developed this idea after seeing an apple fall from a tree) and the three laws of motion. This laid the groundwork for classical mechanics, which dominated the scientific view of the physical universe for the next three centuries.

**Albert Einstein**

Einstein was a German physicist noted for his flowing white hair, irascible nature, and genius. He made many contributions to physics but is best known for his theory of relativity and specifically mass-energy equivalence, expressed by the equation $E = mc^2$. Einstein received the 1921 Nobel Prize in Physics "for his services to Theoretical Physics and especially for his discovery of the law of the photoelectric effect". Einstein's special theory of relativity reconciled quantum mechanics with electromagnetism, and his general theory of relativity and gravitation.

**Galileo Galilei**

Galileo was an Italian physicist and astronomer. His achievements include improvements to the telescope and consequent astronomical observations, and support for Copernicanism (the revolutionary idea that the earth revolves around the sun). Galileo has been called the "father of modern observational astronomy", the "father of modern physics", and the "father of modern science".

**Leonardo da Vinci**

He was a "polyscientist", an expert mathematician, engineer, inventor, anatomist, painter, sculptor, architect, botanist, plus a musician and writer. Da Vinci has often been described as the archetype of the "Renaissance man", a man whose seemingly infinite curiosity was equaled only by his powers of invention. He is revered for his technological ingenuity. He conceptualized helicopters, tanks, concentrated solar power, calculators, the double hull for ships, and he outlined a rudimentary theory of plate tectonics.

**Marie Curie**

A Polish physicist and chemist, Marie Curie was a pioneer in the field of radioactivity (she coined the term). The first female professor at the University of Paris, she was honored with Nobel Prizes in two different sciences. She discovered two new elements (radium and polonium), and founded the Curie Institutes in Paris and Warsaw where she was the first to treat cancers with radioisotopes.

**Nikola Tesla**

Tesla was a Serbian engineer and inventor who is sometimes described as the most important scientist and inventor of the modern age. He is best known for many revolutionary contributions in the field of electricity and magnetism in the late $19^{th}$ and early $20^{th}$

centuries, and is regarded by many as the "Father of Physics". You might see a few "Tesla" electric cars on the roads these days.

**Alan Turing**

You may have heard of this pioneering English computer scientist if you are a movie buff (his story was told in *The Imitation Game*) and he is usually considered the father of modern computer science. This is the man who broke the military code or cipher used by the Germans to send their radio messages during World War II. Turing is credited with shortening the war by at least two years, thereby saving millions of lives.

**Niels Bohr**

Bohr was a Danish physicist who made fundamental contributions to understanding atomic structure and quantum mechanics, for which he received the Nobel Prize in Physics in 1922. Bohr's work helped solve the problems classical physics could not explain about the nuclear model of the atom.

**Max Planck**

A German physicist, Planck is considered to be one of the most important physicists of the twentieth century. Planck made many contributions to theoretical physics, but his fame rests primarily on his role as originator of the quantum theory, which is the theoretical basis of modern physics and explains the nature and behavior of matter and energy at the atomic and subatomic level.

**Stephen Hawking**

Hawking is probably the greatest living scientist (as of 2016) and theoretical physicist and the author of one of the bestselling books ever, *A Brief History of Time*, in which he uses physics to describe how the world works by discussing black holes and other astronomical phenomena. In spite of contracting ALS Hawking held the position of "Lucasian Professor" at Cambridge; the chair once held by Isaac Newton. Check out the movie about Hawking's life, called *The Theory of Everything.*

**Francis Crick and James Watson**

Francis Crick was a British molecular biologist, biophysicist, and neuroscientist, most noted for being a co-discoverer, with James Watson, of the structure of the DNA molecule in 1953. Together with Watson he was awarded the 1962 Nobel Prize for Physiology and Medicine "for discoveries concerning the molecular structure of nucleic acids and its significance for information transfer in living material". This was a foundational discovery of our understanding of how proteins are constructed in our bodies.

**William Harvey**

A 17th century English physician, Harvey is acknowledged as the first to describe how the heart pumps blood to our brains and throughout our bodies.

**Alexander Fleming**

Most Canadians may have heard about Fleming who is primarily known for discovering penicillin and the concept of how anti-bacterial agents work. This discovery has saved untold numbers of lives and first came to prominence in World War II when soldiers dying from infections were given antibiotics that saved their lives. He won the Nobel Prize in Physiology and Medicine in 1945.

**Antoine Lavoisier**

Antoine-Laurent de Lavoisier was a French nobleman and chemist central to the 18th-century understanding of how chemical reactions occur, and a had a huge influence on the history of chemistry. He is widely considered in popular literature as the "father of modern chemistry".

**Johannes Kepler**

Kepler was a German mathematician, astronomer, and astrologer. A key figure in the 17th century scientific revolution, he is best known for his laws of planetary motion which provided one of the foundations for Isaac Newton's theory of universal gravitation.

**Linus Pauling**

Rated by one source as the 16th most important scientist in history, Pauling is one of only four individuals to have won more than one

Nobel Prize. He was an American chemist and biochemist who expanded our knowledge of the DNA structure and became interested in how quantum mechanics might be applied to the electronic structure of atoms and molecules. Later in life he was controversial after promoting megavitamin therapy and dietary supplements.

**Edwin Hubble**

We hear quite a bit about the use of the Hubble Telescope, which was thrust into space to explore the structure and expanse of the universe. Hubble was an American astronomer who played a crucial role in establishing the field of extragalactic astronomy and is generally regarded as one of the most important cosmologists of the $20^{th}$ century. Hubble is known for showing that the universe is expanding and consists of many galaxies.

**Hans Selye**

An Austrian-Canadian endocrinologist, Selye pioneered research into the effects of stress on human health, and he demonstrated that stress-induced breakdown of the hormonal system could lead to various conditions such as heart disease and high blood pressure. I once heard him speak in Montreal.

**Antonie van Leeuwenhoek**

Commonly known as "the Father of Microbiology", Leeuwenhoek was a Dutch tradesman and scientist best known for his work on the improvement of the microscope and for his contributions towards the study of microbiology.

**Louis Pasteur**

A French chemist and microbiologist, Pasteur is renowned for the principles of vaccination, microbial fermentation, and, of course pasteurization of milk and other products. He demonstrated that killing bacteria could prevent diseases; his findings have saved countless lives.

**Joseph Lister**

A British surgeon, Lister pioneered antiseptic surgery by applying Pasteur`s advances in microbiology by sterilizing instruments and cleaning wounds.

**Charles Darwin**

I don't really think that Darwin belongs on this list, although some rank him very high. While he certainly was influential, his *theory* of evolution has generally been disproved by many scientists even while being uncritically accepted by other scientists and the public. An English naturalist and biologist, Darwin attempted to demonstrate that all species of life have evolved over time from common ancestors through the process he called natural selection. However, serious problems with Darwin's theory have been raised. Michael Behe, a respected biochemist, wrote a book called, *Darwin's Black Box*, which presents a compelling case against evolution, including Darwin's acknowledgement of deficiencies in his own arguments. Check out respected scientists such as Hugh Ross, Guillermo Gonzalez, Stephen Meyer, and Gary Habermas, or Lee Strobel's book, *The Case for a Creator*, where scientific evidence is presented for creation.

You probably are thinking that this list of famous scientists and their contributions to society is much too long, and yet I have barely scratched the surface. Perhaps the list should have started with Archimedes, the 3rd Century BC Greek philosopher, mathematician, physicist, engineer and inventor, and 4th Century Aristotle who is the father of Western Science and the inventor of formal logic and the scientific method.

## How Many Houses Have You Lived In?

In many respects, my sweetie and I are fairly normal middle-class Canadians. I'm not sure if my multiple answers to this question are similar to your situation even though we live in a relatively mobile society.

Let me start with the time before I was married. I lived with my family in a tiny house in central Alberta, and then when I was five we moved to another farm where I lived until I finished high school. I then moved to Edmonton where I lived with my sister and her family for several years in two different houses while attending university. Eventually I moved to a little room closer to university for a year, followed by one year when I roomed with another guy. When I completed my undergraduate degree I moved to a nicer basement apartment. My parents moved to the city while I was working on my MSc, and I lived with them until I was married. That brings me to eight places so far.

A few weeks after we were married, my new bride and I moved to Ottawa to work for Health Canada. There we lived in a one-bedroom apartment for a year. The federal government was kind enough to send me back to university at half salary plus paid tuition and books. We lived in a one bedroom married students' apartment decorated with early Salvation Army furniture and moved on to a two-bedroom apartment when our baby came along. After I obtained my PhD we moved back to Ottawa to a townhouse and a couple of years later we bought our first, very own house, which was a three-bedroom, semi-detached bungalow costing $23,000. This was in 1972. That's five more places I've lived.

I eventually decided that I was not strong at doing research, so when a laboratory management position came open in Vancouver, British Columbia, we sold our little house in Ottawa for $46,000 and bought an older house in the city of Richmond for $60,000. After five years we bought a nice new house, also in Richmond. A few years later we moved to Surrey and bought a house there for $132,000 while at the same time reducing our mortgage. By this time our three kids had all grown up and even bought houses of their own, so we decided to downsize. We also wanted a view, even though senior citizenship was drawing inexorably closer. We found a townhouse in Abbotsford B.C. with a spectacular view of the Sumas prairie and Mt. Baker in the U.S. The main challenge was that it was at least an hour's drive from two of our three kids and our grandchildren. I write this, I realize that I have added four more homes for a total of seventeen, which is still a lot but better than "no fixed address".

The key thing is, my sweetie and I have been happy and blessed in every place that we have lived. Can this be a coincidence? Or is God determined to bless us even as we try to be faithful to Him? Our babies were born in these places, they went to school, we all went to church together, and they met their life mates while living wherever we happened to be when they were at that stage of their lives. And now that we are again on our own, in a beautiful townhouse, empty-nesters, as they say, we have been immeasurably happy and blessed with new friends and some continuing friends, plus a church that absolutely knocks our socks off because it keeps blessing us so much.

Now there is another question: how many more houses will we live in before we occupy that great mansion in heaven with our Lord and Savior? We realize that eventually we will become less mobile and may want to move to a condo apartment or, heaven forbid, a senior citizens' care home. At this point, such a decision or a necessity to move seems far away, and it's true that many couples continue to live in their own homes until well into their eighties or even nineties. But we do need to be realistic and do some planning to be able to make a smooth transition when necessary. I hope that you will think about this question as well—not just when you might have to move for job, or family, or health, or other reasons, but think about the big question of where you will move when your adventures here on earth are completed. Make a specific decision for Jesus and choose heaven!

## A Whale of a Story

Whales are mammals—very large mammals. Although they live in the ocean, they are not fish. Like other mammals whales are warm-blooded, breathe air and feed their babies on mother's milk. They breathe through two blowholes on the top of their heads when they come up for air. When whales breathe out, the water vapor in their breath turns into mist which is called the whale's "blow".

Gray whales are humungous. The females can be fifty feet long and weigh more than thirty-eight tons and may live to be sixty years old. The males are almost as big. Gray whales migrate, that is, they live in different places for part of the year, and they travel farther than most animals. In summer they live in the Arctic Ocean where there is plenty of food. In fall, the Arctic Ocean becomes very cold and the gray whales swim thousands of miles to warmer waters in the Pacific Ocean as far as Mexico. In one year a gray whale can travel up to 12,500 miles. They sleep on the surface of the ocean with their blowhole just above the water. Killer whales or sharks sometimes attack gray whales.

Once they reach warmer water they mate, and in spring the pregnant whales swim north again at a rate of about five miles per hour. The female whales swim in groups called pods. Although the Pacific Ocean is warmer than the Arctic Ocean, the mother whale always returns to the Arctic Ocean because more food is there and they require a lot to nourish the growing fetus. Once the weather becomes colder, again the gray whales start south and when they find a quiet place they give birth. Born tail first, the calf is about fifteen feet long and feed on their mother's milk immediately after birth. In spring they return north again, which takes a couple of months, so they grow a layer of blubber to keep warm in the colder waters. Calves stop feeding on mother's milk at about seven months and begin to eat krill, and at about twelve months they leave their mothers' sides.

The white patches on gray whales are barnacles, which are small sea animals with a hard shell that also attach themselves to rocks, ships, and large animals. The barnacles, often more than 400 pounds of them, live on the whales but are harmless. Unlike some other whales that have teeth and can eat fish, gray whales have baleen plates, which are like a bony comb that strains the seawater. The whale gulps seawater that is full of tiny animals called krill, and then squeezes the water out of its mouth leaving the krill behind. These krill are tiny so gray whales spend a lot of time feeding.

A moratorium on commercial whaling was endorsed in 1986, although a few countries ignored world opinion. Whale watching subsequently became a popular tourist industry, although sometimes scientific and educational objectives also exist. There is concern that the rapid growth of the number of whale watching trips and the size of vessels used to watch whales might affect whale behavior, migratory patterns, and breeding cycles. Environmental campaigners urge whale-watcher operators to contribute to regulations governing whale watching. Common rules include "no wake" speed, minimize noise, no pursuing of whales or coming between them, and minimize the number of boats at any one time and on any one day.

## The Northwest Passage

The term "Northwest Passage" should trigger an emotional, even romantic, response for Canadians over the age of fifty, and a concerned response for every Canadian citizen because of both historical and sovereignty issues. The Northwest Passage is a sea route through the Arctic Ocean, along the northern coast of North America via waterways through the Canadian Arctic archipelago, connecting the Atlantic and Pacific Oceans.

Let's address the history part first.

The search for a water route through the Arctic, north of the Canadian mainland, to the supposed wealth of the Far East was a chapter fraught with frustrations in the history of Canada. For over 300 years, after it was realized that North America blocked the route from Europe to the Orient, expeditions probed the inhospitable sea and land environments seeking a commercial route to the Pacific. Martin Frobisher in 1576 was the first to encounter the obstacle of Baffin Island and the ice-blocked westward-leading passages.

The Northwest Passage was finally traversed 1903-06 by Norwegian adventurer, Roald Amundsen. The first west to east passage by the RCMP vessel St. Roch under Henry Larsen followed a similar route through the relatively shallow channels along the mainland coast in 1940-42. During the summer of 1944 the St. Roch also became the first to traverse the passage from east to west in a single year. Finally, in 1954, the first ship to achieve the passage from west to east in a single year was the Canadian government icebreaker, Labrador. The first commercial transit of the Northwest Passage didn't occur until 2013 (saving time and money since they didn't have to go through the Panama Canal). At first only a few icebreakers and tankers made full transit. However, rising temperatures and shrinking ice coverage have opened the once-impenetrable passage to the point where a luxury cruise ship made a two-month passage in 2016. Travelers can now experience the mystique of this region, but there are serious concerns due to the environmental sensitivity and some have used the term "extinction tourism". Recognition of Canadian sovereignty was acknowledged by these cruises by the acceptance of two Canadian ice pilots, and by making stops in Canada's Northwest Territories, and two stops in Nunavut.

In May 1845, 129 men and officers under the command of Sir John Franklin set sail on a three-year expedition to explore the Northwest Passage—that is, to find a safe and reliable route from Europe to the Orient. The ship was well stocked with food (including the newly developed concept of canned food), clothing, tobacco, liquor, and other necessities. The ship was lavishly outfitted with luxury items such as an organ for entertainment, mahogany writing desks, school supplies for the men to learn while out at sea, and even a camera. After eighteen months at sea, the men and the two ships disappeared. Numerous expeditions set out to rescue the expedition, but few clues appeared, until 1850 when some desks and tools were found, plus sealed tins of food, leading to speculation that the men died either from lead or food poisoning or after leaving the ships in an effort to go overland to safety.

After many failed attempts by Parks Canada and others to find the ships, Prime Minister Stephen Harper announced in 2014 that one of the ships, HMS Erebus, from the Franklin expedition had been located. The second ship, HMS Terror, was located in 2016. Although the HMS Terror was found in good shape, no bodies were found. How the men died remains a mystery.

Now, let's consider the concerns of the Northwest Passage regarding Canadian sovereignty.

Canada's claim to its far North rests first on the charter granted to the Hudson's Bay Company (HBC) by Charles II in 1670. In June 1870 the HBC transferred title of its lands to Canada, which acquired sovereignty over all of the present-day Northwest Territories and Nunavut except for the arctic islands. This sovereignty has never been questioned, but where doubt has risen over Canada's claims to arctic sovereignty is in the islands north of the Canadian mainland since some of the arctic islands were discovered and explored by Scandinavians or Americans.

An August 2011 news article quoted a French diplomat as indicating that Canada could lose out to Russia regarding Arctic shipping routes because Canada is too small to finance the costs involved in defending its claims in that area or to finance the infrastructure costs to permit commercial shipping. I'm not sure why the French are poking their noses into these icy waters, but this is indicative of Canada's concerns regarding the Northwest Passage. In 1969, the American oil tanker, Manhattan, with the assistance of a Canadian icebreaker, traversed the Northwest Passage, and later the American Polar Sea also traversed it, raising the question of Arctic sovereignty. In early 1988 Canada and the U.S. reached an agreement to permit American icebreakers access to arctic waters, including the Northwest Passage, on a case-by-case basis, without settling the question of sovereignty.

Although Americans made no formal claims in the early years, they were particularly active around Ellesmere Island, and in 1909 Robert Peary reached the North Pole from his base on northern Ellesmere. One of the greatest dangers to Canada's claims came from the expedition of Otto Sverdrup, who between 1898 -1902 discovered a number of islands and claimed them for Norway.

Beginning in the 1880s the Canadian government sponsored periodic patrols to the eastern Arctic in order to establish a presence there in support of its claims. One prominent explorer was Captain J. Bernier who carried out numerous voyages between 1904 and 1925 including setting up a plaque on Melville Island, claiming the Arctic Archipelago for Canada from the mainland to the North Pole. From 1913-18, Henry Stefansson discovered the last of the arctic western islands and claimed them for Canada. But these symbolic acts of raising flags and erecting plaques carried little weight in international law since they were not accompanied by effective occupation or administration.

The first vigorous assertion of Canadian sovereignty in the Arctic came with the establishment of a North West Mounted Police post at Herschel Island in 1903 to control the activities of American whalers in the western arctic by enforcing Canadian laws and showing the flag in the region. After WWI the Americans and Danes still ignored Canada's claims to the high arctic. Canada responded to this challenge to Canada's arctic sovereignty with a plan for effective occupation of Ellesmere and other islands. Though there were no Canadians living within hundreds of kilometres, the RCMP operated a post office there—with mail delivery of once a year—because operation of a post office was an internationally recognized proof of sovereignty. The RCMP also continued its extensive patrols. The RCMP visited each Inuit camp on Baffin Island annually, took the census, explained the law, and reported to Ottawa on local conditions as demonstrations of sovereignty. Norway formally abandoned its claim to the Sverdrup Islands and Ottawa paid Sverdrup for the records of his expeditions, making Canada's formal claim secure.

Controversies regarding Canada's claims now arise from two regions. Although Canada's claim to its arctic lands seem secure, the fact that large areas are uninhabited and virtually undefended raises the possibility that it may not always be secure. While there is international consensus about the land area, the channels and straits, particularly the Northwest Passage, are not universally recognized as Canadian even though Canada regards them as internal waters through which foreign vessels must request permission to pass. With the prospect of bringing home oil from arctic discoveries off Alaska, the U.S. has increasingly seen these passages as international waters, so Canada has offered to submit the matter to the International Court of Justice. Canadian concerns here are an indication of Canadian nationalism rather than an active interest in the region since we generally ignore the north at all other times. It's noteworthy that the Prime Minister has made it a priority to visit the area at least once a year and there are plans for modern icebreakers and submarines. Some have even suggested using commercial heavy lift "modern day blimps" to transport heavy equipment to mines and other locations since this could also be used to establish Canadian sovereignty in the Arctic.

Under international law, no country currently owns the North Pole or the region of the Arctic Ocean surrounding it. The five surrounding Arctic states, Russia, the United States, Canada, Norway and Denmark (via Greenland), are limited to an exclusive economic zone of 200 nautical miles adjacent to their coasts. Upon ratification of the United Nations Convention on the Law of the Sea a country has a ten year period to make claims to an extended continental shelf which, if validated, gives it exclusive rights to resources on or below the seabed of that extended shelf area. Norway, Russia, Canada, and Denmark all launched projects to provide a basis for seabed claims on extended continental shelves beyond their exclusive economic zones. At present, American plans are unclear.

# The Price of Diamonds is *Hard* to Understand

Diamonds are the most beautiful and perhaps the most expensive gems. Women in particular love them. Up to the mid-18th century, India led the world in diamond production and Brazil became a major producer about 1725. Today there are huge diamond deposits in South Africa and other African countries, and now Russia and Canada also produce diamonds. About 30 million carats of cut and polished diamonds are sold every year and over 100 million carats of industrial diamonds.

The price of diamonds, influenced by quality and weight, was largely controlled by the De Beers company in the past. They controlled a substantial portion of the world's rough diamond production by having an exclusive distribution agreement with all the major diamond mines in the world. De Beers regularly invited its major clients, those with diamond and marketing expertise, to London and offers self-sorted batches of rough diamonds for sale. De Beers decided who received which batches of various classifications, quantity, and quality of diamonds, and at what cost. The clients needed to agree or they apparently were not invited back. Without these controls diamonds would have been worth much less. These clients then re-sell the diamonds or cut and polish them into individual gemstones.

A class action lawsuit was filed alleging that De Beers operated as a monopoly and fixed diamond prices by suppressing competition and reducing supply by restricting sales. De Beers subsequently consented to a historic injunction that prohibits them from monopolizing the world supply of rough diamonds and from fixing the price of polished diamonds, and while this hasn't had a dramatic impact on the cost of diamonds market forces now drive the diamond market. De Beers and its legal entities had controlled up to 85% of the world diamond supply, but this has been reduced to about 35% due to various legal and regulatory problems in a number of companies.

The prices of cut diamonds depend on the 4 Cs - Carat, Color, Clarity, and Cut. The difference of one grade in color or clarity could affect the price of diamonds by as much as 25%. Famous diamonds, such as the Hope diamond, are priced because of their prominence and uniqueness. In addition to the 4 Cs, unusual shapes and cuts may also reflect in the price. The clarity and color of the diamond depends on personal perception and is open to interpretation.

A Carat is equal to 200 milligrams and the diamond's weight is calculated to the nearest 1/100th of a carat, expressed as a 'point'. Other parameters being equal, the price of a two-carat diamond could be double that of a one-carat diamond, but could be much higher as larger diamonds are rare and much more in demand. Color is a significant factor when buying diamonds. A perfectly transparent diamond with no hue, or color, is considered a perfect diamond. The color grading scale ranges from D (Colorless) to K (Faint Yellow) to S (Very Light Yellow) to Z (Yellow). The absence of color makes the diamond more valuable and its price changes significantly with each color grade.

Clarity is the clearness or purity of a diamond, that is, the presence or absence of internal flaws. The clearer the diamond, the higher the price. A perfect diamond having perfect clarity is rare. The clarity scale measures the severity of these inclusions or imperfections. Clarity grades are described as Flawless (the rarest, most beautiful, and highest priced) and Internally Flawless. Cut is the 4$^{th}$ C. A good cut adds to the inherent beauty of a diamond and refers to its shape and proportion since a well-cut diamond will reflect light evenly across its surface, maximizing its brilliance while a deep-cut or a shallow-cut will take away from its beauty. Diamonds are cut in a wide variety of shapes, such as round, oval, marquise, pear, emerald, radiant, princess, and heart, with the round brilliant cut being most in demand. Small diamonds (called the melee size) have become more expensive due to increased demand.

## A Brain Testing Trivia Quiz

In my first classic, *100 Vignettes* book, I wrote an essay called, "The Ultimate Trivia Quiz" with this caveat: My brain stores all sorts of trivial information, much of which is eminently useless and impractical. As I get older my brain often seems to be full, so as I acquire more information I randomly lose an equivalent amount of data. For example, even when I periodically watch the television show, *Jeopardy,* I do spectacularly poorly, plus when someone asks me a question, I remember the answer sometime later. If you can answer most of the following questions in this second edition of my trivia quiz, it doesn't necessarily mean that you are brilliant; it may simply indicate that your brain is as unusual as mine. And if you do poorly that may show that you reserve your brain function to process more useful information.

1. What is a standing eight count?
2. Are baby Dalmatian puppies born all black, all white, or with spots?
3. Who is the only heavyweight boxer in history to retire undefeated (49 – 0)?
4. Who is the only player in NHL history to score goals in all five possible ways (even strength, power play, short-handed, penalty shot, and empty net) in one game?
5. Who said, "Friends, Romans, country men, lend me your ears"?
6. What is the capital of Nepal?
7. What is the most popular colour when buying a new car?
8. Which ocean is saltier, the Atlantic or the Pacific?
9. Who defeated Bobby Riggs in the "Battle of the Sexes"?
10. Which is the only country that has a flag that is one solid color?
11. What Vietnamese City changed its name to Ho Chi Minh City?
12. What is the earth's largest continent?
13. What country, in 1893, was the first to give women the vote?

14. Which nursery rhyme was apparently inspired by the plague?
15. What were the two things that Neil Armstrong dropped on his moon walk to test the moon's gravity?
16. Which planet is not named after a classical god?
17. Who was Elvis Presley's long time manager?
18. What kind of shop did Orville and Wilbur Wright operate while they were building and flying their airplane?
19. How many players are typically on a cricket team?
20. Name the three main constituents of poutine.
21. What is Pogonophobia?
22. What is the speed of light?
23. What world-class city is a regular location for meetings negotiating standards or conventions about the rules of warfare?
24. In using dirigibles or blimps, why was hydrogen replaced with helium?
25. What is the most common length of a standard semi-truck trailer?
26. What is a toque (also spelled tuque)?
27. In golf, what is an albatross?
28. Besides Queen Elizabeth, who is the only English monarch to reign for more than sixty years?
29. Why did the English people start driving on the left side of the road?
30. What is the chemical compound that makes tree leaves green?
31. What is a palindrome?
32. What is an erythrocyte?
33. What is a blue moon?
34. In soccer, what does FIFA stand for?
35. Who was the Canadian Winter Olympic athlete (a snowboarder) who inhaled marijuana but didn't smoke it and was part of a joke about President Clinton who smoked pot but didn't inhale?
36. Who was the founder of McDonalds?

37. In the Papa & Mama burger fast food chain, what do the A and the W stand for?
38. What is the fastest land bird?
39. How many earth years does it take the "dwarf planet" Pluto to circulate around the sun?
40. What is an opposable thumb?
41. What is a black light?
42. What is the name of the awards show that recognizes the best commercials?
43. In sports, what is a repêchage?
44. What are the five colors of the Olympic rings?
45. To be designated as the world's fastest man, what race must be won?
46. What kind of work does a farrier do?
47. What is the Southern Cross?
48. We often hear about "Third World" countries. What are the "Second World" countries?
49. In U.S. college football, what is the difference between a true freshman and a red shirt freshman?
50. What is the name of the ring that surrounds the face of a wristwatch?

**Answers:**

(1) A boxing term used where the referee counts to eight when a fighter is woozy but not knocked out and cannot be hit (2) born all white (3) Rocky Marciano (4) Mario Lemieux (5) Marc Antony (6) Kathmandu (7) silver or white (8) the Atlantic (9) Billie Jean King (10) Libya (it's green) (11) Saigon (12) Asia (13) New Zealand (14) Ring around the Rosy (15) an eagle feather and a hammer (16) Earth (17) Col. Tom Parker (18) a bicycle shop (19) 11 (20) cheese curds, gravy, fries (21) the fear of beards (22) 186,000 miles per second (23) Geneva (24) hydrogen is explosive (both elements are lighter than air) (25) 53 feet (26) a knitted tapered cap with no brim often worn by many Canadians in winter (27) an albatross (a rare bird) is three below

par on a given hole, the same as a double eagle (28) Queen Victoria (29) knights were mostly right-handed so those involved in jousting always rode on the left side as they raced towards each other (30) chlorophyll (31) a word or phrase that reads the same forward as it does backward (32) a red blood cell (32) a month which has two full moons, or a rare event (35) Federation of International Football Associations (35) Ross Rebagliati (36) It seems that there are two correct answers; Ray Kroc managed its worldwide expansion after purchasing the chain in 1955 from Richard and Maurice McDonald (37) Allen and Wright (38) The ostrich (39) 248 (40) Some say an opposable thumb is what separates us from the lower animals. Human thumbs move in a different direction than the other digits and are called opposable because the thumb can be moved around to touch the other fingers, which gives people the ability to grasp things (41) an ultraviolet light (UV), is a lamp that emits long-wave ultraviolet radiation, and little visible light (42) The Clio Awards (43) In sports, such as rowing, this is a trial heat in which first-round losers are given another chance to qualify for the semifinals; from the French word meaning second chance or re-examination for a candidate who has failed (44) red, black, green blue, yellow (45) The Olympic 100 M race (46) A farrier trims the hooves of horses and puts horseshoes on them, if necessary (47) The Southern Cross is a constellation or group of stars that is found in the southern region of the night sky. It is the most easily identifiable of all the southern constellations (48) While developed countries are referred to as "First World" countries, those nations in the Soviet Bloc in the late 20th century were called Second World countries since they were reasonably developed but were different in character (49) U.S. college football players are allowed to play for four years. A freshman is a first year player, typically right out of high school. In some cases a coach may decide that he isn't ready to play or won't make the team, or is injured, so they are held out for one year or "red shirted" and the next year they are still considered a freshman for eligibility purposes (50) a bezel.

## The Most Interesting School in Canada

It's highly unlikely that you have ever heard of L'École Nationale d'Horlogerie in Trois-Rivières, Quebec, and it's possible that by the time you read this vignette the last surviving watchmaking school in Canada may no longer exist. The school was established in 1946 as one means of offering returning Canadian World War II servicemen an opportunity to re-establish their lives and learn a valuable skill. I'm paraphrasing and summarizing Wikipedia's story of this fascinating insight into our history and, if you will pardon the pun, how time changes things. You can even learn about a new word, namely "horology" which is the art of measuring time or of making, or repairing, clocks and watches.

These first horology soldiers sat down at their workbenches and learned how to maintain and repair timepieces. This training has continued until recently, with at least fifteen students and two or three teachers. The students are mostly from Quebec but some come from elsewhere in Canada. They are mostly twenty-something year-old men, along with a few women, who see beauty in clock springs, poetry in moving pendulums, and ballet in the movement of gears. The training lasts up to two years and teaches everything from humankind's history of trying to measure time to precision soldering and repairing. "When you see these watches tick, it's like you're seeing their heart, their soul ...the tick-tick-tick brings me to a different time, a different world. It's just so mysterious," one student reported.

The teachers and the students at the Trois-Rivières school, who service the world's clocks and watches while hunched over microscopic pins and springs in the school workshop, say that this is still a valuable vocation. The school says ninety per cent of its graduates find jobs in places like jewelry stores and after-sale service centres, or working on timing mechanisms for vaults and safes.

The place has a magical and fascinating quality to it. One door off the main hallway opens onto a storage room with shelves brimming with vintage alarm clocks; banks of drawers display glistening vials of minuscule watch parts. Another door gives way to dark, wood-encased clocks lined up in rows along the wall. Near the entrance door, a brass-pendulum French clock rings out, oddly, nine times an hour. The school is "a cacophonous testament to the march of time. Cuckoo clocks trill. Grandfather clocks chime. Stout-faced wall clocks mark the passing seconds a tick at a time".

But today, clocks glow from cellphones to microwave ovens and we view watchmakers in the same sentimental way as milkmen and telegraph operators. The introduction of quartz-regulated, battered-operated watches in the 1970s was seen as the death knell of mechanical movements. Watchmaking schools across Canada and the U.S. began closing so that by 2013 the USA had gone from forty-four schools to eight, and Canada down to one. The Trois-Rivières school, halfway between Montreal and Quebec City, had only two full-time teachers in 2013. A committee of the Quebec education department examined the Trois-Rivières trade school in 2013 and concluded that the watchmaking program should be abolished due to declining enrollment. At this writing, that decision is being reviewed. In the meantime, the school is pleading that, while it may suffer from a low profile, it continues to have a raison d'être. "They'd be closing the last school in Canada. We're going to fight for it," said Luc Galvani, the school-board official who oversees the program.

The Trois-Rivières school benefits from a good reputation and, with its mostly bilingual students, offers opportunities to work in watchmaking's "mecca", Switzerland. Graduates on top of their game can make a good living. With an aging workforce the watchmaking world offers opportunities for new blood.

One person who wanted to see it survive is Conrad Gilbert, a Second World War veteran and a former teacher at the École Nationale d'Horlogerie. A regimental sergeant major during the war, Mr. Gilbert learned watchmaking as a young man and devoted his life to it. He said the school served a purpose then, and serves a purpose now. "It showed veterans a trade, a way to earn a living," he recalled from his retirement home in Quebec City. "Why not teach it to the veterans coming back from Afghanistan? The school should stay open. There are always going to be watch repairs to do."

It's a simple message he hopes authorities will heed. It's a matter of time.

## Medical Alphabet Soup

Whether it's from family and friends experiencing various health related procedures, information provided by your doctor, or items in the news, we seem to be bombarded with medical terms that often sound dangerous, painful, or expensive. On the other hand, modern technology has been of tremendous help in enabling us to live longer and more comfortably by detecting and treating disease or injury conditions. Various news sources, our doctors, and websites such as Wikipedia help us find the answers to our medical questions.

Here are some examples:

**CAT Scan**

A CAT scan (Computer Axial Tomography), also called a CT scan, is a medical imaging method that employs tomography (tomo means slice in Greek). The CAT scanner uses digital geometry processing to generate a 3-D image of the inside of an object. The 3-D image is made after many two-dimensional x-ray images are taken—many pictures of the same area are taken from many angles and then placed together to produce the 3-D image (in contrast to x-ray machines which only take flat, two dimensional pictures).

**MRI**

Magnetic Resonance Imaging has been used since the early 1980s. An MRI scanner uses magnetic and radio waves to create pictures of tissues, organs and other structures within the body, which can then be viewed on a computer. The magnetic field that is created of the tissues sends out different signals creating a picture, which enables the doctor or medical technician to distinguish between various structures and tissues.

**ADHD** (Attention deficit hyperactivity disorder)

ADHD describes a problem with inattentiveness, over-activity, and impulsiveness. ADHD is the most commonly diagnosed behavioral disorder of childhood and seems to be set in motion early in life as the brain is developing. It affects almost 5% of school-aged children and seems to be more common in boys than in girls. ADHD should not be confused with depression, lack of sleep, learning disabilities, behavior problems, or consumption of too much sugar.

**Upper body injury** (not to be confused with a lower body injury)

This is the National Hockey League's perverse way of generically describing any injury that's above the waist of an NHL player. It could be a concussion or a broken collarbone or a broken nose or even a bruised ego. Apparently, the NHL brain trust believes that giving any more information about an injured player will provide an unnecessary advantage to opposition teams.

**Ablation**

This is the removal of biological tissue, usually by surgery, although lasers may also be used. Ablation may be used to regenerate skin or remove skin spots and wrinkles, or to remove the tissue that exacerbates snoring. More importantly, ablation is also used to manage atrial fibrillation.

**Coronary Angioplasty**

This is a technique used to dilate an area of arterial blockage with the help of a catheter that has an inflatable small sausage-shaped balloon at its tip. Angioplasty physically opens the channel of a diseased artery and thereby relieves the recurrence of chest pain and reduces other complications of heart disease. Since it is performed through a needle in the groin, or sometimes the arm, it is less invasive than surgery and can be repeated if necessary. A related term is a stent, which is a mesh tube inserted into the body to prevent or counteract a local flow constriction. Stents are sometimes used to ensure that ureters stay open (for example, when a person has a kidney stone) to prevent kidney damage.

**Charley horse**

This is a layman's term for painful cramps or spasms in the leg muscles, which can last from a few seconds to a few hours.

**FAS**

Fetal alcohol syndrome is a pattern of mental and physical defects that can develop in a fetus resulting from high levels of alcohol consumption during pregnancy. Alcohol crosses the placenta, causing stunted fetal growth and resulting in permanent brain damage and distinct facial features and subsequent psychological or behavioral problems.

**MTBI** (mild traumatic brain injury, commonly known as a concussion)

We hear a lot about concussions in sports, but they can happen in car accidents or anytime there is a blow to the head. A concussion is any direct or indirect hit to the head that can cause a change in behavior, awareness, and/or physical feeling. Symptoms, which include headaches, confusion, slurred speech, decreased coordination, and balance and numbness problems, may be evident immediately after the injury or may take days or weeks to appear. Recovery is equally unpredictable. When the head is struck hard, the brain moves violently within the skull so that brain cells all fire at once, much like a seizure. Treatment involves monitoring the symptoms and requiring reduced physical and cognitive activity. Those who have had one concussion seem more susceptible to another. Football players used to call this "having your bell rung" and they were taught to just shake off the cobwebs and keep playing. With new finding, concussions are handled much more seriously now than they were in the past.

**ALS** (Amyotrophic lateral sclerosis) also referred to as Lou Gehrig's disease

This is a debilitating motor neuron disease characterized by rapidly progressive weakness, muscle atrophy and spasticity, and difficulty speaking and swallowing. Eventually most patients are not able to walk. There is no known cause for ALS, and, at this time, no known cure.

**BMI** (body mass index)

Dig out your calculator for a health check. BMI is a measure of human body shape based on an individual's weight and height. It is defined as the individual's body mass divided by the square of their height, which works out to kg/m$^2$. The easiest calculation is your mass in kilograms divided by your height (squared) in metres. For folks who haven't made the switch to metric, the alternative calculation is your mass in pounds divided by your height in inches (squared), and then multiply this number by 703.

BMI became popular for a time because it provided a simple numeric measure of a person's "fatness" or "thinness", which allowed health professionals to discuss overweight and underweight problems more objectively with their patients. A BMI of 20 to 25 is said to indicate optimal weight while a number above 25 may indicate the person is overweight. A BMI over 30 suggests the person is obese and is morbidly obese if it is over 40.

**RSV** (Human respiratory syncytial virus)

This virus is a major cause of infection of the lungs and breathing passages during infancy and childhood. RSV is highly contagious and can be spread through droplets containing the virus when someone coughs or sneezes. It can live on surfaces such as countertops or doorknobs and on hands and clothing (frequent hand washing is key in preventing its transmission). Almost all kids are infected with RSV at least once by the time they're two years old but most are able to fight it off. Two of our grandchildren contacted RSV in the hospital as newborns, and it can be serious for these little ones who have not yet developed sufficient immunity.

## BANANA, Irrationality, and Affluenza

I don't know if he coined this acronym, but Fazil Mihlar wrote a Vancouver Sun column where he explained that BANANA stands for "Build Absolutely Nothing Anywhere Near Anyone". His basic thesis was that we in our modern affluent society are unwilling to take the risks that our ancestors took. We are comfortable, and perhaps, even subconsciously, we don't want to make any changes that might upset the proverbial apple cart. As a result, many of us are opposed to new things and anything that we don't understand.

Most of our fears are irrational in that there is no logical or scientific reason for our opposition to new things or ideas. Mihlar talked about a "culture of fear". Many people are almost automatically, one might say irrationally, opposed to genetically modified foods, electrical transmission lines, offshore oil and gas exploration, and a multitude of other things, without bothering to do any objective research to assess the risks.

Among these folks, there is little recognition that we need to take some risks and incur some costs if our society is to grow economically to support the lifestyle to which we have become accustomed. The basic position for many people seems to be, "I'm okay so don't mess with the status quo." I believe that behind all of this is our affluence and many of us are instinctively afraid that new things or developments will disrupt our comfortable lifestyles. We forget that we enjoy this comfortable life because those that came before us investigated things and took risks.

Mihlar says we "need to dare" and if we don't change our "careful, don't upset anything" attitude we soon will have a lower standard of living. Already Canada has been criticized for having lower than expected productivity, and certainly part of this is due to our reluctance to accept new ideas. Yes, we need to respect and protect the environment, but we can do this with modern technology and appropriate regulations.

A current example of this way of thinking is the opposition by environmentalists and others to gold and copper mining in British Columbia. Suppose that we stop mining exploration and don't develop any new mines, then some products that we need may no longer be readily available. If we extend this opposition to not building any pipelines, or cellular towers, or oil tankers off our coast, or electrical transmission lines, the lost revenue and the loss of jobs would soon mean that more people will be unemployed and the government will not have the revenue to provide the services that we both expect and demand.

Another example is the widespread opposition to fish farming. Never mind that over-fishing and other human activities have decreased the availability of fish in our oceans and rivers or that fish farms currently supply a significant proportion of the fish we eat. It's easier to focus instead on some of the problems observed in fish farms and to listen to those who, for whatever reason, vehemently criticize fish farms than it is to thoroughly investigate the situation, correct any deficiencies and move forward.

For some reason many of us trust the "activists" and "scare mongers" because "everyone knows" that government officials and other experts have vested interests and can't be trusted. Mihlar says that the sight of a few oil-soaked ducks is enough to convince people that we should prohibit oil tankers from entering our waters even though there has not been a major oil spill in British Columbia in the past fifty years. Never mind that we still expect to be able to drive our cars and heat our homes.

Perhaps perversely or irrationally, we are willing to take some risks for things we know about or for some reason, valid or not, that we believe to be necessary but which pose greater risks than some of the things mentioned above. We accept many voluntary risks. For example we are willing to drive our cars even though more than 2,500 Canadians die every year in car accidents. A significant proportion of people are willing to use or abuse alcohol, drugs, or tobacco even though their health will sooner or later be compromised.

BANANA seems to be a first cousin to NIMBY (not in my back yard). NIMBY was first conceived about 1980 to describe someone "who objects to the establishment in one's neighborhood of projects such as incinerators, prisons, or homeless shelters that were believed to be dangerous, unsightly, or otherwise undesirable". However, it has morphed into objecting to even apparently good things that result in neighborhood changes or in a broader area such as a city or province.

Projects likely to be opposed by "Nimbies" include tall buildings, schools, youth hostels, wind farms, golf courses, and mobile telephone network towers, but also "necessary" but more intrusive things like housing developments, chemical plants, industrial parks, desalination plants, landfills, incinerators, power plants, landfill dump sites, and especially transportation improvement plans like new roads or highways, railways, and airports. My favorite NIMBY example is when people move into a new housing development adjacent to a farming area and then vociferously complain about the smell or the noise even though the farms were there for many years before the Nimbies moved in. So it isn't just the fear or reluctance to change that we see in BANANA; for Nimbies it's more about selfishness (and "affluenza") and the refusal to think about the longer-term needs of our neighborhoods and society.

## The Most Dangerous Creatures on Earth

Were sharks or snakes or humans your first thought? Well, if you're judging by how many people are killed every year by dangerous creatures, then the answer isn't any of the above. The correct answer is...mosquitos. And we know this not just because Bill Gates said that mosquitos were the most dangerous creatures in the world. Mosquitos head the list because they spread devastating diseases.

As reported by Mr. Gates, this is a quick summary of some of the world's deadliest animals (according to the number of people killed each year): Sharks (10), lions or elephants (100), crocodiles (1,000), freshwater snails (10,000, by schistosomiasis), tsetse fly (10,000—sleeping sickness), dogs (25,000 –rabies), snakes (50,000), humans (over 475,000) Here's a bulletin: more people are killed by taking "selfies" than by sharks each year, indicating that some people are careless, or stupid, in addition to being evil. And then we come to mosquitoes (725,000 to more than one million through the spread of malaria, dengue fever, yellow fever, West Nile virus, and a dozen or more other dangerous diseases). The Microsoft chairman mentioned these numbers when he delivered a presentation about malaria education and eradication. Malaria is transmitted from person to person via mosquito bites.

Malaria is an infectious disease caused by parasites in the red blood cells. Each year, 350 million to 500 million are infected, according to the U.S. Centers for Disease Control and Prevention, and some reports put the death toll at more than one million per year. The disease is still prevalent on continents such as Africa and Asia, which have tropical or subtropical climates, and there is currently no effective vaccine against malaria. The only good news is that malaria has been eradicated in most countries with temperate climates. Bill Gates asks why we don't talk more about the dangers of mosquitoes when they kill so many more people than do sharks.

Mosquitoes are specially fashioned "little flies" which is what the name means. The term "fly" is a generic word for insects that have only two wings. Mosquitoes can beat their tiny wings at a rate of about one thousand times per second! Their wings are so thin that even the blood vessels show. Only God could have designed this amazing and minute system. So why did a benevolent God create these bothersome and dangerous creatures? We may occasionally wonder why our heavenly Father made certain things, but we should be confident there was a good reason for so doing, recognizing that we don't understand all of the intricacies of nature.

It turns out that mosquitoes actually are a valuable source of food for many creatures that were made to benefit mankind. For example, frogs, lizards, bats, birds, and some fish eat mosquitoes. These insects are an important link in the animal food chain, thus ultimately they are for our benefit as well. Some have suggested that mosquitos prevent overgrazing by animals since they are bothered enough to keep moving when grazing. There is a balance in nature that we sometimes do not recognize or appreciate.

Mosquito-control operations are targeted against three different problems: The first is "nuisance mosquitoes" which bother people around homes or in parks and recreational areas; second are "economically important mosquitoes" which reduce real estate values, adversely affect tourism and related business interests, or negatively impact livestock or poultry production; and third are "public health related mosquitos" which carry and transmit infectious diseases. Some interesting strategies have been proposed to reduce or eliminate the damage caused by mosquitos.

The giant chemical company, Monsanto, among others, is working on genetically modified mosquitos where sterile males would be released into the environment so they would not produce zillions of offspring when they try to mate, with the hopeful result of a dramatic decrease in the mosquito population. This approach has been proposed by the United Nations Office for the Coordination of Humanitarian Affairs to combat dengue fever and malaria. This approach makes environmentalist nervous but environmentalists don't come off well in this area since their furious battle years ago against DDT has resulted in many unnecessary malaria deaths in poor countries. Malaysia and Brazil are also developing strategies to control the mosquitoes that cause dengue fever. In 2014, Brazil's National Technical Commission for Biosecurity approved the commercial release of genetically modified mosquitos, but reports of effectiveness are sketchy.

Some less controversial, and less effective, control methods include the use of chemicals such as DDT (which is still used in some developing countries) and trapping can also be used. Since many mosquitoes breed in standing water, source reduction can be as simple as emptying water from containers and ditches. Biological control or "biocontrol" is the use of natural enemies to manage mosquito populations. This might include the direct introduction of parasites, pathogens and predators (even predatory fish) to target mosquitoes.

## Advent Calendars: From Bible Verses to Chocolates to Beer Cans

Advent is the season observed in Christianity as a time of expectant waiting and preparation for the celebration of the birth of Jesus Christ at Christmas. The term is from the Latin word *adventus*, meaning "coming" and the practice of Advent dates back to the 4th century. Christian denominations start Advent on the fourth Sunday before December 25th. In Western churches Advent is the beginning of the liturgical year, which is highlighted by Christmas, Epiphany, Lent, Easter, and Pentecost.

The theme of readings and teachings during Advent in the Christian church is basically designed as personal preparation for Jesus' second coming while commemorating His first coming at Christmas. Many churches also organize special musical events including singing Christmas carols and even performing the spectacular and inspiring Handel's Messiah. Keeping an Advent wreath is also a common practice in many homes and churches. The first Sunday in Advent remembers the Old Testament patriarchs who looked forward to the coming of Christ, so some call the first Advent candle that of hope. The second Sunday candle is often called the Bethlehem Candle or the candle of preparation where Christians get ready to welcome the Savior. The third Advent candle is the candle of joy, recalling the shepherds' joy as they saw Jesus in the manger. The fourth candle is the Angel Candle or the candle of love announcing the good news of a Savior. On Christmas day, the white Christ Candle in the middle is lit to honour the birth of the spotless Lamb of God.

So what about chocolates and beer cans, and how on earth do they relate to Advent and Christmas? Well, according the Vancouver Sun, the Advent Calendar has come a long way since the early 1800s when German families put a chalk mark on the wall for every day in December until Christmas Eve, as a reminder to prepare with penitence and hope for the coming of Jesus. The first actual Advent calendars date back to 1851 and the first printed calendars were apparently sold in the early 1900s in Germany. Sincere Christians will search for an Advent Calendar where the flap for each day opens to a Bible verse that prepares us for the coming Christ Child. But in 2013, just like much of the secularization of Christmas, one form of the Advent calendar was a cheery cardboard package with twenty-four pictured windows featuring Santa and Rudolph where one flap is opened each day to reveal a sweet chocolate which is a teaser for the big presents that kids of all ages expect on Christmas Day.

But commercialization couldn't stop there. Depending on where you shop, you might find that the "prize" for each day on an "Advent calendar" might be a small container of nail polish or makeup or a small toy such as Lego, or even a diamond. But effective entrepreneurs saw a new marketing opportunity and produced a Canadian craft beer calendar, assembling a collection of twenty-four beers. The Manitoba provincial government liquor stores sold out their supply in just a few minutes the first year and the outlets in British Columbia quickly sold out as well. Other calendars (I now hesitate to call them "Advent calendars") will provide you with small whisky samples.

God gave us the first real Christmas gift in the form of His Son, Jesus, and the Wise Men of the Christmas narrative seem to have started the idea of giving gifts at Christmas. We all now continue to give gifts at this time of year to those whom we love. Certainly, each person is free to celebrate and express his or her "Season's Greetings" in whatever way he or she might choose. But to me it seems sad and a shame that so many people have lost the essence of the Christmas message that God sent His Son Jesus to earth to be born as a baby and subsequently die for our sins. Buy an Advent calendar, even a secular Advent calendar if you must, but why not think about and accept God's great gift to us at Christmas? Then you will not only be able to look forward to Christmas with hope and joy, but also to eternal life in heaven.

## Alfred Nobel – Not a Merchant of Death?

Alfred Nobel was a Swedish industrialist, engineer, and inventor who built bridges and buildings. This construction work inspired Nobel to research new methods of blasting rock and in 1860 he started experimenting with nitroglycerine, which had been recently invented by an Italian chemist. Nitroglycerine is extremely volatile and dangerous in its natural liquid state, and there are stories of massive accidental explosions occurring in the early years of its use. Nobel understood this and he discovered that mixing nitroglycerine with silica would turn the liquid into a malleable, more stable paste now called dynamite. Another advantage of dynamite over nitroglycerine was that it could be cylinder-shaped for insertion into the drilling holes used for blasting rock or for mining.

The Nobel Company built the first factory to manufacture nitroglycerine and dynamite. Nobel also improved the detonator, or blasting cap, so that it could be safely ignited by lighting a fuse, which then detonated the dynamite rods. Nobel held three hundred and fifty-five patents in the fields of electrochemistry, optics, biology, and physiology.

Nobel recognized the destructive power of dynamite but he believed it was a forerunner or portent of peace. However, the invention he naively thought would end all wars, many others saw as an extremely deadly product. When Alfred Nobel's brother died in 1888, a French newspaper mistakenly ran an obituary for Alfred, which called him the "merchant of death." Nobel did not want to go down in history with such a horrible epitaph, so in his will he established the now famous Nobel Prizes. When he died in 1896, Alfred Nobel left behind a nine million dollar endowment fund. His idea was to award five prizes in physics, chemistry, physiology or medicine, literature, and peace (economics was added in 1969) each year to "those who, during the preceding year, have conferred the greatest benefit on mankind." The will didn't spell out the logistics of how the endowment fund would be administered, plus his relatives were shocked they didn't get the money, so it took several years before adequate procedures were developed to make Nobel's vision workable. The first Nobel prizes were awarded in 1901.

Nobel's two executors established the Nobel Foundation in 1900 as a private institution to manage the finances and administration of the Nobel Prizes. The interest from the fund constitutes the monetary prize each year. Each year there are 100 to 250 nominees for each prize. The Nobel Committee sends nomination forms to about 3000 individuals in September of the year preceding the awards, usually to academics working in relevant disciplines. Nominations for the Peace Prize are sent to governments, members of international courts, professors and rectors, former Peace Prize laureates, and current or former members of the Norwegian Nobel Committee.

In addition to the financial knowledge required to manage the funds in the Nobel Foundation, one can imagine that it requires considerable specific expertise in each of the awards committees to ensure the selection of worthy recipients. The Royal Swedish Academy of Sciences awards the Nobel Prize in Physics, the Nobel Prize in Chemistry, and the Nobel Prize in Economics. The Nobel Assembly at Karolinska Institutet awards the Nobel Prize in Physiology or Medicine, and the Swedish Academy grants the Nobel Prize in Literature. The responsibility for awarding the Nobel Peace Prize was initially given to a committee of the Norwegian Parliament, but the ties to the Norwegian Parliament were later weakened to make the committee became more independent.

Each recipient, or Nobel laureate, receives a gold medal, a diploma, and a sum of money, which typically exceeds $1 million U.S. The award ceremonies are held in Stockholm on December 10, the anniversary of Nobel's death, and each laureate is required to give a public lecture on the topic of their prize. The original instructions were that prizes were to be awarded in recognition of discoveries made during the preceding year, but it was found that this didn't allow sufficient time to pass for the impact of work to be recognized and because some discoveries were later discredited or minimized. The awards now recognize scientific discoveries that withstand the test of time. The criterion of the "previous year" is interpreted by the Nobel Assembly as the year when the full impact of the discovery has become evident. This means that some awards are given twenty or more years after the groundbreaking work was done.

The Nobel Committees have periodically been accused of having a political agenda, of ignoring more deserving candidates, and of favouring candidates from Europe, resulting in controversy in the selection of the Nobel laureates. This is less true for the scientific disciplines, but the selections in literature are more subjective and therefore more likely to be questioned. This also applies to the Peace Prize. For example, Mahatma Gandhi, perhaps the strongest symbol of 20th century peace and non-violence, never received the Nobel Peace Prize. When the Dalai Lama was awarded the Peace Prize in 1989, the chairman of the committee said that this was partly a tribute to the memory of Gandhi. On the other hand, the selection of Barack Obama in 2009 led many to question the process of awarding the Peace Prize. Another controversial Nobel Peace Prize award was to Henry Kissinger and Lê Đức Thọ for negotiating a ceasefire between North Vietnam and the U.S even though hostilities were still occurring when the award was announced. Yasser Arafat, Shimon Peres, and Yitzhak Rabin received the Peace Prize in 1994 for their efforts in making peace between Israel and Palestine. After the award was announced one of the five Norwegian Nobel Committee members denounced Arafat as a terrorist and resigned.

## Corruption and the Bribe Payers Index

Webster's Dictionary defines corruption as impairment of integrity, virtue, or moral principle, or an inducement to do wrong by improper or unlawful means such as bribery. Political corruption is the use of legislated powers or opportunities by government officials, or those associated with politicians, for illegitimate private gain.

Corruption is one of the biggest problems existing in the world today. Governments in many countries including government officials at all levels, many private companies, and many unions have some level of corruption. They say that "power corrupts, and absolute power corrupts absolutely". It seems that people with uncontrolled power almost inevitably misuse their decision-making authority for corrupt ends. They are usually able to do this because of the controlled environment in which they work makes it impossible or at least difficult for outsiders to see into how decisions are arrived at, and accountability is thereby obfuscated.

The same political groups that are in a position to obstruct changes also make it possible to line their pockets illicitly. Government corruption at the top levels breeds corruption at lower levels where ordinary people need to pay to obtain even basic services. In some countries, it seems common to do business using envelopes of cash just to get things done. If bribes are not paid, all kinds of problems can occur, such as foot-dragging, missed deadlines, and holding back information on a tendering process so that only favoured companies meet deadlines. Corruption is widespread even in developing countries and has very serious repercussions on their peoples' quality of life, particularly the poor.

Corruption, of course, is not by any means limited to government, and we have some spectacular examples in industry as well. Companies and governments should be concerned about corruption not only because corruption leads to the abuse of resources but also because employees and customers see that this practice is acceptable and eventually the integrity of the organization will be compromised. I heard a story where a CEO asked one of his employees to lie for him, and he first became angry when the employee refused to do so. The CEO then realized he had an employee with integrity when the employee then told him that if he could lie for him he could also lie to him and he was sure that the CEO would not want that.

Transparency International reported that a 2005 study in India found that more than 55% of Indians had first-hand experience of paying bribes or influence peddling to get things done in public offices. The rise to fame in 2011 of anti-corruption activist, Anna Hazare, brought to light the government corruption problems in India, where bribes were required to obtain many government services such as business permits and birth certificates. Hazare quickly became a national figure with a huge following and his campaign illustrated a deep reservoir of discontent among India's growing middle class. He became so popular that the majority government felt massive pressure to take at least some action in developing stronger anti-corruption laws. Apparently his fame, and whatever success he achieved, was fleeting since he rapidly disappeared from public view.

There were several news reports in November 2011 indicating that Canada's reputation for honesty in doing business overseas had slipped from #1 in the world to #6. The anti-corruption group, Transparency International, produces a "Bribe Payers Index" which rates countries from the twenty-eight leading economies in the world on their likelihood to pay bribes to foreign governments or companies. They concluded that Canada's performance (with a score of 8.5 out of 10) in fighting bribery and corruption has been lackluster, although this seems a bit harsh in comparison to other countries. Netherlands, Switzerland, Belgium, Germany and Japan were ahead of Canada. The U.S. was #10 at 8.1. It was no great surprise to see Mexico, China, and Russia at positions #26 to #28, since we hear a lot about corruption in these countries.

A comparable review, called the Corruption Perception Index (CPI) had Denmark, New Zealand, and Singapore tied at the top of a similar list, while Canada was rated second and the U.S. came in at #22. The CPI rated countries according to their level of corruption in bribery of public officials, kickbacks in public procurement, embezzlement of public funds, and strength and effectiveness of public sector anti-corruption. Perhaps not surprisingly, Somalia, which some have called the least governable country in the world, was at the bottom of the list with a score of 1.1 while Afghanistan and Myanmar (Burma) were at 1.4.

The finance industry has seen some spectacular examples of fraud and corruption and questionable ethics. Enron, formed in 1985, used accounting loopholes and creative financial reporting to hide billions in debt from failed deals and projects. The Chief Financial Officer and other executives not only misled Enron's board of directors and audit committee on high-risk accounting practices, but also pressured their accounting auditors to ignore the questionable practices. Shareholders lost nearly $11 billion when Enron's stock price plunged from $90 per share in mid-2000 to less than $1 by the end of November 2001. Some Enron executives were indicted for a variety of charges and sentenced to prison. The financial industry, at least in the U.S. has been the recipient of billions of dollars in taxpayer bail-out funds, but even when companies are doing poorly or even going bankrupt, the executives may be paid extraordinarily huge bonuses. It's a sad day when "business ethics" becomes an oxymoron.

## Childhood and Youth Memories

I was born in the early 1940s, so if you are under fifty you can read the following as ancient history, and if you are under fifty with no farming background you may regard this as a report from some prehistoric civilization.

I spent my first five years on a little farm near New Sarepta, Alberta, which is southeast of Edmonton. My earliest memory is that of a little unpainted house that was icy cold in winter. I can also recall my father branding some calves beside a corral. He and whoever was helping him used a branding iron that was heated in a bonfire; branding apparently was necessary since some of his cattle roamed freely in the summertime by a local lake.

I thought I remembered my Dad building a new barn, but my older brother informed me it was built several years before I was born, so I guess I just recall seeing the barn in our farmyard. I recall my older brother and sister sometimes riding to school in winter in a "one horse open sleigh". I recollect riding to church one Christmas Eve in a horse-pulled, big, flat sleigh with side boards when I was probably four; the sleigh was filled with straw and blankets to keep us warm. Bells on the horses' harness added to the Christmas atmosphere.

My mom liked to maintain the German tradition of lighting real candles in glass or metal holders on the Christmas tree. It's a beautiful sight though we always had water handy in case of a fire.

In the summertime we went to the church festival or picnic, called a "fest". There were heaps of food and lots of running around by the kids, but probably a church service as well.

The spring that I was five we moved to a larger farm near Bawlf, Alberta, east of Camrose. The night before my first day of school in Grade One, my Mom asked me how many sandwiches I wanted. I had no idea. (To me at the time, that was like asking you how many nephrons there are in a human kidney). I think I said eight, but I suspect Mom used her own judgment.

That first year we rode seven miles to school on a bus that had wooden seats. Seats were assigned and I had to sit with two crabby (I thought) high school *girls*! In Grade Four I learned to write using a fountain pen (ball point pens hadn't been invented yet) and had to periodically fill the pen's ink chamber from an inkbottle. Inevitably, a kid would spill the contents of the bottle all over a desk and the floor. I think that I held off until after Christmas before I added to the stains on the schoolroom floor.

Since Alberta winters can be extremely cold, our school would make hot soup for lunch and the farm kids would take turns bringing milk. This was before plastic containers were commonplace, and every once in a while the two quart glass jars would be accidentally broken on the bus, which made a big mess as the milk slopped on the floor.

In our living room we had a four-foot high floor-standing radio that was powered by two batteries of the size used in cars and since the signal gradually weakened, every few months Dad had to take them to town to be recharged. I remember, at about the age of seven, sitting in front of this radio with my little sister listening in awe to some program right after the batteries had been charged.

I remember Dad upgrading and repairing the barn, and along with my older brother I climbed up on the roof. It was a dangerous thing to do unless you were a farmer and used to such activities.

One day in early December when I was in Grade Six, I found out one of my classmates had been promoted to Grade Seven. I thought I generally had better marks than she did, so I reasoned if she could skip the rest of Grade Six then I should be able to do this as well. I talked to my Mom and Dad and they talked to the teacher and in a few days I was also in Grade Seven. For about a month, I had double the homework as I did the regular assignments plus lots of catch up work. Although Bawlf was a small village of only a few hundred, the school had over 200 students from Grades One to Twelve, as buses brought kids to school from the surrounding areas. There were just seventeen students in my Grade Twelve graduating class and only four teachers for the various Grade Nine through Twelve high school subjects. We didn't have a gym so at noon hour we played outside, even in winter. It must have been a sight seeing all the boys play soccer in parkas and winter boots.

The little village of Bawlf was a social centre for the community, especially on Saturday nights. After dropping their kids off to go to "the show" the parents would have coffee with neighbours in one of the two restaurants, or shop at the grocery store, hardware store, and drug store. In addition to a garage or two plus some grain elevators, that comprised the village.

The spring I was eleven, our church had a week of evangelistic meetings and one night Mom and Dad took my sister and me. Both of us kids were impressed by our need to commit our lives to Jesus and on the way home we discussed what to do and how to ask Mom and Dad to help us with this decision. When we arrived at home we finally told them what we wanted to do and we knelt down with them in the living room and asked Jesus into our hearts. The next night we went back to church and made a public commitment by walking to the front when the speaker gave the invitation. That was the beginning, and it's been an interesting walk with the Lord since then!

We had initially gone to a Baptist Church in Camrose after moving to the Bawlf farm, but Camrose was too far away in winter. Because we went to school in Bawlf and some of our neighbours went to church in Bawlf, and because my mom's family had a Lutheran history we soon started attending the Bawlf Lutheran church. When I was fifteen, I started going to confirmation classes, essentially Lutheran theology lessons, on Saturday mornings for a year. At the end of the year I was confirmed. This meant that, along with the other teens in the class, I publicly confirmed my commitment to Christ.

We were relatively poor but we didn`t know it, and we always had plenty of food to eat. Mom had a big garden. I had the jobs of hauling water and weeding for hours on end. I also rode our horse pulling a one-bottom plow while my dad held the plow straight and Mom or my sisters followed behind planting the potatoes.

We had a huge raspberry patch and enjoyed fresh raspberries with rich cream in summer and in winter we ate canned raspberries. Mom and Dad went to Safeway in the fall to buy boxes of peaches, pears, plums, and apricots and the produce man would open each box to show that there were no spoiled ones. Mom would then can dozens of two-quart jars of fruit we enjoyed all winter.

We had plenty to eat because of the animals on the farm. We always had at least a hundred chickens. In spring, Dad would clean an empty granary, buy about 300 chicks and proceed to feed them. By the end of summer the hens were carried off to the chicken barn and the roosters were put into huge crates to be sold. The old hens were either sold or served for dinner; many were canned for consumption in winter.

We had all the eggs we needed for eating and baking. Once a week, my sister and I washed eggs and put them in cardboard cartons and then a wooden box to take to town for sale. Every so often Dad would kill a steer or a pig and the meat was taken to a freezer locker in Camrose where my parents would pick up a couple of packages each week when they went to town.

This was necessary because we had no electricity on our farm until I was about twelve years old. Calgary Power brought electricity to our part of rural Alberta. We continued to use the coal and wood stove to heat the house. Dad brought in a potbellied stove to heat the living room in winter but once electricity came along, we could replace the white gas lantern and the kerosene lamps that we used for light in the house.

When we got electricity Dad installed a milking machine in the barn so we could milk more cows. We used a cream separator to separate the milk and cream; the cream was sold and the skim milk fed to calves that either came from our cows or Dad had bought from dairy farms.

One March we had a terrific blizzard so that we couldn't go to school for a week and after five or six days the snowplow finally came so the delivery truck could take the cream cans to town.

Each August we went to Camrose to buy school clothes and new shoes. The shoe salesman would let us put our feet under a fluorescent light so that we could see the bones of our feet and know that there was lots of room in a shoe for our feet to grow. (Shoe store proprietors eventually realized that this wasn't a wise thing to do.) My mom poured over the Eaton's catalogue and the Simpsons Sears catalogues each fall, and she would order winter clothes for all us kids, plus Christmas presents. (Modern city folks may be horrified to learn that the catalogues served another useful function in the outdoor privy.)

We never did have indoor plumbing in our farmhouse and I often had to lug many pails of water from the pump house to the house on laundry day. My mom loved to read so I had access to many books such as the Hardy Boys, the Bobbsey Twins, and the Sugar Creek Gang series. Since I had five sisters, I also read almost all of the Anne of Green Gables series.

I recall walking from the house to the barn on a cold winter evening and seeing the spectacular Northern Lights splash across the sky with all the star constellations also in sight. The advantage of living out in the country where it's completely dark at night is being able to see this dramatic light display. When I walked into the warm barn I could feel the contentment and peacefulness as the cows ate their hay and chewed their cud.

I always liked fall when I was young because of the opportunity to help with harvesting the grain from our fields. After my big brother left home, my job was to take the tractor and wagon to haul the grain from the combine as Dad drove along picking up the swaths and threshing the wheat or oats. I shoveled the grain off the wagon into an auger that lifted the grain into the granary. It was cool doing this at night, often until late a night when it got too damp to harvest. The engines seem to hum along better at night.

When I was younger, harvesting was done by cutting the grain with a binder, a wonderful tractor-pulled machine that cut the grain, tied it up into manageable bundles that were carried along until five or six had been collected at which point they were dropped on the ground. A man would come along and stand them up in piles or stooks. My dad worked with a local farmer who owned a threshing machine and would take it to several other farms. All the farmers helped each farm in turn to do the threshing. They picked up the stooks by horse and wagon and took them to the threshing machine where the kernels were separated from the stalks or straw. The straw was blown out to make a huge straw pile while the grain was dumped into a granary. My job was to shovel the grain away from the opening of the granary.

Perhaps you can relate to the following memory. A week after I finished Grade Twelve I took the bus to Edmonton and began my pharmacy apprenticeship. About two weeks later I went home for a visit, but it wasn't home anymore. It was the strangest feeling. It used to be my home but now it wasn't, not really. My younger siblings were doing the chores I used to do and I wasn't needed anymore. Someone once said that home isn't a place; it is a relationship. I found my relationship with my parents and siblings had changed. I was still loved but was getting used to the idea of growing up as an independent person.

## Interesting Countries

I suppose that you can make the argument that every country is interesting but I've selected a few that resonate with me for one reason or another.

Some think Canada is pretty dull vanilla known only for hockey and cold weather, but it's interesting to me for several reasons. Canada is the second largest county in the world by area, and it stretches from St. John's, Newfoundland to Tofino, British Columbia, a distance of about 7400 km. Approximately 90% of Canada's thirty-five million people live within 100 miles of the U.S. border. The people who rate such things assert Canada to be the 8$^{th}$ "happiest" country in the world currently (Denmark is #1; the U.S. is only 17$^{th}$). Canada has fantastic scenery including prairies, mountains, oceans, rivers, lakes, and glaciers.

Indonesia is a fascinating and diverse country. It is composed of 17,500 islands, thirty-three provinces and 722 languages with many ethnic groups and religions, and a diverse political agenda. Holding the nation together must be a monumental task but so far they seem to be managing.

Ireland seems special, and it has a certain mystique. Everybody seems to love the Irish (with the exception of some Brits in the past) and their beautiful accent, and many wear green on St. Patrick's Day. On the other hand, Ireland has had a torturous history. Northern Ireland is part of Great Britain, and the Republic of Ireland, which constitutes about 83% of this beautiful island with its rolling green hills, is not. The struggles between Protestants and Catholics and the role of the Irish Republican Army have been well chronicled, but the Irish seem to have moved beyond "The Troubles" now.

I'm considering Russia and Iran together. They both interest me because of their intriguing histories and because I think they are two of the most dangerous countries in the world today. The Czars reigned, sometimes in beneficence and sometimes in cruelty, over the far-flung

Russian empire, the largest country in the world, for many years only to be replaced by the ruthless and ideological communists in 1917. For a while in the 1980s it looked like democracy and capitalism might gain a foothold, but the love of power by government leaders, and widespread corruption soon changed that. And even today Russians seem to be paranoid (everybody is against us) which helps explain why so many of them support ruthless corrupt and aggressive leaders like Vladimir Putin.

Iran is one of the world's oldest civilizations. You probably heard about Persia if you were listening in high school. A Shah ruled Iran after 1925, and in 1979 Iran became a republic with Ayatollah Khomeini becoming symbolic of the radical Muslims who have ruled the country since then. Iran's claim to fame in 2012 was the development of nuclear capability. They claim it is for peaceful purposes, of course, but are also on record as promising to obliterate Israel.

Vatican City is the smallest independent state in the world at 0.2 square miles, with a population of only 770. The tiny country surrounding St. Peter's Basilica is the spiritual centre for the world's Roman Catholics. It's difficult to think of Vatican City as a country, but it is recognized as a sovereign nation and it maintains international relations with at least 174 countries. It even issues its own stamps and coins and tourist mementos, which generates government revenue in addition to fees for admission to museums and the sale of publications.

The U.S. is a fascinating country. While it is often described at the world's only "super power" there is some concern that its political and economic systems are now broken. On the other hand, the U.S. has always been known for its ability and courage to solve tough problems. This nation was born out of revolution and a desire for freedom. The civil war of 1861 to 1865 was a pivotal part in its history, but freeing of slaves came grudgingly. It took the charismatic non-violent resistance leadership of Martin Luther King in the 1960s, and the emergence of black athletes, to push the cause of equality along. The U.S. has a varied climate ranging from the continual summers in

Hawaii, California, and Florida to the snow and ice of Alaska, Minnesota, and North Dakota.

Nepal has a great mystique because it contains eight of the world's highest mountains, including Mt. Everest. The capital city of Kathmandu is a jumping off point for the thousands of mountain climbers who come to tackle these mountains, and the Sherpas have deservedly gained fame as experts for their capabilities in hauling gear up the tough peaks. Nepal was a monarchy for most of its history but is now a democratic republic of thirty million people, led by a President.

You probably have never heard of the Republic of Kiribati. I hadn't either until we took a Hawaiian cruise. Due to the requirements of the U.S. Jones Act, the cruise ship had to visit an international port which turned out to be Fanning Island some 1200 miles away (and only 228 nautical miles north of the equator). Fanning Island is part of the Republic of Kiribati, which has a population of about 100,000 with thirty-two atolls (coral reefs) plus one coral island, all spread over 3.5 million square kilometres. Fanning Island apparently has a supply ship come from Australia twice a year. Kiribati gained freedom from Great Britain in 1979, and is a member of the IMF and the World Bank, and a member of the United Nations since 1999. Kiribati is the easternmost country in the world, so it is always the first to enter a new year. You may have heard about Christmas Island, which is part of Kiribati.

Here's another "daily double" —Greece and Brazil. Brazil isn't only famous for the Amazon River and the rainforest or their extravagant celebration of Mardi Gras. In the 1980s and 90s Brazil's economy was in tatters with rampant inflation, but eventually they summoned the courage to make tough decisions and they grew to become the world's seventh largest economy. But they still have serious problems with poverty and crime and have again experienced economic problems. Greece is in a difficult financial situation and seems on the brink of going bankrupt. Neither the Greek politicians nor the people seem prepared to lower their sense of entitlement and to stop avoiding paying taxes or cut down generous pensions or salaries. They have such an incredible history and it's sad to see the country descend into chaos.

## Stupidity May Be Contagious

There are dozens of "scientific" studies published every day, some of which lead one to consider if they really are scientific and objective or if the authors just have an axe to grind and have set out to prove something after already forming a conclusion.

A new study suggests that stupidity may be, at least temporarily, contagious. (If this is true, you may wish to consider right now whether you should continue reading this vignette). The study in question assessed the effects of watching mindless TV programs and movies. Various studies show that people are subtly but significantly influenced by what they watch and read. While we should be concerned about the effects on children who watch aggressive actions or play violent video games, there also may be a negative effect of watching a lot of mindless or "intellectually challenged" movies. For example, after watching a movie where the characters are excessively stupid or are doing stupid things, it's likely that the watcher's "cognitive skills" may be temporarily impaired.

Another side of this issue is why some people do "stupid" things, like participate in a riot after a Stanley Cup game. Some people just get caught up in the excitement and do dumb things that they otherwise would not think about doing. The "mob mentality" is a powerful force, but one still wonders why some individuals suddenly lose their sense of right and wrong. Generally, our brain has built-in alarm systems to help us be cautious and conscientious, but when this alarm system fails we become careless or do reckless things. Alcohol can turn off this alarm system and is particularly a problem when one's moral compass is a bit loose to begin with.

A considerable amount of work has been done to increase our understanding of why some youth become "delinquents". As individuals grow they demonstrate at least three indications of maturity, namely the ability to learn from mistakes, ability to function as individuals, and moderate expression of thoughts and actions. Delinquents have trouble in these areas. Adolescents require strong emotional relationships, hopefully with their parents, as they develop their sense of personal identity and well-being. In addition to a variety of other issues, the behavior demonstrated by a significant number of young people in the June 2011 Vancouver "Stanley Cup" riot suggests that poor parenting was a factor. Most of the participants, apart from the "professional anarchists" who came prepared to do violence, were not delinquents but clearly fell prey to other internal and external pressures.

This doesn't have anything to do with stupidity or delinquency, but I read about a study that showed that substances such as drugs act differently on the developing brain than on the adult brain. The conclusions in this report were that one in four adults who began using any addictive substance before they were eighteen became addicted, in contrast to one in twenty-five adults who started using drugs after they were twenty-one years of age. Apparently 75% of American high school students have used addictive substances, so the authors suggest it is time we stopped passing off substance use as adolescent behaviour and that ordinary adults, as well as the rich and famous, stop portraying smoking, drinking, plus marijuana and other drug use as glamorous or fun.

Stupidity is defined as the state or fact of lacking intelligence, so I suppose that the opposite of stupidity is intelligence or the ability to learn. Some researchers have determined that the Internet is dramatically changing how we learn and how we remember. They have called this the "Google Effect" since the premise is "why would we try to learn or remember something when we can just look it up by "googling" our question?" Apparently, we are getting better at remembering *where* to find information rather than remembering the facts themselves. Our ancestors used the extended family and friends as sources of information whereas today we use the Internet. On the other hand (there always is another hand), it may be easier to understand an abstract concept if our brain is not concentrating on memorizing facts. I suppose that good teachers have known this for a long time since they encourage students to think, not just to memorize.

## Can You be a Christian Pastor *And* an Atheist?

Could a person, let's call him Roger, who is a dedicated Socialist committed to nationalization of his country's largest businesses and banks expect to be accepted as a member of a right wing political party? Would the party feel obligated to accept the membership of this person to avoid hurting Roger's feelings or avoid being accused of intolerance?

The answers seem to be obvious and yet we see this happening in the United Church of Canada (UCC). Douglas Todd, a Vancouver Sun religion columnist, has written about the changing beliefs of the UCC. The pastor of a small Toronto UCC parish is a self-proclaimed atheist, describing herself as a "minister/writer/atheist", and the author of two best-selling books on atheism's "superiority". Some outsiders are asking why a "Christian" church would allow an atheist to be in the clergy. The interesting thing is that the UCC has allowed this situation to go on for at least fourteen years and only now is the church's Toronto presbytery "politely" asking if this person is performing her religious duties. As of this writing it seems that her dubious employment will continue for the foreseeable future.

In the 1950s the once-influential UCC was frequently considered as the conscience of Canada, and more than 2.5 million Canadians still claim affiliation. But UCC membership has declined precipitously in recent years. One church historian has attributed this in part to the UCC's embrace of secularism, pluralism, and multiculturalism. On their own, these are not necessarily bad things but in a Christian church full bore acceptance of secularism while abandoning basic Christian beliefs seems highly contradictory.

Another historian claimed that the UCC faltered because it has promoted personal freedom above morality. The UCC has become so freedom fixated and so focused on accepting everyone and being ultra-inclusive that it seems to have lost its reason for being. If the UCC has stopped being Christian they should say so and become a social organization that at least would help feed or house people without giving anyone a false impressions of being Christian. The problem at the UCC apparently is that there are many pastors and lay members who also have these vague but contradictory pseudo-Christian views.

Douglas Todd stated that one of the problems is that "atheist UCC pastors" and many UCC members have lost sight of the Christian concept of God. One UCC member indicated that she was offended by a prayer offered in Jesus name since she was a Buddhist. That seems to me to be pretty incredible and contradictory if the church is Christian. It would be like a person working for Coca Cola complaining that Pepsi wasn't being promoted by them since it was a superior product.

Many individuals today do explore their doubts and curiosity about God. Some leave the Christian faith while others come to know the eternal God through Jesus Christ who created the world and provided a way of salvation for every person who accepts him as Lord and Savior. But it doesn't seem logical or acceptable for a so-called Christian pastor to consistently declare that there is no God. Such individuals should find another line of work. Todd suggested that it's time for the UCC to become more honest (rejecting a personal God if they no longer believe in him) and decide what they really stand for and believe.

The UCC has been in transition for many years. Some congregations have left the UCC and established themselves as Bible-believing, God-honoring churches. Others have continued their liberal drift and now face this identity crisis, trying to decide their reason for being. Do they want to jettison their belief in a God as an eternal being and be an agency committed to social activities such as helping others—a fine objective but not necessarily requiring belief in God? Do they want to be pantheists who believe that the universe, or nature, is identical with divinity? Or will they accept the fact that "everything" constitutes an all-encompassing, immanent personal God?

The short answer, realistically, to the title question is –no! The UCC may be an effective social organization, but its apparent departure from conservative Christian theology is tragic.

## My Retirement Party

I retired from the Canadian federal government after working in Ottawa and Vancouver for thirty-five years. I took early retirement (I started work when I was very young) just before I turned sixty. I had been the Chief of the Food and Drug Laboratories in Vancouver/Burnaby for twenty-six years, first for Health Canada and for the last few years as manager for CFIA (Canadian Food Inspection Agency). My colleagues graciously decided to hold a retirement party for me at a banquet facility in a local hotel. My friend, Dale, was the Master of Ceremonies. He started with the following top ten list, in his own words, in response to the question of how he was picked to be the MC.

"Well, there was a committee to organize a retirement party for Jerry and they got to talking what they needed. Among other details for the party, they decided that the MC had to have certain characteristics to do justice to Jerry's retirement. Bearing in mind that a committee made these decisions, the following list was developed and that was why they chose me.

1. The person needed to know Jerry really well. I hardly know Jerry apart from having lunch with him almost every day and exchanging what he calls jokes.
2. The person had to have worked with Jerry for a number of years. Well, I have never worked with Jerry.
3. The candidate had to be an employee of CFIA. Not me. With all the changes in Health Canada I'm not even sure whom I work for.
4. The person had to relate to Jerry on a scientific level. It is well known that Jerry is a renowned PhD and research scientist [sic]. I on the other hand am the only person in this organization that doesn't have a degree in science. In fact, I am the only person that doesn't have a degree at all.

5. The candidate had to be available on the night of the party. I wasn't, so they changed the date.
6. The candidate had to be as serious as Jerry. Well, you know how serious I am.
7. The person had to be as physically fit as Jerry. The truth is in the eye of the beholder. [Dale tips the scale at a high rate.]
8. The person was to be someone with as much hair as Jerry. I know I have him beat here.
9. The person had to be a Toastmaster. Well, I am a toast master. I can put away a pound of toast at a single sitting.
10. So why did they pick me? Because I came through the door just as they were selecting the MC, and they asked me, "Dale, would you be prepared to be on the organizing committee?" I said "Sure." And they said "Great! ... That will be thirty-six bucks and your job is Master of Ceremonies." So, here we are tonight!"

With that hilarious introduction, the evening got off to a fine start. There were about fifty people there, including my sweetie and all of our kids, and we had a fabulous dinner. Dale presented me with a framed TIME magazine cover that had my picture on it with a few headlines relating to my career highlights. Dale knew how to use Photoshop and other computer tricks, but this picture is a priceless memory from my friend reflecting many hours of work. And one of my senior colleagues gave me a soapstone carving of a dolphin, which I will always treasure. Dale and the organizing committee also presented an informative and intriguing slide show illustrating my career and family life, and there were a few speeches.

Finally, I had to give a speech. I started out by saying that a retirement dinner speech was rather like being at your own funeral where people say all sorts of nice things about you, except that here one is actually able to enjoy all the compliments even if they aren't necessarily deserved. I went on to say that I was reminded of the story of Tom Sawyer and Huckleberry Finn, two scallywag boys well known for their antics. One day they went rafting down the river and when they didn't come back after an extended period the townspeople decided that the boys had drowned so they organized a memorial service. Huck and Tom happened to come back just as the service was being held and when they saw all of the horses and buggies pulled up by the church they quietly sneaked up to the balcony to see what was going on. They heard a bunch of speeches about two wonderful boys who had demonstrated such great character and devotion. Tom and Huck couldn't figure out who was being honoured, but finally someone saw the boys and after much consternation things returned to normal. Anyway, I thanked my friends and colleagues for their kind wishes and recalled some of the good times that we had together. It was a great evening culminating my working career.

## Service Organizations

Many men and women use their spare time, or their retirement years, to "give back" to society as a gesture of thanks for the freedoms and the "stuff" that most of us enjoy in Canada. Service organizations, and I'll include churches in this discussion, are a significant part of the glue that holds communities together. In a Vancouver Sun(?) article, Stephen Hume estimated that Canadians contribute two billion hours, which is perhaps equivalent to about one million fulltime jobs, each year to make our communities better places in which to live. And today, "community" doesn't just mean our local neighborhood; it also means the entire globe.

The list of what services Canadian organizations provide is long. This includes funding expensive equipment for hospitals and other health care initiatives, helping boys and girls go to summer camp or to a weekly activity during the year, providing meals for the homeless, helping veterans cope with the transition to civilian life, helping new Canadians adapt to our culture, visiting with seniors, helping physically challenged and burned kids, providing donations to food banks and helping distribute donated food, and so on and so on! Besides churches, service organizations include the Canadian Legion, Rotary, Lions, Kinsmen, Kiwanis, and Shriners (the guys with the funny hats). There are many more, too numerous to mention.

The Royal Canadian Legion is the largest volunteer organization in British Columbia; their list of activities includes supporting Remembrance Day through poppy sales, sponsoring housing and social interaction, providing health care information to veterans and their families, plus scholarships to young people. A major emphasis for the Lions is blindness prevention as well as sight and hearing conservation. Among other activities, the Kiwanis target iodine deficiency, which is a leading cause of physical and mental disability in developing countries. They also provide affordable housing for seniors plus support youth activities, and they donated the land for the G.F. Strong Rehabilitation Centre in Vancouver that develops prosthetics for kids and adults. The Salvation Army provides food and shelter for many individuals and raises much of their revenue through the "Christmas Kettles" each December. The Union Gospel Mission in Vancouver has recently expanded its facilities and programs to assist the homeless and those with addictions.

One of the best-known charities is the Canadian Red Cross. For over 130 years the Red Cross has responded to tragedies by providing medical and logistical care as well as equipment and money. Dr. George Ryerson created the Red Cross flag in 1885 while caring for the sick and wounded during the Northwest Rebellion led by Louis Riel in Saskatchewan and Manitoba. Since then the Canadian Red Cross has responded effectively to many tragedies, including the 1917 Halifax Explosion, the 2010 Haiti Earthquake (where their support included providing temporary transition shelters), the 2013 Lac-Megantic rail disaster, and the 2016 Fort McMurray wild fire. Another major focus of the Red Cross has been water safety.

While over 90% of adult Canadians make charitable donations to service organizations, one study reported that less than one-third of them volunteered their time. There is the further concern that fewer Canadians are volunteering today; Statistics Canada reports that the decline is as high as 15%. Some organizations are struggling to retain or recruit members while others seem to be doing fine. The decline may be in part to our aging population where young people may have more demands on their time and are more preoccupied in carving out a living in our global complex modern world. Perhaps the need for social interaction is being met more through Facebook and Twitter than by meeting regularly with other like-minded folks. One of the keys is getting people to be active in their communities and to look beyond themselves and their families.

One church that I know about has a variety of community related programs. These include helping families by having programs for handicapped children to give their parents a break, working with men and women to deal with loneliness and frustration after divorce, planning activities for seniors, helping men address issues relating to pornography, bringing eligible minimum security prisoners to church and small group meetings, providing activities (and baby-sitting) for young moms so they can get out of the house at least once a week, and providing a place for teen agers to hang out, get a meal, or do laundry.

Many churches and individuals support the Samaritan Purse "Christmas Shoe Boxes" which are distributed to children in poor countries around the world.

One last thought – if you are not sure to which agencies you should donate, it would be good to contact CanadaHelps, which is an online umbrella organization that helps people donate to Canadian charities. CanadaHelps provides charities with a framework to communicate their goals and measure progress and impact. It's important to be aware of administration costs for any charity but it is also useful to know what they have done.

# House Churches and Three-Self Churches in China

Christianity in China (the PRC) is a growing minority religion that comprises Protestants, Catholics and a small number of Orthodox Christians. Although Christianity in China is not as ancient as the institutional religions of Taoism and Buddhism, and the social ideology of Confucianism, Christianity has existed in China since at least the seventh century. The growth of Christianity has been evident in China for about 200 years. Chinese adults are permitted to be involved with officially sanctioned Christian meetings through the "China Christian Council" (an umbrella and support organization for all Protestant congregations), the "Three-Self Patriotic Movement" or the "Chinese Catholic Patriotic Association", but many Chinese Christians also meet in independent "unregistered" houses or "underground" churches. These unofficial non-registered churches generally cannot own property so they usually they meet in private houses, often in secret for fear of arrest or imprisonment. There was a period in the past when the Three Self church actually served as the Communist government's informant and helped it persecute the underground church.

China's churches started experiencing very significant growth after the conclusion of the Cultural Revolution in 1976. A successor to Chairman Mao, Deng Xiaoping, reformed politics, liberalized the economy, and opened China to foreign countries. The Chinese house church movement developed after 1949 as a result of the Communist government policy requiring the registration of all religious organizations. This supervision may involve interference in the church's internal affairs either by government officials or others who are approved by the Communist Party. During the Cultural Revolution of 1966-1976 all Christian worship was forced underground after the official churches were closed, so the house church movement was solidified as an ongoing phenomenon.

Because house churches operated outside government regulations and restrictions, local government officials frequently harassed their members and leaders. This persecution could take the form of a prison sentence or re-education through labor. Heavy fines were also not uncommon, with personal effects being confiscated in lieu if payment was refused or unavailable. House churches were outlawed officially from the 1950s right up until the late 1980s.

Since the 1990s there have been cases of increasing official tolerance in various regions of house churches. Some, but not all, believe that the opposition of house churches by the government is less from an ideological opposition to religion and support of atheism, and more out of fear of potential disturbances to orderly society from mass mobilization of people.

The three pillars of the Three-Self Patriotic Movement, now just called Three-Self Churches, are self-governance, self-support and self-propagation, which respectively reject foreign church leadership, foreign financing, and foreign missionaries, while "Patriotic" indicates loyalty to China. These three rejections have kept divisive Western denominationalism out of China, which is good, but the concern is that this "movement" tries to restrict various aspects of Christianity. For example, the Communist Party may decide who can preach and may require that preaching focus on the social rules and the social benefits of Christianity. Evangelizing or giving out Christian materials is generally forbidden and printing Bibles without authorization is prohibited even if they are to be given away. In addition, government officials, schoolteachers, police officers, as well as children and teens cannot become Christians. Thus the Three Self Movement reflects the Communist government's attempt to keep Christianity out of key segments of its society and to reduce the gospel to a set of moral rules that serve its social objectives. Many Christians justifiably distrust the Three-Self Church, calling it a puppet of the PRC government's designs to control the gospel. (China ranks 29th on Open Doors' list of places where it's hardest to be a Christian). Some ambitious and self-serving pastors have used the government to save themselves in times of oppression, to the point of betraying other Christians. On the other hand, many who read the Bible and become Christians at the Three Self churches leave to worship in an underground church, although some remain to evangelize.

Some observers suggest that the Communist party overestimated the political threat from the church and say that Christianity has brought positive changes to China. In spite of restrictions, the Chinese church today is several thousand times bigger than a hundred years ago. Indeed, what has happened in China in the last century is one of the most marvelous stories in the history of the Christian church.

There is considerable question about the number of Protestant Christians in China. Estimates a few years ago ranged between low figures of 10-13.5 million to 67 million (which is the estimate given by the Pew Research Center in 2010) to over 100 million. This number eclipses the 87 million members of the ruling Communist Party. The low figure may count only Christians in the "registered" churches; others say that the numbers of Christians is extremely underestimated intentionally because the increase of religion would reflect negatively on government officials. Part of the problem is that most congregations, even Three-Self churches, usually don't have membership lists. Some say that the majority of all Christians in China could be called "evangelical", including provincial and national church leaders, even if they prefer not to use this label themselves.

The good news is that within fifteen years, China may become the country with the most Christians in the world. This explosion of Christianity in China will upend the traditional Christian powerhouses of the world. In 2010, the U.S. had around 159 million Protestants, and some observers say their congregations are in decline.

## My Favorite Summer Jobs

I only had two summer jobs if you don't count working on the farm while growing up in Alberta. When I graduated from a small town high school my parents gave me ten dollars, a bus ticket to Edmonton, and a suitcase, so I figured out that I was supposed to leave home. My sister and her husband met me at the Edmonton bus depot and dropped me off at the nearest drug store since I had decided to go into pharmacy at university. The requirement was that each pharmacy student had to do a twelve-month apprenticeship and since I was a farm boy as green as grass I wisely decided to do the apprenticeship before going to university.

This was a good decision and I'll always be grateful to Rose and George for helping me adjust to city life, plus I learned a lot that year about being a pharmacist. As an apprentice I earned the grand salary of thirty dollars per week and from this I paid forty dollars a month for room and board. I even managed to save a few dollars.

Anyway, when my twelve months of indentured service were completed my brother arranged to get me a summer job near Jasper, Alberta, as a driver and general go-fer driving vehicles between Maligne Lake and Medicine Lake. Maligne Lake is about thirty miles east of Jasper, Alberta, and is one of the most beautiful places on planet earth. At about fourteen miles long it is the second largest glacier fed lake in the world. Tourists today can drive directly from Jasper to Maligne Lake but in the 1960s they had to take a tour bus from Jasper to Medicine Lake, then a boat across the five-mile Medicine Lake and finally a bus to Maligne Lake. This is where I came in. I drove a sixteen-passenger bus and picked these folks up, usually about 9:00 AM, and drove the eleven miles on an unpaved one-lane road to Maligne Lodge. The tourists typically had lunch on arrival and then were taken on a ninety-minute boat cruise up the lake. I then took the tourists back on the bus to Medicine Lake in the late afternoon.

There were other trips for me to make to Medicine Lake and back since some folks stayed in the Maligne Lodge for a few days, so I often made three or four return trips each day.

One extra trip that I regularly made was to pick up fishermen at Medicine Lake at 7:00 AM to deliver them to a small lake a few miles away. I drove a Volkswagen bus for this trip, and if you can imagine seven overweight men and their gear, plus skinny me, in an underpowered VW bus on a bumpy uphill and downhill road...well let's just say that we didn't go real fast. It was always interesting.

Staff employed by the Maligne Lake Lodge included personnel to clean the cabins, serve in the dining room and cook in the kitchen, drive the tour boats, and do maintenance. Some of these were university students like me, while others were simply individuals who wanted an interesting summer job. Room and board was provided, and I earned some money in tips so I was able to save my entire salary to pay for university.

While driving the bus or a van was my main job, occasionally when it was very busy I also drove the fourteen-passenger tour boat up Maligne Lake after I had obtained a Boatman License from the local Jasper Park Ranger. I was needed to pilot the boat when it was warm and sunny, which meant there were lots of tourists, so I always happy to do this. We stopped at a small dock at Spirit Island about two-thirds up the lake where the snow-capped mountains surround the end of the lake. This is said to be one of the most photographed scenes in the entire world!

The husband of the Maligne Lake Resort manager was an outfitter who kept about thirty horses near Jasper. His main job was to take big game hunters out in fall to hunt bear, elk, and moose for a huge fee, but he was also available in the summer to take adventurous people into the backcountry. On one occasion he had to go a day's journey from Maligne Lake to pick up a lady who had been camping alone and I was able to go along since I had two days off.

We left on horseback early in the morning with about fifteen horses in our party, including the head guy, one helper, eight packhorses (to carry our gear including tents for the night, our food, and horses to carry the lady and her gear back), and me. I would have been lost within twenty minutes of leaving camp, but these guys knew the backcountry. It was a fabulous sunny day as we slowly wound through mountain passes and over summits. We reached the lady about four o'clock, set up camp and cooked dinner over a campfire. If you have lived in the city most of your life you have no idea how dark it gets and how many billions of stars there are in the sky. It was a fabulous day and evening. The next morning we packed everything up and made our way back.

I worked at Maligne Lake for two summers, and the third summer I worked at the Columbia Icefields, located between Jasper and Banff in the Rocky Mountains. I arrived early that spring to do some maintenance, but in the afternoons we early season workers took a couple of snowmobiles and began to carve out a road on the snow covered glacier, the Athabasca tongue of the Columbia Icefields, a huge 150 square mile pack of compressed ice that pushes down into various valleys. The glacier "tongue" is always moving, about nine feet (almost three metres) per year, and this explains why the surface is often rough, especially when it pushes downwards into the valley.

After the surface snow melted we had a full time ice grader to maintain and groom the road and redirect the various small creeks on the ice surface. By late May, tourists began to arrive and we took them onto the glacier. The snowmobiles, which could carry ten adults and had a roof that slid open, had caterpillar-type track in the back and wheels in front (rather than skis); the engine in the back made the front-end light.

The round trip from the ticket office high up on the moraine alongside the glacier, down the gravel trail to the ice took about forty-five minutes. The light in front vehicles could drive right beside small holes two to three feet wide and at least fifty feet deep, called mill holes. Surface streams that had found a weak spot in the ice drilled them. I opened the front door and let the tourists look down to see the deep blue ice below the surface. Fortunately, no one ever fell in, although once my snowmobile had to be towed out after I had driven too far into the hole.

We always stopped at the halfway point of our tour to let people walk on the groomed turn-around area, and since many had never seen snow or ice this was always a hit. Sometimes, in late August, it would snow and we couldn't see more than fifty feet ahead, but since these folks had some from sunny and warm places like Louisiana or Florida to see the ice fields we took them for the tour anyway.

I was classified as a "swing driver" which meant that I drove the other guys' snowmobiles while they had two days off. I liked driving the eight cylinder vehicles much better than the six cylinder weaklings that had a tough time climbing the moraine hill from the ice back up to the ticket office. Being a swing driver also meant that I didn't get many days off but with this great job I didn't mind.

One time, when I had a day off, I went with two other guys farther up the ice fields, past where we could go with the snowmobiles, to the place where deep crevasses as much as a hundred feet deep cut through the glacier. We used crampons, which are spikes that strap onto boots, and with ropes took turns lowering each other down into the crevasses. We were young and fearless, and we took some spectacular pictures. Many years later my kids, and even later, my grandchildren, couldn't believe that I had done such crazy and exciting things.

Each fall I returned refreshed to Edmonton and that last fall in particular, I felt revived and ready to complete my third and final year of pharmacy before entering the normal work world.

## It's In You to Give

Blood is essential to keep the human body healthy. Blood carries oxygen and nutrients to all parts of the body, and takes carbon dioxide and other waste products to the lungs, kidneys, and liver for disposal. Blood fights infections, and helps heal wounds. It is needed to sustain the lives of people whose functions have been impaired by injury or illness. The primary constituents of blood are red blood cells, white blood cells, plasma, and platelets.

Canadian Blood Services is a national, not-for-profit charitable organization that manages the blood supply in Canada. It was created in 1998 as a successor to the Canadian Red Cross. Canadian Blood Services collects almost one million units of blood annually and processes it into the components and products that are administered to thousands of patients each year through blood transfusions. A person can donate blood every fifty-six days, but can donate plasma or platelets more frequently.

There are about thirty recognized blood types. This classification is based on the presence or absence of antigens on the surface of red blood cells. Blood types are inherited and represent contributions from both parents. There are four major blood groups: Type A (36% of Canadians), Type B (8%), Type AB (8%) and Type O (39%) plus there are some other less common blood types as well. In addition, there is the Rh system of specific antigens where individual can be either Rh+ or Rh- . Patients should receive their own blood or type-specific blood products to minimize the chance of a transfusion reaction.

Platelets are small disc-shaped cells that stick to injured blood vessel walls for the purpose of reducing or preventing bleeding and excessive blood loss. The average person has about 150 to 400 million platelets per litre of blood (adults have about four to five litres of blood). Another way to say this is that adults have about 150 to 400 platelets per microlitre of blood. A platelet count of about eighty in each microlitre is needed to prevent excessive bleeding. However, immuno-compromised individuals may have levels as low as only five or ten platelets per microliter, so they urgently need life-saving platelet infusions. Platelet counts below five can result in life-threatening spontaneous bleeding.

Platelets are produced by our bone marrow. Individuals with diseases such as leukemia or aplastic anemia may have dangerously low platelets levels. Chemotherapy treatments for other cancers may also suppress platelet production. After a car accident or other serious trauma individuals may lose a lot of blood and therefore have low platelets counts.

While many people should donate whole blood, some are asked to donate plasma or just platelets. Donating platelets is critical since the shelf life of platelets is only five days compared to whole blood that can be stored for up to forty-two days. Giving platelets takes up to two hours since the blood is separated into its components by centrifugation and the platelets are kept while the plasma and the rest of the blood is returned to the donor. The process is painless, just like donating blood, but it just takes a little longer. The nurses use an anticoagulant when the blood is first removed, and when re-infused this may cause a tingling effect and coolness since calcium is bound up by the anticoagulant. At Canadian Blood Services you'll be given a hot water bottle, a blanket, and hand warmers, plus you can watch a movie during the procedure! The collection of plasma and platelets is called plasmapheresis and apheresis, respectively.

## The Most Evil Men in History

Yes, everyone on this list is male. Perhaps this should be a ten-way tie since it's difficult to rank or prioritize evil or the atrocities that some people commit. There are many examples in history of men who have taken advantage of their position and power to abuse and torture their fellow citizens or the people they have conquered.

Joseph Stalin (1878-1953) often tops this list since he is said to be responsible for killing ten to sixty million people through various policies, purges, and executions of real or perceived enemies of the state until his death in 1953.

However, I would also insert the less well-known name of Joseph Kony (1961 - ?) the quasi-religious leader of the Lord's Resistance Army in Uganda who is responsible for mass rapes and other atrocities in Uganda, Sudan, and Congo. I also include him in first place because of the unspeakable modern day acts that he has perpetrated. He has forced young kids to kill their parents and family members and to watch while other family members and friends are tortured and killed. He has raided villages and forced young boys to join his "army" and wage mayhem against their own people. And the rest of the world sits by and lets this happen because they have no economic or strategic interest in this poor little country.

Chairman Mao Tse Tung (1893-1976) was a Chinese Communist revolutionary, guerrilla warfare strategist, Marxist political philosopher, and leader of the Chinese Revolution. His rule from 1949 to 1976 is believed to have caused more deaths than any man in history (forty to seventy million people). He orchestrated these deaths in part by being responsible for severe starvation during the Great Chinese Famine, mass suicides as a result of his "reform movements" to rid China of so-called enemies of the state, and political persecutions. His campaigns and their varying disastrous consequences are further blamed for damaging the culture and society of China.

Adolf Hitler believed in territorial conquests and racial subjugation, leading to the deaths of tens of millions of people including six million Jews. He died by suicide in 1945 to avoid being held responsible for his heinous acts.

Pol Pot was Prime Minister of Cambodia from 1976-1979. He initiated "extreme communism" policies including forcing city dwellers to move to rural areas under slave labor conditions, and his policies resulted in malnutrition and extreme lack of medical care, causing the deaths of over two million Cambodians. And who can forget seeing pictures of the stacks of skulls of Cambodians that Pol Pot killed in some of the most egregious rampages against his fellow citizens?

Idi Amin (1925-2003) of Uganda ruthlessly killed up to half a million of his people. Amin's rule was characterized by gross human rights abuses, political repression, ethnic persecution, extrajudicial killings, nepotism, corruption, and gross economic mismanagement.

Ayatolla Khomeini (1902-1989) was an Iranian religious leader and politician, and leader of the 1979 Iranian Revolution, which saw the overthrow of the Shah of Iran. Khomeini enforced extreme Sharia (Islamic) Law in Iran in the 1980s and killed and massacred anyone who opposed him. The decade of his ruling in Iran was marked with extensive violations of human rights.

Osama Bin Laden would likely be near the top of this list for many people since his immense wealth and complicated organization sponsored acts of terrorism that killed many innocent people.

Mafia leaders who killed opponents and innocent people in cold blood also should be on this list. It's not really possible to understand how a Mafioso could blatantly kill people on a given day and then go home and bounce his kids on his knee while waiting for dinner.

Some other dishonorable men, from earlier times, could also be on this list. Leopold II, King of Belgium (1865-1909) epitomized everything that was wrong with colonialism. Desiring the rubber and ivory of the Congo, he was responsible for the deaths of more than three million Congolese.

Ivan IV of Russia, known as Ivan the Terrible, proclaimed himself the first Tsar in the 16th century. He is most known for his brutal ruling and killing of fellow citizens and executions of conquered people as he expanded the boundaries of the Russian Empire.

Attila the Hun in the 5th century has been described as the epitome of cruelty and rapacity. Nero, Caligula and some other Roman Caesars also established well-deserved reputations for cruelty.

As of this writing, nameless brutal men leading ISIS are causing mayhem in the Middle East and impacting the rest of the world by their heinous barbaric acts, apparently in the name of Allah.

Why do I even think about some of the most evil people in history? One reason is we all need to be vigilant in guarding what's right and having the courage to speak out when we see evil and wrongdoing, whether it's by our neighbors or our government or business or other nations.

The situation in pre-World War II Germany is an example where ordinarily good citizens looked the other way and convinced themselves that things were going to be fine instead of trying to stem the Nazi tide.

They say that power corrupts, and in some way we saw this in Canada when Jean Chretien was Prime Minister for many years. I don't suggest, by any means, that he was evil or corrupt, but my impression is that he changed over the years. Early in his political career he was known as the "little guy from Shawinigan" because of his humble origins and his ability and desire to help ordinary people. But as he got used to the trappings of power I think he became the "little bully from Shawinigan". I think this happens to many people when they gain power and influence but have far less conscience than Chretien.

We have a late entry onto the list, namely Vladimir Putin of Russia, who is alleged to have ordered the deaths of many opponents. If you think that's unfair or unwarranted, I invite you to read *Red Notice* by William Browder. Putin's invasion of Ukraine is just one small example, and he has been reported to set in motion a process of "re-Stalinization" in Russia where the killing of millions of innocent victims is ignored and Stalin is praised as an economic modernizer and great leader. For economic and political reasons, the West is reluctant to push back against Putin, so it may be many years before we have a better understanding of Putin's crimes.

## The Teflon Kingdom

The Teflon™ Kingdom is the name given to Saudi Arabia by Jonathan Manthorpe in a September 2010 Vancouver Sun article. Manthorpe is an internationally recognized correspondent specializing in international affairs. He believed Saudi Arabia to be the primary source and support of global Islamic terrorism, but for various reasons this country has escaped relatively unscathed from American or international criticism.

Conspiracy theorists have had a field day in proposing alternate theories about who caused 9/11, the destruction of New York's World Trade Center buildings by terrorists, but some strange things involving Saudi Arabia happened before and after that tragedy. It has been established that the attacks on New York and Washington on September 11th had the characteristics of an Osama bin Laden led al-Qaida terrorist operation and that fifteen of the nineteen hijackers were Saudi citizens. Some questionable Saudis had been in the U.S. for some time and had been receiving Saudi government money, even including the Saudi ambassador to the U.S. Members of the bin Laden family and the Saudi royal family who were in the U.S. at that time were understandably concerned and even panicked about American reaction to their presence in the states immediately after 9/11.

For some unexplained reason, President Bush and his government apparently authorized four planes to take these Saudis out of the U.S. without anyone being questioned even though all regular flights had been grounded.

Another strange thing happened between the U.S. and Saudi Arabia. Manthorpe reported that three senior Saudi royal princes were named by bin Laden supporters as al-Qaida members and as advocates for the 9/11 attacks. All three of these princes died within one week in 2002; the suggestion has been that Saudi authorities orchestrated their deaths to placate American officials and maintain good relations.

Saudi-U.S. relations were particularly tense right after 9/11 but had been somewhat rocky since 1996 when Saudi Arabia refused to cooperate with the U.S.-CIA special unit that was set up to deal with bin Laden/al-Qaida terrorism concerns.

Is it possible, a cynic might ask, if this Teflon™ property relates at all to the fact that, after Canada, the U.S. imports more oil from Saudi Arabia than any other country? The Middle East has more oil reserves than any other area in the world and it just happens that the U.S. is still dependent on foreign oil.

Saudi Arabia is an intriguing country. The Kingdom of Saudi Arabia, as it is officially known, has a population of about twenty-six million people, although at least five million are non-citizens. The two holiest places in Islam, namely Mecca and Medina, are in Saudi Arabia. This country is the world's largest oil exporter, with oil accounting for more than 90% of exports and about 75% of government revenues. A major concern about Saudi Arabia is the lack of human rights, particularly for women whose rights are said to be no different from that of children.

Abdul-Aziz bin Saud, leader of the House of Saud, took power in 1902, eventually leading to the creation of the modern state of Saudi Arabia in 1932. His main weapon for achieving these conquests was the Wahhabist-Bedouin tribal army. The new kingdom was one of the poorest countries in the world until 1938 when vast oil reserves were discovered, which provided Saudi Arabia with economic prosperity and substantial political leverage internationally. After the Iraqi invasion of Kuwait in 1990 Saudi Arabia invited American and Coalition soldiers to be stationed in Saudi Arabia, since they feared an Iraqi invasion. This is said to be one of the issues that has led to an increase in Islamic terrorism in Saudi Arabia, as well as Islamic terrorist attacks in Western countries by Saudi nationals.

The government is an Islamic absolute monarchy, and the royal family dominates the political system. The family's vast numbers allow it to control most of the kingdom's important ministries and other important posts and to have an involvement and presence at all levels of government. The number of princes is estimated to be more than 7,000 with most power and influence being held by about 200 male descendants of the first King. The Saudi government and the royal family have often been accused of systemic and endemic corruption and that they run the country as if it belongs to them (they even say the country is named for them), and the distinction between state assets and the personal wealth of senior princes is indeed blurry.

## Pearls of Great, or Modest, Price

Pearls have long held a special place in the world of jewelry. Cultured pearls are one of the most intriguing, stunning, and beloved gems. A pearl is a hard object produced within the soft tissue of a living mollusk. Just like the mollusk shell, a pearl is made up of concentric calcium carbonate layers which have been deposited in minute crystalline form. The ideal pearl is perfectly round and smooth, but many other shapes of pearls occur. The finest quality natural pearls have been highly valued as gemstones and objects of beauty for many centuries, and because of this, the word pearl has become a metaphor for something rare, fine, admirable, and valuable.

The most valuable pearls, called natural pearls, occur spontaneously in the wild but they are extremely rare. Cultured or farmed pearls from pearl oysters and freshwater mussels make up the majority of pearls that are currently sold. Imitation or fake pearls are also widely sold in inexpensive jewelry, but the quality of their iridescence (the property of certain surfaces which appear to change color as the angle of view or the angle of illumination changes) is usually poor, and artificial pearls are generally easily distinguished from genuine pearls. Pearls have been harvested and cultivated primarily for use in jewelry, but in the past they were also stitched onto lavish clothing. Pearls have also been crushed and used in cosmetics, medicines, and paint formulations.

Mother of pearl is the common name for iridescent nacre, a blend of minerals that are naturally secreted by oysters and other mollusks and deposited inside their shells, coating and protecting their bodies from parasites and foreign objects. Nacre is the same substance that is deposited around an object that becomes lodged in the mollusk—either naturally or inserted by pearl farmers to form a pearl. The depth of the nacre coating depends on the type of creature involved, the water it lives in, and how long the intruder is left in place before it is removed. As nacre thickness increases, so does the quality and durability of the pearl. Whether wild or cultured, gem quality pearls are almost always iridescent, as is the interior of the shell that produces them.

You may have seen the classic pictures of pearl farms in Asia where China and Japan are large pearl producers, or in the Pacific—Tahiti, for example—where pearls are cultured in mollusks in salt water. These two areas set the world quality standard. Workers typically insert tiny pieces of mussel tissue inside live mussels' shells and this "irritant" helps create a pearl that takes about two years to reach full size.

There is a now new player in the game. China has been busily developing a freshwater pearl farming industry; these new Chinese pearl farms are often in fields formerly used to grow rice. Chinese entrepreneurs are using new scientifically sophisticated techniques that can produce one-half to up to one-inch pearls of reasonable quality at substantially lower costs than usual. A strand from Tahiti may have a wholesale price of $14,000 while a comparable freshwater Chinese strand of perfectly round blemish-free pearls may have a price tag of less than $2,000, since the objective is to make peals available to the average woman. One company has also started producing bright purple, pink, and bronze pearls in sizes of one-half inch or more. These "Edison" pearls are the result of genetic research where tiny beads are used instead of mussel tissue, and using a special still-secret technique. Further automation is expected to yield pearls of high quality but relatively low price.

Taking good care of your pearls is important. Pearls are more fragile than most other gemstones, so they must be handled carefully to keep them in the best condition. Pearls will stay cleaner if one puts them on after applying makeup and perfume or hand and body creams. Wipe pearls with a soft, lint-free cloth as soon as they are taken off. Dirty pearls can be cleaned with a mild soap and water solution but should not be placed in an ultrasonic cleaner.

## The Middle Wife and Other Tales

I believe that I first heard this story by an anonymous Second Grade teacher on CBC radio, and it has also been on the Internet, but it's so funny I wanted to share it with you.

"I've been teaching now for about fifteen years. I have two kids myself, but the best birth story I know is the one I saw in my own Second Grade class a few years back. Since I always used to love Show and Tell as a kid, I always have a few sessions with my students. It helps them get over shyness and usually Show and Tell is pretty tame. Kids bring in pet turtles, model airplanes, pictures of fish they catch, things like that. And I never, ever place any boundaries or limitations on them. If they want to lug it to school and talk about it, they're welcome.

"Well, one day Erica, a bright, outgoing little girl, takes her turn and waddles up to the front of the class with a pillow stuffed under her sweater. She holds up a snapshot of an infant, and says, 'This is Luke, my baby brother, and I'm going to tell you about his birthday. First, Mom and Dad made him as a symbol of their love, and then Dad put a seed in my Mom's stomach, and Luke grew in there. He ate for nine months through an umbrella cord.'"

"Erica's standing there with her hands on the pillow, and I'm trying not to laugh and wishing I had my camcorder with me. The kids are watching her in amazement. She continues, 'Then, about two Saturdays ago, my Mom starts saying, "Oh, oh, oh, oh!'" She puts a hand behind her back and groans. "Mom walked around the house for, like an hour, moaning "Oh, oh, oh!"' At this point, this girl is doing a hysterical duck walk.

"'My Dad called the middle wife. She delivers babies, but she doesn't have a sign on the car like the Domino's Pizza man. They got my mom to lie down in bed like this.' Then Erica lies down with her back against the wall. 'And then, pop! My mom had this bag of water she kept in there in case he got thirsty, and it just blew up and spilled all over the bed, like psshhheew!' She has her legs spread with her little hands miming water flowing away. It was too much!

"'Then the middle wife starts saying, "Push, push," and, "Breathe, breathe." They started counting, but never even got past ten. All of a sudden, out comes my brother! He was covered in yucky stuff that they all said was from Mom's play-center, so there must be a lot of toys inside there.' Then Erica stood up, took a big theatrical bow and returned to her seat. I'm sure I applauded the loudest. Ever since then, when it's Show and Tell day, I bring my camcorder, just in case another "Middle Wife" comes along."

**Bone Button Borscht**

I am a fairly regular listener to CBC's *As It Happens*, a program that provides in-depth interviews with people describing major and minor current events. Every year in late December they take some airtime to read stories of peace and good will. Long-time listeners will recognize the name of "Fireside Al," who has since gone to the big studio in the sky. The *As It Happens* co-host, Barbara Budd, however, read one of the most memorable and heart-warming stories, called "Bone Button Borscht." I can only give you a short summary and urge you to purchase the book, written by Aubrey Davis and published by Kids Can Press.

The story is about a beggar who comes to a dark, unfriendly village. When he asks for food and help he is refused. He claims he has the ability to make delicious borscht from the bone buttons on his ragged coat. The people are skeptical but they do want to see this supposed miracle. The beggar is given a big pot and when he adds his buttons to the boiling water, he announces that the borscht is good, but needs something. The villagers are eager to see a miracle so someone adds a few carrots. This happens again and again. Each time someone is convinced to add something, the beggar says that the borscht is good but still needs something. Finally, beets are added, and onions, and cabbage and so on until they have superb borscht. Because of the "magic" of the bone buttons and the winsome beggar, the previously insular villagers, who didn't share anything with each other or with strangers, are now excitedly enjoying wonderful borscht. Eventually, after the passage of time, they realize that sharing is the key and they can make borscht for the community anytime even without the magic bone buttons.

**Mom's Role**

The child was a typical four-year-old girl—cute, inquisitive, and bright as a new loonie. When she expressed difficulty in grasping the concept of marriage, her father decided to pull out his wedding photo album, thinking visual images would help. On one page after another, he pointed out the bride arriving at the church, the entrance, the wedding ceremony, the reception, and more.

"Now do you understand?" he asked.

"I think so," she said. Then she asked, "Is that when mommy came to work for us?"

## The Tragedy of Mexico

Mexico is the thirteenth-largest independent nation in the world, with a population of over 112 million, and the most populous Spanish-speaking country. Mexico is a federation comprising thirty-one states plus the capital city, which is a Federal District. Mexico has one of the world's largest industrial economies, and is considered an established upper-middle-income country and an emerging power. It was the first Latin American member of the Organization for Economic Co-operation and Development (OECD).

Various cultures, including the Mayans and the Aztecs, are part of Mexico's early history. In 1521 Spain conquered and colonized the territory until independence was gained in 1821. This was a turbulent period that included a civil war and territorial expansion. Texas achieved independence and was annexed by the U.S. A border dispute led to the Mexican-American War in 1846; the settlement forced Mexico to give over half of its land to the U.S., including Alta California, New Mexico, and the disputed parts of Texas and southern Arizona.

Porfirio Díaz, a Republican general, ruled Mexico from 1876 to1880 and then from 1884 to 1911 in five consecutive re-elections. These years were characterized by remarkable economic achievements and investments in the arts and sciences, but also economic inequality and political repression. Electoral fraud during Diaz's fifth election, and his dictatorial style, sparked the 1910 Mexican Revolution that finally ended with the adoption of the 1917 Constitution and development of the country's current political system. The Institutional Revolutionary Party (PRI) then held power in every election until 2000.

Between 1940 and 1980, Mexico experienced a substantial economic growth that some historians call the "Mexican miracle." Although the economy continued to flourish, social inequality remained a factor causing widespread discontent. Moreover, the PRI rule became increasingly authoritarian and oppressive. In December 1994 the Mexican economy collapsed, but then-U.S. President Clinton authorized a rapid rescue package and the new President Zedillia initiated major macroeconomic reforms so that the economy rapidly recovered.

In 2000, after seventy-one years, the PRI lost the presidential election to Vicente Fox of the opposition National Action Party (PAN). Felipe Calderón, also from PAN, won the 2006 presidential election but Enrique of PRI was declared the winner in 2012.

The Tropic of Cancer divides the country into temperate and tropical zones. Land north of the twenty-fourth parallel experiences cooler temperatures during the winter months, but the area south of the twenty-fourth parallel experiences temperatures that are fairly constant throughout the year, giving Mexico one of the world's most diverse weather systems.

Mexico has become a popular attraction for sun-seeking tourists. Guadalajara, the second-largest city, is one of the most visited cities in Mexico. It is home to some of Mexico's best-known traditions, including tequila, mariachi music, and charros (Mexican cowboys). Its similitude with western European countries, mixed with modern architecture and infrastructure, makes Guadalajara appealing to tourists, as do Mexico City and beach destinations, such as Cancún and Acapulco.

As of this writing, Mexico is the sixth-largest oil producer in the world. Energy production in Mexico is managed by state-owned companies such as Pemex, which is in charge of exploration, extraction, transportation, and the marketing of crude oil and natural gas, as well as the refining and distribution of petroleum products and petrochemicals. It is one of the largest companies in the world by revenue. According to a study by the Carnegie Endowment, Mexico is among the developing countries best prepared for rapid adoption of foreign technologies largely because of relatively high levels of educational attainment and supportive infrastructure.

Although it has a remarkable history, wonderful people, and many natural resources, there is a dark side to Mexico. Drug trafficking and narcotics-related activities are a major concern. President Felipe Calderón made fighting drug trafficking one of the top priorities of his administration, but rival gangs continue to kill each other and murder innocent citizens. Public safety in some Mexican cities is almost nonexistent; sometimes police and government officials are intimidated and controlled by drug gangs because of corruption.

The city of Monterrey, founded in the late 16th century, is one such example. Monterrey, close to the border of Texas, was once a powerful, wealthy city built by Mexicans in the steel, glass, petrochemical, cement, and banking industries. The per capita income was nearly double the Mexican average but by 2011 this once prosperous city was dominated by violent gangsters. Criminals routinely set up roadblocks and violent car thefts increased ten-fold in one year. Schools were forced to train students to dive under their desks at the sound of gunfire.

Casino Royale was built in a posh area near BMW and Mercedes dealerships, but it was set on fire in an extortion action, killing fifty-two people. Extortion and bribery commonly include police officers. Open warfare between rival gangs was common and homicides increased from 200 in 2009 to over 1200 in 2011.

The situation has improved in recent years but violence is still a key concern and Monterrey's status as a safe first-class city is questionable. In 2011, authorities in northern Mexico, which includes the city of Monterrey, fired over 260 police officers for various offenses and arrested sixty-six of them because of suspected links to drug gangs. Many police officers fear for their lives and succumb to pressures and threats from gangs.

Some companies are attracted to doing business in Mexico, but there are hazards. Theft in 2015, following several mine robberies, equalled about $10.7 million worth of gold, highlighting the risks. One policy analyst said, "It's a part of doing business." Kidnappings and murder, as well as intimidation of international workers, are also major concerns, largely as a result of organized crime.

Corruption at many levels of government, including the police forces, certainly contributes to Mexico's problems (Mexico ranked 103rd out of 175 countries in a 2014 Corruption Perceptions Index). Another serious issue is poverty, affecting at least sixty per cent of the population. The gap between the poor and the rich seems to get ever wider.

In spite of this, there is some hope. It seems contradictory, but at the same time there are reports that the middle class is growing in Mexico. If corruption and drug problems could be solved, Mexico has the potential of being a truly wonderful country.

## Make Babies, Not Money

The birthrate or the replacement fertility rate (RFR) in developed countries is often below the replacement level. There seems to be an inverse relationship between fertility and socio-economic status. The ideal RFR is generally recognized as being about 2.3; that is, each couple must have 2.3 children to maintain the population in any given country. This figure is derived from that fact that there needs to be two babies to replace the parents, plus the extra .3 to account for infant mortality and the probability of more males than females. The RFR is significantly higher than 3.0 in countries with higher mortality rates. Some experts are predicting a decline in the world population in the near future due to falling energy resources, food shortages, and declining birth rates in many countries.

The world population has been increasing continually since the Middle Ages, with an occasional decrease related to events such as the Bubonic Plague, but countries are now expressing concern that their populations are declining. Some have sub-replacement rates but still have growing populations due to immigration, while other countries such as Germany, Ukraine, and Japan have severe and sustained sub-replacement fertility rates and expect a population decline.

Economic development, leading to a higher cost of living and increased costs in raising children, is said to have a negative effect on population growth. In many developed countries, more females are in the workplace today, and bearing children is seen as less of a social duty. Some European governments have developed policies such as family allowances or tax allowances for working parents, albeit with limited success, to encourage women to have more children.

Countries like Nigeria and Kenya have a RFR of five or more, while other countries like France (1.9), Argentina (2.3), Brazil (1.9), Australia (1.8) and Russia (1.3) have much lower reproduction rates.

The RFR in the U.S. was as high as 3.8 in the 1950s but by 1999 it had dropped to about 2.0.

The fertility of the population of the U.S. is below replacement among those born in the country but is higher now due to recent immigrants and Hispanics. Canada's RFR is presently at about 1.5, but Canada also depends heavily on immigration, with about half a million immigrants coming to Canada each year. Significant factors for low fertility rates are said to include instability of modern relationships and changes in moral values.

The increase in the aging population is a serious concern for the future of the Japanese society and economy. About 3.6 people in the workforce, aged twenty to sixty-four, currently support a person at age sixty-five, but this is projected to decrease to less than two in approximately forty years. The population of Japan in 2009 was 127 million, but there has been a net population decline in recent years due to a falling birth rate and a significantly larger older population. Japan has one of the highest life expectancies in the world, combined with almost no immigration. Japan's RFR was over 4.0 in 1947 but had dropped sharply by 1960, stayed stable at about 2.0 during the economic growth periods of the 1960s and 1970s, then decreased to about 1.3 by 2002. Some have projected that Japan's population could fall to less than half of its present total within three generations, by 2100.

As mentioned, some developed countries encourage immigration to maintain or increase their population and workforce. Another population management issue that isn't politically correct to mention is abortion. According to the U.S. Center for Disease Control, about fifty million abortions have been performed in the U.S. since 1973. The rate has dropped from over 1.2 million per year until 1994 to the current 800,000 per year. Canada is one of the few nations with no legal restrictions on abortion since the Supreme Court ruled in 1988, in a case brought by Dr. Henry Morgentaler, that existing laws were unconstitutional. The rate has been decreasing, but each year there are just under 100,000 abortions performed in Canada. This translates to about thirty abortions per 100 live births.

For some reason, Russia, with 2.7 million abortions per year, has by far the most abortions of any country in the world except China, which had 7.9 million abortions in 1996. Interestingly, the small country of Viet Nam had 1.5 million abortions that year. It seems that abortion rates in Eastern Europe are higher than many countries. But for one year in Western European countries like France (160,000), Italy (134,000) and Germany (130,000), rates are still high but less than in other parts of the world.

The reasons women give for having an abortion include: wanting to postpone childbearing (25%), not being able to afford a baby (21%), having relationship problems or a partner who does not want pregnancy (14%), being too young, having parents or others object to their pregnancy (12%), not wanting any more children (8%), risk to fetal health (3%) and risk to maternal health (3%). Cases of rape or incest account for only 1% of abortions.

There is another incredible issue involving abortions, namely sex-selective abortions. According to a 2012 Christianity Today report, Asia would have an additional 163 million females if gender selective abortions were not happening. This practice has carried over to the U.S. and Canada, although laws are being considered to prohibit female feticide. In some societies hearing, "It's a girl" is a death sentence since males carry on the family name, are easier and cheaper to marry off, have better access to education and influence. In some societies the sons are more able to provide for aging parents.

More girls have been killed in the past fifty years than men in all the wars of the 20th century. A massive part of this problem is related to China's one-child policy and forced abortion policies (which has only recently changed), which disastrously resulted in a population of nine males for every female. Access to modern technology also plays a role since parents can readily determine the sex of the fetus.

Governments and citizens, especially Christians, need to rise up and protest these evil actions.

## SNOWBIRDS

There are various kinds of snowbirds. When you hear this term you might think about Canada's flight demonstration team that visits airshows across the country and around the world to demonstrate the skill, professionalism, and teamwork of Canadian Forces personnel. But I'm thinking of the kind where Canadians flee the misery and rigours of the cold Canadian winter to find sun and solace in the southern United States.

Most of these snowbirds are age fifty-five or older and have the resources to spend a few months in a warmer climate—if they have good health or can afford the insurance. Health care is a significant issue for many, and the rule generally is that a person cannot remain outside of Canada for more than six months for their health insurance to be valid. Even then, the cost of health insurance may be prohibitive for those of modest means and who have pre-existing conditions that drive up the cost of insurance.

There are other complications for Canadians staying in the U.S. for more than 183 days in a calendar year, since they may be considered resident aliens for U.S. tax purposes and could be required to file a U.S. tax return. If snowbirds regularly stay in the U.S. for up to six months each year they could meet what is called the "substantial presence" test and be subject to U.S. tax. Uncle Sam is in dire financial straits these days and will look for tax revenue wherever possible.

There even is a "Canadian Snowbird Association," which provides information to prospective snowbirds on issues ranging from health insurance (recommending everyone have a "personal health record" to facilitate proper care by an unfamiliar health care professional) to finding places to rent or buy, to finding campgrounds for those with recreational vehicles to describing local attractions. They even have "Lifestyle Presentations" for those who feel they need assistance in making sure they get the most out of their southern sojourn.

There are various kinds of snowbirds, including Florida snowbirds (primarily from Ontario and Quebec), Texas snowbirds, Arizona snowbirds, and California snowbirds. Some American citizens may resent the Canadian invasion each fall, but when they stop to think about all the money that Canadians spend, they tend to relax and make friends—and even some extra income.

The state of Florida, for example, does much advertising to make Canadians aware of what is available and provide lots of information, including where to find approved accommodation, deals offered for golfers, and local advice such as, "Do not feed the alligators." Other southern states also advertise consistently to attract and inform potential snowbirds since they often constitute a substantial portion of revenue for the local and state governments.

Many snowbirds leave the rapidly cooling Canadian climate in October or November but face the dilemma of wanting to be back home in Canada for Christmas. Some are fortunate enough to be able to afford to fly home for ten days or so or to bring their family south for the Christmas break. A return to Canada may then enable them to stay in the U.S. for a longer period of time.

Some mini-snowbirds may go south for only two months or so, either for financial considerations or because they don't want to be real snowbirds and stay away from home for an extended period of time. In these cases, there is the question of when to go and what type of accommodation may be available. The high season down south consists of the coldest months from January to March, so costs are higher during this period. Many rental accommodations want lease agreements for the whole season and aren't interested in a one or two month stay. The same may apply to those with RVs since many RV parks want folks to stay longer and parks that provide short-term spaces are generally full. Some mini-snowbirds will flee to the U.S, from late September to early December when both RV parks and rental accommodations are more available and less expensive. Of course, the disadvantage of this approach is that the coldest months of the Canadian winter are still ahead, but at least they are able to enjoy every 85-degree sunny day while down south. Driving back home from Arizona or southern California can be a discouraging feeling in November or December since these mini-snowbirds are likely to see many real snowbirds heading south!

## The Law of Unintended Consequences

None of us is prescient so we don't know how things will eventually turn out when we make a decision or take an action. The best thing is to do our homework by assessing the information, looking at whatever historical data is available, talking with experts and those who will be affected by our actions, and then making a decision. Politicians at all levels, from local to national, and managers of large companies in particular, need to exercise due diligence in making decisions.

The law of unintended consequences is what happens when an apparently or relatively straightforward or uncomplicated action tries to regulate a complex system. We see this fairly often in politics where decisions may be influenced by pressure groups or for political rather than practical reasons. Politicians sometimes operate with limited information, or more often with short-time horizons and poor or misguided incentives. The law of unintended consequences is a cousin to Murphy's Law, which is often used as a humorous warning against the somewhat arrogant supposition that we as humans can fully control the world around us.

Unintended consequences may sometimes involve positive, unexpected, or windfall benefits, but more often have negative, unfortunate results, or a perverse effect, contrary to what was originally intended. The solutions sometimes make a problem worse. The following examples generally fall into one of these categories.

A favorite illustration is the introduction of rabbits into Australia for food. This was followed by an explosive and damaging growth in the rabbit population so large that they became a major pest. Another modern-day example out of Australia was the 2012 law mandating that cigarettes be sold only in plain packages, presumably in an attempt to discourage teenagers and others from smoking. The unintended result was that contraband tobacco consumption increased by 21%, even though the smoking of legally produced cigarettes remained about the same.

One of the Australian states made wearing safety helmets mandatory for all bicycle riders. While there was a reduction in the number of head injuries, there was also an unintended reduction in the number of juvenile cyclists, which at least partially accounted for the fewer injuries. Young cyclists considered wearing a bicycle helmet unfashionable, just as in Canada today, a fact that wasn't considered before the law was passed.

The publicity and subsequent ban on DDT, a synthetic insecticide, has had tragic unintended consequences in poor countries, leading to the resurgence of malaria and thousands of unnecessary deaths.

Most drugs have unintended consequences and side effects associated with their use, and often this is not determined until they are fairly widely used. It has turned out that sometimes these side effects were beneficial as in the case of aspirin, which is a pain reliever but is also an anticoagulant that can help prevent heart attacks and reduce the severity of strokes.

African bees were released in Brazil in 1957 in an attempt to increase honey production there, but these bees proved to be dangerous in their new environment as they expanded into both North and South America.

Entertainment stars have attempted to censor or remove personal pictures or documents from social media but this action often had the reverse effect by causing that information to become more widely known and distributed since the public perceived it as more interesting than they would have if nothing had been done.

Increasing the penalty for drunk driving in the U.S. led at first to an increase in hit-and-run accidents because many drunken drivers tried to avoid prosecution. Legislators had to pass another law that increased the penalty for leaving the scene of an accident.

A debate that is still raging in the U.S is the subsidization of biofuels such as ethanol because it is alleged that this leads to the destruction of rainforests, increased greenhouse gas emissions and increases in the price of food, which hurts the world's poor by converting crops like corn from a food source to a fuel.

Non-aggressive fire management policies in the United States led to the rapid buildup of forest fuel, causing bigger and more destructive forest fires.

It may make sense to bail out banks and financial institutions that are in trouble and avoid financial meltdown, but if governments offer this guarantee then banks have a greater incentive to take risks knowing they will be bailed out.

Rent controls may be desirable at first glance, and often there is considerable public pressure to enact such controls in an effort to make housing more affordable for lower income tenants. However, such controls may reduce the quantity and quality of housing since landlords can't get sufficient return on their investment.

Governments across Canada and the U.S cut the railway infrastructure in the 1960s and built roads to facilitate car and truck transport, but by the 1990s there was increased demand for trains because of congested roads, which created huge problems as many good rail lines no longer existed.

On the positive side, the medieval policy of setting up large hunting reserves for the nobility throughout England and other places in Europe has resulted in the preservation of green space, often as parks.

## THE DOMINION OF CANADA

We Canadians live in one of the greatest countries in the world. Americans routinely tell anyone who will listen that *they* live in the greatest country ever and they are partly correct, but we also know about their problems and excesses and their tendency to jingoism.

Only a few years ago Canadian banks told us they needed to become bigger and even to merge with American banks to survive, but the Canadian government and people told the banks to keep on doing what they were doing and instead work at improving. We saw the wisdom of this approach at the start of the 21st century when huge American banks were in imminent danger of failing and needed to be bailed out by their government, which was already in crippling debt. This was in contrast to the Canadian economy and Canadian banks, which were relatively stable.

According to Wikipedia, the British North America Act of 1867 provided that there should be four provinces in the new Dominion of Canada—Ontario, Quebec, New Brunswick, and Nova Scotia—and that others could join later. Each province was to have its own seat of government, its own lawmaking body, and its own Lieutenant Governor to represent the Crown. In addition, the BNA Act established a federal government in Ottawa, composed of an elected House of Commons, an appointed Senate and a Governor General as the Crown's representative. The Act described the matters on which the provinces could make laws and listed those that were the responsibility of the federal government.

Canada's form of government is a constitutional monarchy under the British Monarch, and the Canadian founders wanted their confederation to be known as the "Kingdom of Canada." However, John A. MacDonald, our first Prime Minister, and the British Foreign Secretary believed that the phrase "Kingdom of Canada" was too provocative to the anti-monarchical neighboring United States, so they determined that Canada was to be called a "Dominion."

There has been an ongoing debate regarding the precise motivations for using the word "Dominion" as the country's formal title. Sir Leonard Tilley, a religious man from New Brunswick and one of our founding fathers, is said to have suggested the word "Dominion" which he saw Psalm 72:8 in the Bible in which refers to God in this way: "*He shall have dominion from sea to sea*" (RSV) and these words are actually carved into the Parliament buildings' tower. Canada was not the first country to be described as a Dominion; the root of this word stems from the Latin word, meaning master. The term "Dominion" also had a long history of use by the British government as a generic title to refer to any of its extraterritorial possessions.

The Canadian government, however, no longer regards "Dominion of Canada" as the country's proper name, and has deliberately not used the title in several decades. The phrase was gradually phased out from the 1940s to the 1960s, largely a result of growing post-colonial Canadian nationalism which triggered a desire to downplay terms and symbols that were considered excessively imperial in nature. Curiously enough, the phrase "Dominion of Canada" does not appear as the formal name anywhere in the original 1867 BNA Act, now known as the Constitution Act. Basically, the document says that Canada is a dominion and its name is Canada.

It is interesting to me that at least some of our country's founders had a Christian faith, and that the name of our country, or at least the original informal name, had in part a biblical basis. It's fairly evident that Canada is now a secular society and can no longer be called a Christian country in that we have largely departed from accepting the Christian values that once were a significant component of our society. Some would applaud this, but it remains to be seen whether our society is weaker because of these changes in values.

As a side note, it turns out that Americans also have a solid Christian heritage and beginning. The rule in designing Washington D.C. was that no building could be higher than the Washington

Monument, which is just over 555 feet high. On the aluminum cap, atop the Washington Monument overlooking the sixty-nine square miles which comprise the District of Columbia, capital of the U.S., are displayed two Latin words: *"Laus Deo"* meaning "*Praise be to God!*"

This giant obelisk was opened to the public in 1888. Visitors can take in the beautiful panoramic view of the city with its division into four major segments. One can see the plan of the designer, Pierre L'Enfant, which is a cross imposed upon the landscape, with the White House to the north, the Jefferson Memorial to the south, the Capitol to the east and the Lincoln Memorial to the west.

While the separation of church and state has been interpreted to be stated in the First Amendment in the U.S. Constitution, it seems that there still is a substantial Christian presence. The cornerstone of the Washington Monument was laid on July 4th, 1848 and deposited within it were many items, including the Holy Bible presented by the Bible Society. This illustrates the discipline, moral direction, and the spiritual tone given by the founders of America. Another indication of this is George Washington's prayer for America asking for God's blessings and protection for the new nation, to enable its citizens to do justice and to love mercy.

## We Need Sweet Honeybees

While there is no clear evidence to support this, Albert Einstein is reported to have once said, "If the bee disappeared off the face of the Earth, man would only have four years left to live."

Bees provide us with honey but, even more importantly, they provide vital pollination to plants. You may have seen row upon row of hive boxes lined up in a farmer's field. Often an apiarist will rent space in rural fields or be paid to install hundreds of hive boxes. But if you're a city slicker you may well think of bees as an irritating nuisance or a serious allergy concern when you encounter them buzzing around your head. Could a reduction in the number of bees be an early warning sign of a larger problem in the environment? Are they the "canary in the coal mine" for the health of planet earth?

Yes.

At least one-third of our food supply relies on honeybees for pollination, which is essential for the reproduction of the plants the bees service. The honeybee is a major pollinator of many food crops such as almonds, apples, avocados, blueberries, cantaloupes, cherries, cranberries, cucumbers, sunflowers, watermelon, and many others totaling billions of dollars' worth of crops. So if honeybees disappear and plants are not pollinated, these crops will not grow and cannot provide food to feed our families. Finding replacements that can do the work of bees is problematic. While there are perhaps 20,000 different species of pollinators, scientists have found that bees and other pollinators such as butterflies and hummingbirds may be on a path to extinction, but they have been unable to find a primary cause.

Honeybees do provide a second service: they make honey. There are seven species of honeybees that produce and store honey and build nests out of wax, but only two are commonly used by beekeepers. Beekeepers often transport beehives and bees from field to field as crops need pollinating and they usually charge for the pollination services they provide. Honey is a thick liquid produced by certain types of bees from the nectar of flowers. While many species of insects consume nectar, honeybees refine and concentrate the nectar to make honey. Indeed, they make lots of honey so they will have plenty of food during winter when flower nectar is unavailable. Honey is the complex substance made when nectar and sweet deposits from plants and trees are gathered, modified and stored in the honeycomb as a food source for the colony.

A colony generally contains one queen bee, a fertile female, and up to a few thousand drone bees or fertile males, and a large seasonally variable population of sterile female worker bees. Eggs are laid singly in a cell in a wax honeycomb, produced and shaped by the worker bees. Drones develop from unfertilized eggs. Females (queens and worker bees) develop from fertilized eggs. There is only one queen in a hive and her main purpose in life is to make more bees. She can lay over 1,500 eggs per day and will usually live less than two years. She is larger and has a longer abdomen than the workers or drones.

Young worker bees clean the hive and feed the larvae. When their royal jelly-producing glands begin to atrophy, they begin building comb cells. They progress to other within-colony tasks as they become older, such as receiving nectar and pollen from foragers, and guarding the hive. Later still, a worker takes her first orientation flights and finally leaves the hive and typically spends the remainder of her life as a forager. Older workers are called field bees. They forage outside the hive to gather nectar, pollen, water, and certain sticky plant resins used in hive construction. Workers born early in the season will live about six weeks while those born in the fall will live until the following spring. Worker bees cooperate to find food and use a pattern of "dancing" to communicate information regarding resources with each other. Worker bees of a certain age will secrete beeswax, which is used to form the walls and caps of the comb. As with honey, beeswax is gathered by humans for various purposes.

All honeybees live in colonies where the worker bees will sting intruders as a form of defense, and alarmed bees will release a pheromone that stimulates the attack response in other bees. The worker bee dies after the stinger is torn from its body. A bee sting can be serious or even fatal if a person is highly allergic.

While most beekeepers have medium to large operations, some brave city dwellers are installing one or two beehive boxes in their back yards. If done properly, these folks receive a double benefit in that they obtain all the honey they can consume, or perhaps sell at a local farmers' market, plus effectively helping to pollinate plants in their neighborhood.

One odd note: Killer bees are Africanized honeybees or a subspecies of bees that were released accidentally in Brazil in 1957. They were imported from South Africa by a researcher who was attempting to produce a variety of honeybee better adapted to the tropics than the European honeybee. Africanized honeybees produce honey better in hot climates, but, unfortunately, they are also much more aggressive at defending their nests. Many people have been killed by mass stinging, resulting from getting too close to a nest of Africanized honeybees.

## Think Tanks

Organizations commonly referred to as "think tanks" have become increasingly prominent in recent years in the policy-making arena, and in the arena of influencing public opinion. The thing about think tanks, I believe, is that many of them have an ideological basis while trying to give the impression that they are objective. More often this is not the case, but the newspaper reader or the TV newscast watcher may be misled to think that an objective opinion is being presented.

One knows, for example, that if the Fraser Institute speaks out on a given policy issue, they will give us a conservative perspective, while conclusions from the Canadian Centre for Policy Alternatives will generally have a left-leaning bias. This is not to say that think tanks are not doing useful work; it's just that their philosophical approach to issues should be stated up front to help citizens reach their own conclusions by considering all available viewpoints. While think tanks may do lots of research, it is important to realize that most of them also function as lobby groups. The following is just a thumbnail sketch of some of the think tanks in Canada.

The Council of Canadians is described as Canada's pre-eminent citizens' watchdog organization and claims to be non-partisan but instead leans left of centre and is supported by a range of activists. The Council lobbies Members of Parliament, conducts research, and runs national campaigns aimed at putting some of the country's most important issues into the spotlight.

The conservative Fraser Institute has strong views on limiting the role of government and the role of markets in presenting ideas on economic and social policy. Although this is a minor portion of their work, each year it stimulates considerable angst by rating the quality of schools in British Columbia.

We don't hear as much from the C.D. Howe Institute as we used to but it is a respected independent, non-profit, economic and social policy research institution. The Institute derives the majority of its funding from individual and corporate members, who are given the opportunity to attend public policy roundtables and conferences featuring prominent Canadian and international policymakers, business leaders, and public servants.

The Canada West Foundation is said to be an independent, non-partisan and non-ideological, non-profit research institute that introduced western perspectives into Canadian policy debates. A major objective is to give the people of the four western provinces a voice on Canadian issues.

The Canadian Centre for Policy Alternatives is a center-left think tank that offers an alternative to the message that Canadians "have no choice" about the policies that affect their lives. They concentrate on economic policy, international trade, environmental justice and social policy.

The Institute On Governance (IOG) is a non-profit organization that attempts to promote effective governance described as the "traditions, institutions and processes that determine how power is exercised, how citizens are given a voice, and how decisions are made on issues of public concern."

The mission of the Pembina Institute is to advance sustainable energy solutions through innovative research, education, consulting, and advocacy. It provides policy research leadership and education on climate change, energy issues such as oil sands and coal bed methane, green economics, and energy efficiency.

The Canadian Institute for Advanced Research (CIFAR) works to enhance Canada's knowledge base by allowing Canada to think ahead of the rest of the world in the development of new technologies and insight by bringing together distinguished thinkers from across Canada and around the world. They enable Canadian researchers to work on multidisciplinary international research teams that built to develop ideas that advance Canada's research community and drives innovation. CIFAR supports about 400 researchers in sixteen countries.

The International Institute for Sustainable Development advances policy recommendations on international trade and investment, economic policy, climate change, measurement and indicators, and natural resource management to make development sustainable through collaborative projects with global partners and rigorous research. A range of environmental activists from around the world supports it so the Canadian input may be fairly small.

The National Citizens' Coalition advocates free enterprise, individual freedom and personal responsibility under limited government, and basic political and economic freedoms. Founded in 1967, the NCC is a registered, non-profit corporation that is independent of all political parties. Their mantra is "more freedom through less government."

The Policy Research Initiative (PRI) works to strengthen the federal government's policy research capacity. While PRI was created by the Clerk of the Privy Council, it has links to the broader policy research community, including academics, policy researchers, and independent organizations.

The Canadian Council on Social Development is a non-profit social policy and research organization focusing on issues such as poverty, disability, cultural diversity, child well-being, labor markets, and housing. Their emphasis initially was on children and the well-being of families but the focus has shifted more broadly to the development and promotion of effective and progressive social policies.

I haven't listed all of the think tanks in Canada, but you get the idea. I'm sure most of them do good work, some even do great work; it's just a good idea to find out where they are coming from before accepting their conclusions.

One thing that can be said is, many Canadians care passionately about our country and work to make it better.

# Things You Don't Want to Hear

**Things you don't want to hear in a laboratory:**

Oops!

Has anyone seen my gum?

Didn't we bring ten rats in here this morning?

Where is the fire extinguisher?

I hope that we're insured.

Well, I'm not cleaning *that* up!

This rash just won't go away.

Protocol – Shmotocol!

How many times have I told you not to eat anything here in the lab!

**Things you don't want to hear while in surgery:**

Oops!

Someone call housekeeping. We're going to need a mop!

Wait a minute; I thought we were supposed to amputate the other leg!

Oh no! I just lost an earring!

Better save that—we'll need it for the autopsy.

Darn, there go the lights again.

I wish I had remembered to bring my glasses.

Wow, if that's his spleen, then what is this?

**Things you don't want to hear from your airplane pilot:**

Oops!

Ladies and gentlemen, there will be a slight delay of two hours before we can take off.

Is there a doctor on board?

Ladies and gentlemen, severe weather is reported in [Vancouver] so we are diverting to [Regina].

Ladies and gentlemen, has anyone seen our navigator?

Our landing gear won't work so we need to circle the airport for about an hour.

**Things you don't want to hear at work:**

There's no easy way to say this…

Everyone in your unit just signed a complaint against you.

Did you really just say that?

Can I speak to you in private?

We have a crisis on our hands.

Do you really think that your presentation went okay?

I can't find your document; I must have accidentally deleted it.

I know it's the long weekend but you need to work tomorrow.

Are you familiar with our harassment policy?

**Things you don't want to hear about losing weight:**

You just need to put more effort into it.

Just buy this plan. I lost fifty pounds in five weeks.

It's easy; you just need to eat properly.

It's easy; you just need to get more exercise.

You can't lose weight overnight.

Dieting is a lifelong commitment.

**Things that school teachers don't want to hear:**

My child is really bright; it's just that he's bored in your class.

I know I agreed to drive kids for the field trip today but something came up.

You give too much homework.

Our computer crashed so my daughter's homework isn't done.

Our dog ate my homework.

Our old teacher didn't make us do that.

You get three months' vacation each year so you should be able to stay late once in a while.

**Things you don't want to hear at a gun shop:**

Can I buy, like, just one bullet?

Will this pistol show up on a metal detector?

Do you know what time that bank across the street opens?

Can I just rent this gun for a few hours?

Why do I need ID to buy a gun?

**Things that traffic policemen don't want to hear:**

I pay your salary.

Shouldn't you be busy catching real crooks?

I'm sorry officer; I forgot that my radar detector wasn't plugged in.

Excuse me but I had to call my office.

Hey, I didn't think that police cars could go 125 kph!

My brother-in-law is a judge.

You're not going to check the trunk, are you?

I thought you had to be in good shape to be a police officer.

Your breath smells really bad.

Honest beer, there's no officer in the trunk.

Don't you think I drive real good even if I'm drunk?

Do you know who I am?

## Women's Rights

Morocco approved a new constitution in 2011, granting new rights to women and minorities. This was a first for an Arab monarchy and many wondered if it would be a model for other Arab nations. The new constitution also gave more power to the elected Parliament and established an independent judiciary, but the King still has controlling authority in many areas. All of this was, at least, a first step and is in contrast to what has been happening in other Arab nations. Morocco is different from most Arab countries largely because its proximity to Europe means that many Moroccans travel back and forth to Europe to work or go on vacation. Plus, it established political parties and unions when it gained independence from France in 1956.

The situation is starkly different in Saudi Arabia where no woman can travel, work, get married, get divorced, gain admittance to a public hospital, or live independently without permission from a male guardian. A few brave women were trying in the spring of 2011 to organize a protest defying the ban on women driving, with the result that they were charged and forced to stand trial. Apparently, there are more than 750,000 male taxi drivers or chauffeurs in the country.

The Saudis are anxious about the possibility of women having unrestrained mobility and the regime demands the exclusion of women from the public sphere. They say this is required for religious reasons, but others have failed to find this requirement in the Koran and state that Muslim women used to ride camels for centuries so they should be able to drive a car today. We don't hear much about this women's campaign for the right to drive It will be interesting to see if it gains traction along with other freedom issues in the Middle East. If so, it may produce an overhaul of the Saudi political system.

Some progress is being made since King Abdullah, who was actually regarded as a bit of a reformer by Saudi standards, suggested that he may allow women to vote in the future and even be candidates in local elections. Time will tell if this is too radical for Saudi males.

Iran tried to implement strict driving prohibitions in 1978 after the revolution, but the ruling Ayatollahs were unable to push these rules through in part because women had already been driving there for decades. Riding bicycles and motorcycles was deemed to be "un-Islamic" and sexually provocative. It may take decades to change this fundamental attitude of male domination and excluding women, but when it does there will be a dramatic change in the way these countries work. Already we have seen men and women protesting together in countries like Tunisia, Egypt, Bahrain, and Syria. Sometimes these changes happen quickly while other times it takes a long time.

It may be easy for us in North America to sit back and say that women's rights should be improved in the Middle East as well as in other countries around the world so as to be equal to those of men, but things get more complicated when we look at our own examples.

In the majority of mosques in the U.S., for example, Muslim women are forced to worship and pray separately from men, as is the case around the world. U.S. law says that "private organizations" cannot discriminate based on gender but here is where things become complicated. The doctrinal position of the Catholic Church and Orthodox Jewish synagogues is that only men may be priests, and some evangelical/conservative denominations require that senior pastors be men. Governments are loath to wade into theological or doctrinal or worship issues, and rightly so. It will take a lot of thinking to ensure that denominations and churches are free to worship as they feel led, and yet treat women fairly.

## TIBET

Tibet is a modern-day tragedy ever since China, by brute force, simply took over this country and now calls it a province of the People's Republic of China (PRC). Perhaps if Tibet had huge oil resources, the western world would not stand by while China works to assimilate this unique people and culture.

Chinese authorities say Tibet has always been part of its territory but many Tibetans insist the region was virtually independent for centuries and that Beijing's control is draining Tibetan culture. For at least 1500 years, the nation of Tibet has had a complex relationship with its large and powerful neighbour to the east, China. When the Mongols' Yuan Empire fell in 1368 to the ethnic Han Chinese Ming, Tibet reasserted its independence and refused to pay tribute to the new emperor.

In 1950, the People's Liberation Army (PLA) of the newly formed PRC invaded Tibet. Having stability re-established in Beijing for the first time in decades, Mao Zedong sought to assert China's right to rule over Tibet as well. The PLA inflicted a swift and total defeat on Tibet's small army, and China drafted a "Seventeen Point Agreement" incorporating Tibet as an autonomous region of the People's Republic of China. Much of majestic capital city of Lhasa subsequently lay in ruins by March 1959. An estimated 800 artillery shells had pummeled Norbulingka (a palace and surrounding park), and Lhasa's three largest monasteries were essentially leveled. The Chinese rounded up thousands of monks, executing many of them and ransacking monasteries and temples all over Lhasa. The remaining members of the Dalai Lama's bodyguard were publicly executed by a firing squad. The Dalai Lama has remained in exile ever since. The end result in 1959 was a failed attempt to liberate Tibet from China.

By the time of the 1964 census, 300,000 Tibetans had gone "missing" in the previous five years, either secretly imprisoned, killed, or in exile. In the days after the 1959 uprising, the Chinese government revoked most aspects of Tibet's autonomy, and initiated resettlement and land distribution across the country. China's central government, in a bid to dilute the Tibetan population and provide jobs for Han Chinese, initiated a "Western China Development Program" in 1978. As many as 300,000 Han Chinese now live in Tibet, two thirds of them in the capital city, and ethnic Chinese hold the vast majority of government posts. The Tibetan population of Lhasa, in contrast, is only about 100,000. In a five-year period ending in 2012, almost one hundred Tibetans set themselves on fire to protest Chinese oppression; the Chinese government responded by arresting many who had been associated with the people who died.

An era ending in 2011 in a rainy temple courtyard in the northern town of Dharamsala when Harvard-educated lawyer, Lobsang Sangay, took the oath of office as Prime Minister of the Tibetan "government-in-exile," and the Dalai Lama ended his formal role as a political leader. The move has been parsed in various quarters as either a break from Tibet's feudal past, a modest stepwise change, or an attempt to outsmart the Chinese occupation of their Tibetan homeland.

Polls opened in Tibetan community centres around the world on March 20, 2011. By the end of that day some 100,000 Tibetans living in exile voted in the historic election to replace "Prime Minister" Tenzin who had served two five-year terms. In Tibet itself, however, an estimated six million Tibetans were not permitted to cast ballots because of Chinese control.

Voting stations were also set up in four Canadian cities: Toronto (with 1,089 registered voters, the country's largest Tibetan voting bloc), Montreal, Vancouver, and Calgary. The sealed ballot boxes were sent to the Central Tibetan Administration's New York office, where they were counted and the results forwarded to Dharamsala, which is the seat of the government in exile. The formal transfer of Prime Ministerial "power" occurred that August.

India has the largest contingent of exiled Tibetans, and they of course were free to vote, but the fate of some 20,000 Tibetans living in Nepal was problematic. During preliminary run-off votes for Prime

Minister last year, Nepalese authorities bowed to pressure from China and prevented voting. Some 15,000 Nepalese police were deployed to break up rallies of Tibetan refugees in Kathmandu who were seeking to mark the 52nd anniversary of the Tibetan uprising. Nepal's official one-China policy precludes the possibility of an independent Tibet. China's repressive actions in Tibet continue even though U.N. human rights investigators called on China in 2011 to halt repression of Tibetan Buddhist monks and voiced concern that many had been arrested or had disappeared during a recent crackdown on religious freedom.

Lobsang Sangay was a senior fellow in the East Asian Legal Studies Program at Harvard Law School. He wrote his doctoral dissertation on "Democracy and the History of the Tibetan Government in Exile from 1959-2004." In 2003 he organized five conferences between Chinese and Tibetan scholars, including a meeting between the Dalai Lama and thirty-five Chinese scholars at Harvard University.

China insists they must appoint the next Dalia Lama, which would be like having the fox appoint the security guards for the hen house. An expected visit by a Chinese-appointed Tibetan Buddhist leader to a prominent monastery raised new fears of repression among monks loyal to another person named by the Dalai Lama.

A proposed trip by a Beijing-chosen Panchen Lama to the Labrang Monastery in the northwest was seen as an attempt by China to boost his credibility among Tibetans over the Dalai Lama selection. The Panchen Lama is the second-highest religious leader for Tibetans after the Dalai Lama, and traditionally has a role in both the identification and education of any new Dalai Lama after the current one dies.

## ACADEMIC FREEDOM - IS IT A MYTH?

I studied pharmacy and then pharmacology in university, so I dealt with questions of how a given drug works and other basic scientific matters. My master's thesis dealt with how the stereochemistry of certain compounds affected their ability to induce a disease called porphyria. I therefore rarely ventured into topics where academic freedom would be an issue. I was once told in a graduate student seminar that I was a "teleologist" (the belief that purpose and design are apparent in nature, or the belief that final causes exist), which I took as a compliment since it meant this professor seemed to recognize that I believed that God had created the universe and designed how intricate things such as the human body work.

Academic freedom is a big issue in universities, especially on the arts or philosophy side of academic studies. Academic freedom is the belief that university faculties and even students must be free to pursue, express, and teach any and all ideas, even if those ideas are unpopular, without fear of losing their jobs. Some people love to say, "I disagree with what you are saying but I will defend your right to say it," but when pressed, the situation becomes a lot more complicated.

Universities generally strongly advocate the concept of academic freedom but there are numerous examples where the concept runs into practical difficulties. Few, if any, universities today would hire a Philosophy Department faculty member who advocated conservative Christian views, for example, even if couched in terms that suggested their comments were "evidence-based research".

It is my view that most university departments or faculties undeniably operate from a secular humanist perspective. When asked, most professors would probably say that they are not religious, not recognizing that secular humanism is also a belief system. Many would say they are agnostics or atheists, which are also belief systems or religions. At the same time, both science and arts departments would not readily accept a potential faculty member who presented him or herself as a Christian. For example, a geologist or anthropologist who presented research evidence that indicated the likelihood of a creator, while rejecting evolution, would find it very difficult to be hired at most universities, regardless of the quality of his scientific research.

My impression is that university professors feel free and entitled to propagate secular or even anti-Christian world views but they are not, in fact, tolerant of anyone with a Christian perspective. This is quite a contradiction since these academics are defending academic freedom while actively rejecting an alternative way of looking at things. I suppose they defend their approach by saying (incorrectly) that the Christian perspective is not credible or that the research is of such poor quality that it doesn't deserve to be considered. However, making premature or uninformed decisions rather than seriously assessing the evidence is neither an indication of academic freedom nor a true scientific approach.

# My University Stories

It seems like a hundred years ago, or at least a lifetime, that I first registered at the University of Alberta (UofA) in Edmonton, Alberta, in 1960. We didn't register online like students do today and we didn't have advance notice about what courses we would have to take. Instead, all seventy-five of us hopeful pharmacists met in a large classroom and the faculty led us through all of the forms as we completed the schedule of classes and laboratories. We only had one elective, so the process went pretty quickly.

I sat next to a fellow who became my best friend the entire three years until we graduated, and we are still friends today. We had thirty hours of classes per week, partly because of the eight hours of labs attached to three of the courses. We found that many students in Arts or Commerce had only seventeen or eighteen hours. Probably one of the most interesting courses was Pharmaceutical Latin, which was only one hour per week, but the professor was a real character in teaching us basic Latin so that we could learn how to read prescriptions.

Back in those days, all freshmen were required to take Physical Education, which was three hours per week. We started with badminton for about three months then took swimming. I remember swimming because they had an interesting way of deciding who would go into the advanced class and who was relegated to the beginner's class. Every person had to jump into the deep end of the pool, and those who desperately struggled to reach the side of the pool quickly were classified as the beginners while those who swam to the other end were the advanced group. After a quick shower, we ran with our wet heads across the campus—in winter—to Zoology and Botany.

I worked as a pharmacist for almost two years, and then was accepted into graduate school at the UofA where I still had to take a number of courses such as chemistry and calculus. I particularly remember calculus since anything related to math was generally a major challenge for me.

The first day I walked into class I found the professor barely spoke English. I thought, "I'm going to have enough trouble with the material and, if I can't even understand what the prof is saying, I'm going to be in worse trouble." I was able to switch to another section where the prof spoke English well and was an excellent teacher, plus he gave fairly easy progress exams so I actually had a reasonably good average. My friends who stayed in the other section struggled. The final exam applied to all sections and counted for fifty per cent of the final grade. I followed my usual practice of trying to answer the easy questions to build momentum and confidence, but to my consternation I didn't find a single easy question! I struggled on, and ended up with a final average of sixty-six per cent, just one point above the mark required to pass.

My master's thesis involved studying the effects of chemicals on porphyria, which is a disease passed down through families where a precursor of hemoglobin, called "heme," is not made properly. We used a tissue-culture technique of red blood cells from chicken blood because chicken blood contains high levels of the enzyme that stimulates hemoglobin formation. An excellent place to obtain fresh chicken blood is a Kosher slaughterhouse, so every two weeks or so I would visit one, where the Rabbi would cut throats of about ten chickens and I would hold my little beaker (stored in ice) and collect as much blood as I needed while two little Polish babushkas took care of the chickens.

I had just started dating the beautiful lady who would eventually become my wife, and she tried to explain to her father the kind of work that her new boyfriend was doing. Her dad wasn't very impressed that his daughter's boyfriend was frequenting slaughterhouses collecting blood, but I guess he understood enough that I was allowed to continue seeing her. My thesis professor was astonished when I eventually told him that I was getting married. He assumed that because I was quiet and devoted to my work, I must not have a social life or time for girls.

A year after getting married and moving to Ottawa to work for Health Canada, the government sent me to Michigan State University in East Lansing, Michigan, to get my PhD. We enjoyed university life in the U.S. but some things were noticeably different. I was on half salary from my government job, and while we were happy, we were pretty poor.

I used rabbits in my thesis research (they didn't seem to be as prolific in captivity as everyone believes) but periodically I brought home a control untreated rabbit for dinner. As they say, it tastes like chicken. We made friends at church and my sweetie would do hair for some of the ladies, which provided some income. When we invited another student couple over, we could generally afford only popcorn and coffee. One Christmas we received $50 from each of our parents, which had never happened before or since, and this enabled us to provide a nice Christmas for some relatives who happened to visit.

We lived in married-student housing; every cracker box apartment was exactly the same with early Salvation Army furniture, except that some students had nicer stereo systems than others. Then our baby came along, so the lady who lived next door lady babysat for us. The walls were so thin than she could hear our little girl cry when she woke up from her afternoon nap.

One of my grad student colleagues was quite a talker. He was the only grad student I knew who had a post-doctoral position lined up while there remained a distinct possibility that he would be kicked out of grad school. One day he was setting the controls on the large oven to dry some tissues when he said to me, "Tell Dr. X (who was Jewish; the name is changed to protect the innocent) that his shower is ready." It happened that Dr. X had walked into the lab right behind the loquacious grad student and heard his inappropriate comment. Let's just say they had a few words.

I had a tiny office adjacent to my lab and mounted a large Canadian flag on the wall. My office was close to the back entry of the building so many Americans saw this huge flag as they came into the building. Some of them didn't appreciate my patriotism, but for most, if they stopped, it was a great conversation starter.

My thesis prof was great and his research grant paid for me to give papers at different scientific meetings. I was able to visit Stanford University, which I enjoyed immensely, but I also went to the University of Pittsburgh and to the University of Michigan. Early on at MSU, I spend two days writing comprehensive exams, which I had to pass to stay at grad school. Then after three years of study and work, I successfully defended my thesis and we packed up and moved back to Ottawa. While studying at MSU was a marvelously rewarding experience, I felt that the U.S. was a nice place to visit but I wouldn't want to live there. I came back to Canada with a renewed appreciation of being Canadian.

## Important and Intriguing Sentences

William Watson once suggested in the Vancouver Sun that the following four sentences should be identified as important: "Love thy neighbor as thyself," "Honor thy father and mother," "Two plus two equals four," and Adam Smith's "The division of labor is limited by the extent of the market."

Watson went on to write about division of labor, the industrial revolution and various other economic issues. I'm more interested in pursuing the idea of other important sentences. Here are some suggestions:

"In the beginning, God created the heavens and the earth." (Genesis 1:1).

"I love you; will you marry me?" is a pretty important sentence with a lot of implications.

"It was a dark and stormy night." (Edward Bulwer-Lytton, *Paul Clifford*)

"It was the best of times and the worst of times." (Charles Dickens, *A Tale of Two Cities*)

"If you were to die tonight, do you know for sure that you would go to heaven?" (D. James Kennedy, Evangelism Explosion)

"Being a Christian is more than just an instantaneous conversion—it is a daily process whereby you grow to be more and more like Christ." (Billy Graham, who has led hundreds of thousands of people to make personal decisions to accept Jesus Christ into their lives.)

"I am not a crook." (Richard Nixon)

"Political power grows out of the barrel of a gun." (Mao Zedong) This crude sentence seems to summarize fairly accurately the philosophy of the Chinese communists and helps explain the carnage and suffering that occurred in China after Mao and his cohorts took over.

"Grab them by their [anatomically obvious reproductive organs] and their hearts and minds will follow." (Joseph Stalin, the USSR's brutal dictator)

"If you have it [love] you don't need to have anything else, and if you don't have it, it doesn't matter what else you have." (James M. Barrie) This philosophy, opposite to the above two entries, is much more attractive; the only thing missing is a commitment to accept the love of Jesus Christ.

"Loneliness and the feeling of being unwanted is the most terrible poverty." (Mother Teresa)

"Are we there yet?" (Anon—Every child who as ever travelled any distance in the back seat of a car.)

"It is hereby recognized and declared that in Canada there have existed and shall continue to exist without discrimination by reason of race, national origin, color, religion or sex, the following human rights and fundamental freedoms, namely, (*a*) the right of the individual to life, liberty, security of the person and enjoyment of property, and the right not to be deprived thereof except by due process of law; (*b*) the right of the individual to equality before the law and the protection of the law; (*c*) freedom of religion; (*d*) freedom of speech; (*e*) freedom of assembly and association; and (*f*) freedom of the press." (Canadian Charter of Rights and Freedoms)

"Teacher, which is the greatest commandment in the Law?" Jesus replied: "Love the Lord your God with all your heart and with all your soul and with all your mind. This is the first and greatest commandment. And the second is like it: Love your neighbor as yourself." (Matthew 22: 36-39)

"The truth is incontrovertible. Malice may attack it, ignorance may deride it, but in the end; there it is." (Winston Churchill)

"We, the People of the United States, in order to form a more perfect Union, establish justice, insure domestic tranquility, provide for the common defense, promote the general welfare, and secure the blessings of liberty to ourselves and our posterity, do ordain and establish this Constitution for the United States of America." (Preamble to the U.S. Constitution)

"If you believe in God and God does exist, you will be rewarded with eternal life in heaven, thus an *infinite gain*. If you do not believe in God and God does exist, you will be condemned to remain in hell forever, thus an *infinite loss*. If you believe in God and God does not exist, you will not be rewarded, thus a *finite loss*. If you do not believe in God and God does not exist, you will not be rewarded, but you have lived your own life, thus a *finite gain*." (Blaise Pascal defining "Pascal's Wager")

"John Newton, Clerk, once an infidel and libertine, a servant of slaves in Africa, was, by the rich mercy of our Lord and Savior Jesus Christ, preserved, restored, pardoned, and appointed to preach the faith he had long labored to destroy." (Epitaph on John Newton's tombstone)

"Even though large tracts of Europe and many old and famous States have fallen or may fall into the grip of the Gestapo and all the odious apparatus of Nazi rule, we shall not flag or fail. We shall go on to the end. We shall fight in France, we shall fight on the seas and oceans, we shall fight with growing confidence and growing strength in the air, and we shall defend our island, whatever the cost may be. We shall fight on the beaches, we shall fight on the landing grounds, we shall fight in the fields and in the streets, we shall fight in the hills; we shall never surrender, and if, which I do not for a moment believe, this island or a large part of it were subjugated and starving, then our Empire beyond the seas, armed and guarded by the British Fleet, would carry on the struggle, until, in God's good time, the New World, with all its power and might, steps forth to the rescue and the liberation of the old." (Portion of a 1940 Winston Churchill speech)

"Recommend to your children virtue; that alone can make them happy, not gold." (Ludwig van Beethoven)

## Driving Miss Daisy and Mr. Attitude

I used to ride the bus every day to work, although I rarely ride buses now. I told one of my friends a few years ago that it must be nice to be a city bus driver. At that time I had just been on a new electric bus as it hummed and clicked along with the driver controlling an impressive dashboard console. I told him I thought that his job was just like riding in a nice little office with the scenery continually changing and always presenting the opportunity to meet new people and regular friends. My bus driver friend wasn't too impressed with my enthusiasm and he intimated that driving a city bus would be a great occupation if it weren't for some of the passengers.

One of the big things about being a city bus driver is the shift work. Of course, seniority plays a huge role so junior drivers get the less desirable shifts. This includes split shifts, which may account for thirty per cent of the work. Typically a driver might start work around 6:30 AM and work to 9:30 AM, then be off until 2:00 PM and work until 6:00 PM. This makes for a long day even though they are paid for only seven or eight hours. Straight shifts might begin at 5:00 AM and go to 12:30 PM or from 2:00 or 3:00 PM until 9:00 or 10:00 PM.

There even are "owl shifts" which might not end until 2:00 or 3:00 in the morning. A related complication is getting to the bus depot or to the street location where you relieve a driver and start your shift, or need to take a bus at the end of your shift to get back to your car or back home.

Straight shifts typically do not have coffee breaks or lunch breaks. Some routes have sufficient "reco time" built in at the end of the line, but sometimes the traffic is extra heavy or there are other problems and the driver has no option but to turn around and head back the other way with no break at all. If the bus is late people complain and blame the driver even if he or she hasn't had a break for several hours.

Planning for vacation is another complicated challenge for city bus drivers. Drivers often need to sign up in September for the following year's vacation time off. Again, this is done by seniority so junior drivers may need to be satisfied with February or October holidays. Drivers also need to make lots of compromises to get the days off that they want, or the routes that they want.

City bus drivers need to watch carefully for car drivers. Drivers know that they can easily beat a bus across an intersection and then they may cut right in front of the bus and stop suddenly if they just spotted a parking spot or a pedestrian. Many car drivers are courteous but others seem to need to use their finger or car horn to demonstrate their displeasure when a bus pulls out of a bus stop and back into the traffic flow on a busy street.

Successful and happy bus drivers adjust to all of this by maintaining a professional attitude so they can drive safely and smile when people get on and off. Other tests of patience for a bus driver are little old ladies who slowly get on and off the bus and get upset when there are no seats left during rush hour, and harried young mothers with three little kids and a baby carriage. Drivers need to just keep driving and answer questions politely, and not go home and take their frustrations out on their families.

Transit drivers have no shortage of hair-raising, and harassing, stories so having thick skin is a requirement to succeed at the job. In Winnipeg, a passenger made a gun gesture to a driver with his fingers before revealing an actual gun in his jacket. In another case, an older man walked up to the bus driver and started screaming for a schedule. When told that the driver didn't have one the passenger started yelling obscenities. Another driver said he gets sworn at all the time just for following the bus route rather than taking an arrogant passenger to his or her front door.

One report indicates that five bus drivers are physically assaulted every day in Canada. A media release from Winnipeg Transit said there were seventy physical assaults on drivers in 2009, with about forty per cent of those involving a passenger spitting or throwing an object at the driver. One B.C. driver suffered mild brain damage and short-term memory loss after he was sucker-punched in the head. Some cities have tested or used plastic shields to protect drivers, but these shields have some disadvantages. Drivers also often deal with people with mental illness, addictions and drunkenness.

Police investigate serious incidents and often have videotapes from bus security cameras. Women make up at least ten per cent of bus drivers, and sexual assaults against female drivers are especially troubling. While unions may call for more transit police to provide security on buses, it doesn't seem feasible to provide police on every bus. In Metro Vancouver, the number of assaults on bus drivers has actually decreased from 240 in 2006 to 143 in 2008, but this is still far too many. Of the assaults in 2008, sixty-three involved physical violence and twenty-three charges were laid or recommended.

Bus drivers face another problem, namely that of passengers who refuse to pay. Transit companies say they try to eliminate or at least dramatically reduce fare evasion, but it's the driver who is at the frontline. Drivers are in a no-win situation in confronting fare evaders, especially from a safety perspective—some riders not only beat the fare—sometimes they beat the driver, too.

Still, driving a bus can be a good job if you are willing to work unconventional hours, at least at the start of one's career. One needs to have a responsible attitude, good time-keeping skills, good verbal communication skills, and of course, good vision and hearing. Applicants must demonstrate that they possess these and other key qualities. Transit companies have developed an extensive battery of tests to assess applicants. They typically conduct a "trainability test" which involves spending time with an instructor from the training department, and the opportunity (requirement) to drive a bus on the city streets in the area. The driving test also measures the ability to remember a specific set of instructions. A video test presents a wide range of scenarios, which are frequently encountered by transit operators, and the applicants are asked to select the most appropriate response. These tests measure an applicant's customer service skills and their ability to defuse potential conflict situations.

It may seem odd, given that a city bus driver deals with hundreds of people during a shift, that driving a city bus is basically a lonely job. Drivers often feel alone, except when some other lonely person sits in the "yacketty seat" across the aisle from the driver and chats when things aren't too busy. The only contact a driver might have with a supervisor might involve being called to his or her office to respond to a complaint. The positive side is that there is quite a lot of independence, and one is not stuck in a stuffy office.

So remember, when you ride the bus, please be considerate of the driver! It's not an easy job.

## It's a Digital Technological World Out There

Technology seems to be moving along faster than our ability to control it or at least recognize all of the implications of these changes. Many of these changes are good but some may prove problematic. For example, we have a store in our community that sells all kinds of spy gadgets so you don't need to hire a private detective to find out what your neighbour or competitor is doing. Written messages and phone calls can be easily monitored and recorded, and it seems inevitable that some enterprising physicist, physician, or engineer will invent a device that records our thoughts as we walk past their detectors or when they surreptitiously bug our house and telephone.

A practical application of this idea has already occurred in the medical field where technology is continually proving to be advantageous. Neuroscientists have used brain implants to send out signals that enable paralyzed patients to maneuver their arms or prosthetic devices just by thinking that this is what they want to do. The patients "just imagine" moving an arm and the brain implant picks up this signal. This is a fabulous development for people suffering from spinal cord or brain injuries, or strokes. Some brain implants can control computer cursors.

One change that techies are already discussing is how our approach to banking will soon change even more than it already has. We won't need to go to a bank since technology enables us to scan or take a picture of a cheque and deposit it into our account. We can pay our bills or even take out a mortgage just by using an electronic signature. ATMs will soon be obsolete, and wallets as well, since smart phones will replace debit and credit cards. Perhaps passports will soon be obsolete if we are implanted with a micro-sized chip in our arm to positively identify ourselves.

When you get up in the morning and go to the bathroom, your toilet will be able to perform a quick health checkup, store the results in your home computer and send the results to your doctor (or other family members if you wish, or even to Twitter). Your hormone levels, and your weight, can be broadcast as widely as you wish. The coffee maker, which has your favorite brew all ready for you, is also communicating with the security system so that your house will be all locked up when you leave. The house temperature and the lighting are both monitored automatically, and if the sun starts to shine into any of the rooms the blinds will automatically close. You will be able to monitor humidity and carbon monoxide levels and activate alarms when certain levels are reached. If you later fall asleep the TV is programmed to shut off after a number of minutes. The courier will be able to leave a message on the pad at your front door, or communicate directly with you wherever you happen to be.

Privacy in a digital world is relative. Privacy experts have asked students if they knew that text chat services owned the communications sent out by the students, and the answer often was yes but they thought this was more private than a phone call that could be overheard by their parents!

Governments appoint privacy commissioners to protect privacy issues for the public. Some companies, such as Microsoft, also have strong policies relating to the creation of online services that customers can trust, while other well-known companies have clashed with privacy commissioners over privacy violations.

One thing that the digital age does not stimulate is community or personal interaction. The Internet may stimulate communication and information exchange and it encourages a virtual type of interaction between individuals. But instead of handshakes and hugs when "meeting" there is often isolation and even loneliness. For some people that's okay since they enjoy solitude with no personal obligations.

Human beings are naturally social beings with a built-in desire for connectedness, but our digital advances seem to be thwarting fulfillment of this need. Many "one person" families, if honest, would admit that being alone sucks, and it is an open question as to whether our modern digital communication advances help or hinder this. We can send out e-mail on a lonely weekend or blog about our visit to the art gallery, or tell our 321 Facebook virtual "friends" how work is going, but we're still alone.

It's ironic, but that while people may be interested in saving the Great Bear Rain Forest or plaintively worry about the fate of Tibet, this lifestyle doesn't seem to encourage individuals to be good neighbors or to volunteer for a local charitable organization. We haven't yet seen much of the fallout from this lifestyle, but eventually plummeting marriage and birth rates will have a dramatic impact on our society. Perhaps our technological quality of life is increasing, but this seems to be happening at a huge personal costs.

One good thing about the digital age is that young families are no longer subjected to intimidating high-pressure encyclopedia salespeople who used the line that "you don't want your kids to grow up ignorant". Still, it is a bit sad that the encyclopedia Britannica has closed down its printed book version and computerized its operations. On the bright side, millions of feet of bookshelves will be freed up. Britannica used to say that its volumes contained the sum of all human knowledge, and now even more knowledge can be contained on one tiny disk or thumb drive.

Douglas Todd, a Vancouver Sun columnist, has asked the question, "Can we adapt to a world in which labor is infrequent and occupations aren't as important as leisure?" Todd is referring to the exponential rise in the use of robots to perform repetitive tasks, including applications in warehouses, store checkouts, manufacturing, fast-food deliveries, and even driverless cars.

If you "Google" drones, you will find many uses for them ranging from photography to military spying and bombing to geographical mapping to mineral exploration to firefighting to search and rescue. Farmers may use drones for controlling irrigation and monitoring crops and the medical community is developing many applications including robotic surgery.

All of this leads to the issue of artificial intelligence (AI) in machines and computer software. One of the big areas of research involves how to have computers reason, plan, learn, and perceive changes. AI is already used for logistics, data mining, medical diagnosis, and other technology applications. Science fiction writers have long created scenarios where computers take over the world.

## Amazing Stories From 9/11

My sweetie and I were in Kansas City, Missouri on 9/11 (September 11, 2001, when the World Trade Center was struck by hijacked airplanes) at a scientific meeting, and we experienced the fear and concern felt by Americans and other conference attendees from countries around the world.

I was scheduled to teach a course on 9/13 and 9/14, and we struggled through the first day but prematurely ended the course on the morning of the next day. Everyone was thinking about other things and wanted to go home, but this wasn't easy since air travel in those first few days was complicated. Many Americans rented cars to get home but this wasn't an option for us Canadians.

I was scheduled to fly to Ottawa on the Friday after my conference, but my meeting was cancelled. After many phone calls, my sweetie and I were able to arrange for flights home, via Toronto, on the Saturday. We were told to get to the Kansas City airport four hours early, but it turned out that the airport was virtually deserted except for those also waiting for our flight.

Toronto was another story. Thousands of beleaguered travelers crowded the airport and the lineups snaked through all the concourses. When we finally got to the airline check-in desk the agent was unable to print out a boarding pass for me, apparently because of the changes in my flights. After about fifteen anxious and frustrating minutes he just wrote out a boarding pass and we rushed onto the plane as they were about to close the door. We were happy to safely and finally reach home.

While waiting to leave Kansas City we were bombarded over and over again with TV pictures of the collapsing twin towers, and endless speculation about the terrorists. Unknown to us at the time were some fascinating stories emerging in Canada. The following is a summary of one such story.

On the morning of Tuesday, September 11, a Delta flight out of Frankfurt flying over the North Atlantic was informed that all airways over the continental United States were closed to commercial air traffic. There were no further details but the flight crew knew that this was serious. The captain was told to land ASAP at the nearest airport, which turned out to be Gander, Newfoundland/Labrador. While the flight crew prepared the airplane for landing the passengers were simply told that the plane had an instrument problem and they needed to land in Gander to have it checked out. The passengers were, of course, unhappy. It turned out already about twenty other airplanes from all over the world were on the ground having taken this detour on their way to the U.S. After a few more hours about fifty-three airplanes had landed at Gander.

After landing, the captain's brief real explanation of why they had landed was greeted with loud gasps of disbelief. More news gradually became available and the air travelers learned more details about what had happened at the World Trade Center in New York and the Pentagon in Washington DC. That evening further news came about the collapse of the World Trade Center buildings and the fourth hijacking that resulted in a crash. People tried to use their cell phones but soon found that connections to the U.S. were either blocked or jammed.

All of the passengers though emotionally and physically exhausted, not to mention frightened, were cooperative. They were safe and realized many others were in the same predicament.

The Delta flight passengers had to spend the night on the plane and finally disembarked at 11:00 the next morning. They were then taken by school buses to the terminal to go through Immigration and Customs and to register with the Red Cross. Flight crews were taken to the local hotels.

Since Gander has a population of only about 10,000 and more than 10,500 visitors had suddenly arrived, they had a few logistical problems. All of the high schools, meeting halls, lodges, and other large gathering places in Gander and surrounding areas were closed and converted into mass lodging areas for the stranded travelers. High school students volunteered their time to take care of the guests. The 218 Delta passengers were taken to a high school in Lewisporte, a small town about forty-five kilometres from Gander.

Phone calls and e-mail to the U.S. and around the world were available to everyone once a day and guests were offered excursions to local lakes, harbors, and forests. Local bakeries stayed open to make fresh bread, and food was prepared by residents and brought to the schools. People were driven to restaurants of their choice and offered wonderful meals. Everyone was given toiletry items and tokens for local Laundromats to wash their clothes since their luggage was still on the aircraft.

When the U.S. airports finally reopened some two days later, everyone was delivered to the airport. The Red Cross had all the information about the whereabouts of every passenger and knew which plane they needed to be on and when each flight was to depart. When the Delta passengers and crew were reunited at the airport, many passengers cried while telling their stories to the crew. When passengers came back on board, it was like they had been on a cruise. Everyone knew each other by their first names and they exchanged phone numbers and email addresses. They swapped stories of their stay, impressing each other with who had had the better time. The flight back to Atlanta looked like a chartered party flight.

Another unusual thing happened. One of the passengers asked if he could make an announcement over the PA system, which was something that was never allowed. But this time was different, so the man picked up the PA and talked about what they had just gone through. He reminded them of the hospitality they had received and announced he would like to set up a Trust Fund to provide college scholarships for the high school students of Lewisporte. They ended up collecting more than $28,000! This heart-warming story shows that tragedies and difficulties often bring out the best in people.

## Highway Adventures

My sweetie and I lived in Ottawa for five years when our kids were small so several of our summer vacations were spent driving from Ottawa to Edmonton where both of our families lived.

On one trip we left after work and the plan was to drive through the first night and all the next day (we were young then), stay one night in a motel and then arrive in Edmonton the following day. It didn't exactly turn out that way.

Forty-five minutes out of Ottawa, our six year-old barfed all over the back seat. We cleaned up the mess as best we could and motored on. We had a big station wagon and had fixed it up so that child could sleep in the back beside the luggage while the two little ones slept on the filled-in back seat. The kids enjoyed the freedom and extra room during the day.

I hasten to add that this was in the pre-seat belt days so we didn't know any better. Anyway, about 11:00 PM we heard a loud noise under the hood. It seemed the cowling around the radiator fan had broken. This was in the days before cell phones but we somehow contacted a tow truck and soon all five of us were huddled together in the truck along with the driver. He took us to Blind River, Ontario (it's not the end of the world, but you can see it from there) where we found a motel and a garage and by 10:00 AM the next morning we were on our way again. Driving straight through after this little adventure, we arrived in Edmonton on schedule.

I don't remember if it was on this return trip, or another time, but on our way back to Ottawa we stopped in Winnipeg for gas. About fifty miles past the city, the car started choking and wheezing and the fastest we could go was about fifteen miles per hour. We sputtered on until we got to Dryden, Ontario where we found a garage. It seemed that we had purchased some dirty gas. It was a holiday Monday and the mechanic was supposed to be digging a grave (I'm not making this up), but he grudgingly cleaned out the carburetor. (For you young folks, you will need to look this up in the dictionary; let's just say that cars now use fuel injection systems.) We continued on towards home.

Some years ago my sweetie and I zoomed from Edmonton, Alberta, to Chicago in our brother-in-law's car for a family wedding. Gordon is an excellent driver and loves to speed, (for him it isn't speeding if you don't get caught), and we arrived relatively quickly.

Gordon loves cars, especially clean cars, and at that time he also loved Plymouths. His car was cleaner that the average hospital operating room. We had a great time, staying up late, visiting and eating, and after a few days we headed home, starting out late one evening. After an hour or two Gordon actually let me drive and he quickly fell asleep, as did the rest of the passengers. I was motoring along minding my own business (not speeding) when all of a sudden there was a loud FLOUSH that sounded like an explosion. Gordon almost put a dent in the roof he woke up and sat up so fast.

I pulled over to see what had happened. It turned out that some kids on an overpass had scored a direct hit with a large water balloon that had been filled with slough water. Naturally, Gordon carried cleaning cloths so we mopped up the mess on the windshield and roof as best we could. Gordon started driving again. The next morning he had thoroughly cleaned the car back to show room specifications.

For many years I belonged to the organizing committee for a technical organization in the Pacific Northwest. This position involved a three-hour trip to the Seattle area twice a year to participate in the planning. I was motoring along early one morning in 1986 to get to the 9:00 AM meeting when the news reported the explosion of the Challenger spacecraft where seven astronauts lost their lives. This was a seminal event in U.S. space history and it's the sort of event that you remember for years where you were when it happened.

I used to take two or three of my staff to the annual June meeting I had helped set up. We used to leave work early from Vancouver for the drive to either Olympia or Tacoma, Washington, and after crossing the border into the U.S. we would stop for dinner so that we wouldn't be driving through Seattle at rush hour. It so happened that I had discovered a fabulous pie restaurant north of Seattle so we always stopped there before eventually getting to our meeting destination. It became a bit of a joke that I always wanted to stop at this restaurant. I would even stop there on my way home even if just for soup followed by ice cream and pie.

My sweetie and I drove our motor home across Canada in 2006 (that's another story) but then we drove much of the way home through the U.S. We were in Missoula, Montana, one night when we phoned our daughter in the Vancouver, B.C. area. She and her husband were expecting the birth of their first baby in the next few days. They seemed a bit discombobulated that we had called that night but we attributed this to the first baby syndrome.

My sweetie, however, was concerned enough that she phoned our daughter again when we arrived near Spokane the next day, and had scheduled a two-day stop. We discovered the baby had decided it was time to make an early appearance. We concluded that we wouldn't sleep or rest properly anyway so we made the decision to drive right through to Vancouver that day. We drove 575 miles or over 900 km, which is no small feat in a motor home towing a car, and we arrived at the hospital about 10:00 PM.

When the nurse informed our daughter that we were at the hospital she was told that this was impossible since we were on vacation. But we were there, and the baby arrived about a half hour later. Arriving at home is always rewarding, but was especially so in this case.

I worked at the Columbia Icefields near Jasper one summer while going to university and half way through the summer I decided that I needed to go back to Edmonton to retrieve my car. I met some friends of friends visiting the Icefields and they volunteered to take me to Edmonton on their way home. We left the Icefields after work and everything was going great until we got near to Lake Wabamum about fifty-five miles east of Edmonton.

My chauffeurs decided they were going to stay at their cottage by the lake so they dropped me off at a truck stop along the highway. It was 2:00 AM. I was concerned about getting the rest of the way to Edmonton at that time of the night.

I never was much of a hitchhiker but I bravely tramped into the restaurant and asked the lone visitor, obviously a trucker, if he was going to Edmonton. He was happy to have some company, and since the good Lord was helping me the trucker dropped me off in east Edmonton not far from my destination.

## How Old Would You Be If You Didn't Know How Old You Are?

This is a serious question and every person's answer is critical. We should all be capable of providing a good answer, but to get your thinking juices started permit me to give you a scenario.

Suppose, for example, that you wake up one day after being in a coma for a long time and you have absolutely no recollection or memories of the past. You are apparently healthy and among strangers who can't fill you in on your past. How old would you decide that you are? Well, in some ways you decide that question every day of your life.

I heard an interview with a public figure recently and he was asked if he was considering retiring since he was about sixty years old. His response was that, in his head, he was still a young man. I thought that this was a fabulous response, and I asked myself if I was still young "in my head".

"In my head" is the key determinant. Yes, some people are blessed with extraordinary physiology and can remain healthy and active even as they grow "older". The rest of us, if we decide in our deepest being that we are young and capable, are much more likely to keep on being young, active, and healthy.

I asked the "how old would you be" question to some of my friends. One of them, who is around sixty-five replied, "probably in my fifties" while another one said, "between twenty-five and thirty" even though she is over sixty. One fellow, who is at least seventy-five answered, "about ten or eleven", which in his case might be almost accurate.

A related question is this: when did you decide that you were an adult? For me, there seem to be several answers. In retrospect, the first time that I decided I was an adult—and this wasn't any specific conscious thought—was shortly after I graduated from university with a Bachelor's Degree in Pharmacy. I had a profession and a job; I could rent my own apartment and spend my time more or less as I wished.

Upon reflection, I suppose there were several updates in subconsciously deciding I was an adult. Getting married was one of those times and having our first child was another.

Being young at heart, or in our heads, and recognizing we are adults is wonderful, but we also need to realistically consider that time marches on. The first time that I actually realized that I was getting older was a few days after my 35th birthday. For some reason I had to complete a questionnaire, and it asked into what age range I fit. The applicable age range was thirty-five to fifty years old. I was shocked! I was well on the way to fitting into the same category as old people!

All of this is well and good when we are young and healthy. Inevitably, as we grow older we are forced to stop thinking that we are young and could live forever, or at least for the foreseeable future. This started to happen to me after I became a septuagenarian. I had cycled over 1,800 miles, or 3,000 kilometres, the previous year and in winter I rode ten km every day on the stationary bike. I wasn't exactly a couch potato. But I found that I wasn't thirty-five anymore either and there were some things that I no longer could do.

Someone I know told me that you know you're starting to get old when you begin getting aches and pains not experienced in youth, when it becomes difficult to get up from the floor, or when not being able to put on a sock while standing on one leg. But I was told, it's still possible to feel young while doing something you really enjoy. For this person, this happens while leading singing at church services.

Arthritis, or osteoporosis, or, heaven forbid, Alzheimer's disease, are pretty clear indicators that we have passed our prime and best before date. Keeping active in body, mind, and soul is still the key, along with good physiology and genes. Not dwelling on feeling old is pretty important as well. We live each day as it comes and try to enjoy it to the fullest in seeking to please God and serve others. It's up to us then to decide how old we feel. A positive attitude, combined with some regular exercise and good nutrition, can go a long way to helping us feel younger than our chronological ages. Feeling comfortable in your own skin and being content with yourself is so important.

John Wayne apparently said, "The older you get, the further out you go and the more alone you are." People who feel old, or who may suffer various physical or mental limitations, or who have always had a limited social life often become more isolated and don't spend much time with other people. This situation can make one feel, and become, old pretty quickly.

Being satisfied with whom we really are and what we have accomplished in life is another key. Some folks are generally unhappy because they don't differentiate between "want" and "need". If we dwell on "what if" or on why family members or others have slighted us, we are more likely to feel older than the calendar indicates. A happy family life also influences how old we feel.

## Ordinary Adventures of an Ordinary Guy

I have limited athletic ability I have never made any great discoveries as a scientist. I have always been shy and reserved, so you might be wondering what kind of adventures an ordinary guy like me could have.

They may be ordinary adventures but God has blessed me with a wide variety of different experiences and I am determined to share some of them with you.

One year when I was working as a research scientist for Health Canada in Ottawa I needed to attend a meeting in Atlantic City, New Jersey. The plan was to fly to Philadelphia and then take a shuttle bus some fifty miles to Atlantic City. My well thought out plans went awry when we arrived late in Philadelphia about 10:30 PM. I had missed the last bus to my destination so I stood around the baggage carousel for a few minutes trying to decide what to do.

A few minutes later a scruffy looking fellow walked up to me and said, “Hey, are you trying to get to Atlantic City? I can take you there, not quite all the way, but close to the main hotels.”

I thought, *yah, right, you’ll drop me off along the highway after punching me out and taking my money.* I politely said no thanks and called the airport hotel for a room and cancelled my Atlantic City hotel for that night. I took the first bus out the next morning and learned a lot at my technical meetings.

It doesn’t snow often in the general Vancouver area but when it does there is serious traffic chaos. I left for work early one morning in my trusty little Honda Civic after it had snowed a foot or more overnight. I was crossing a six-lane bridge when I noticed that only one lane was being used so I decided that I would try the almost unused curb lane. I soon found out why no one else was using this lane since I quickly became stuck in deep snow. I had a shovel along so I could clear a pathway back to the center lane. Traffic was light enough as most people had sense enough to stay home, so I was never in any danger. I crossed the bridge and then the next decision was what hill to take northward to get to my destination. I tried one hill but had to back down since the snow was too deep (I guess the snowplow drivers couldn't make it to work) and drove several miles to a street that was manageable. Suffice to say that I was one of the first to arrive at work and that most employees either stayed home or came several hours later.

My sweetie and I went on a seven day Alaska cruise out of Vancouver a few years ago with most of her brothers and sisters plus spouses, and we had a fabulous time. Upon our return, as we walked into our house about 9:30 AM, I heard the telephone ringing.

"Please, please," the caller said. "We are short of players today for our slow pitch softball team. Can you come by 10:30?"

I had been playing for this team, as a pitcher or on first base. They knew that I had been away, but they desperately needed me that day. I got ready and drove twenty-five minutes to the playing field. I pitched a magnificent game, if I have to say so myself, and we won handily. It was a great feeling to make a contribution and especially, to be needed and appreciated.

After graduating from university I worked as a pharmacist in a small drug store for about a year. Even though I enjoyed the work, I had decided to go back to university to earn a Master's degree. I changed jobs and went to work for a large chain of stores for the summer, the same chain where I worked as a relief pharmacist in various stores for two or three weeks while the regular pharmacist went on vacation. In one case, I went on a Friday to a pharmacy dispensary located in a ten-storey medical building to be briefed by the sole pharmacist about her procedures.

Everything seemed in place on the following Monday morning except that I couldn't open the safe. I had been given the combination but the pharmacist neglected to tell me that I had to hold my tongue just so and that the combination was sensitive. Embarrassed, I had to call headquarters to ask for a safe cracker to be sent out. The fellow managed to open the safe with the combination I provided and then showed me the intricacies of opening it on my own. I enjoyed working in a dispensary as opposed to a retail drug store, and the next two weeks passed without incident.

My sweetie and I frequently go camping each summer at Birch Bay, Washington, just an hour's drive from our home in British Columbia. I enjoy the various bike routes available there, even though most of them involve cycling up a particular hill to return to our campground. I was following my cycling buddy one morning and, in a moment of carelessness, I came too close to the pavement edge. I tumbled into the bramble bushes, my bicycle on top of me and my friend wondering why I had inexplicably disappeared from his rear view mirror. My arms and my pride were scratched but not too seriously and we continued on to our campsite. I later posted this little poem on a telephone post near the site of the incident: Hey, hey hey / here Jerry lay. For a few moments he didn't take care / He biked on a shoulder that wasn't there.

My sweetie and alleged friends wanted to put up a cross with flowers to mark the spot, and they laugh hilariously each time we drive past the infamous site.

My first real experience in a competitive team sport didn't occur until I was in Grade Twelve and joined the high school curling league. In a draft of all the players I was selected by arguably the best curler in the school to play lead and throw first rocks. We had a successful season and ended up winning the school championship bonspiel. My sweetie and I later curled for a couple of years in Ottawa with a church league and I later played in Vancouver with periodic success, which came in the form of impressive trophies. We didn't take it too seriously and always had a good time.

Along with another fellow, I taught a two-day laboratory quality assurance course one to three times a year in places ranging from Winnipeg to Los Angeles, Cincinnati to West Palm Beach, and even Saskatoon and Kansas City. I was even sent to Tallinn, Estonia, and Port of Spain, in Trinidad and Tobago. We stayed in a Holiday Inn in Tallinn, which doesn't sound like an adventure but it was situated across the street from the old walled city, which originated almost a thousand years before.

The hilly, cobblestoned streets wound around brightly coloured buildings with three-foot wide stone walls. Some of the magnificent churches were almost a thousand years old. I went for a walk early one morning and saw a little old lady sweeping the street with a broom made from twigs, looking like she was part of a scene from an old movie. I asked to take her picture but she shyly demurred.

The day after the course we took the streetcar into the main city, which consists of miles of faceless, nondescript apartment buildings that reminded us of films we had seen of the iron curtain countries.

It must not have been tourist season on the island of Trinidad since there was almost no one around. A young fellow gave us a personal tour. He even showed us the beach where two Canadians had been killed the week before, which was rather unsettling for us even though the scenery was beautiful. Six-feet wide, 1960s Cadillacs taxis drove through ten-feet wide cobbled streets. Meeting another taxi was always an event.

We visited a friend of a friend whose house was wide open at each end above the walls and up to the roof peak. The annual temperature never varied more than seven degrees in the low eighties. After the course was over, my sweetie and I took a 20-minute flight to the second island of the country, namely Tobago, which is perhaps the most beautiful place that I have seen. Our one-day tour guide was a little mama who drove us around in her van showing us the beautiful beaches. We even went snorkeling in the most fabulous blue-green water you could imagine.

## Camels: Would You Like One Hump or Two?

I have always been confused about which camels have one hump and which have two humps.

It turns out that one-hump camels are called dromedaries and are found in Africa and the Middle East. They often weigh more than 1500 pounds.

Bactrian camels are more rare and are native to the Gobi Desert in Mongolia and other parts of Central Asia. Besides having two humps they grow a thick coat of hair each winter (which they lose each spring) to deal with the extreme variations in temperature. Bactrian camels generally are more mild-mannered than dromedaries.

Now that we have that cleared up we can talk about some of the characteristics that make camels interesting. In addition to the architecture of the big hump, I found, upon visiting a camel farm, the most obvious feature is their teeth along with the nastiest case of plaque imaginable. No camel I have ever seen has been anywhere near a toothbrush or a plaque-removing product.

Female camels are generally preferred for riding since they have a calmer temperament than males, and interestingly, better endurance. And of course females give milk, an important source of nourishment for desert families. Males are more aggressive and tire more easily, though they can carry larger loads for shorter distances. Camels have remarkable dexterity and can kick violently with a large range of motion with both their front and back legs.

Camels can drink more than twenty-five gallons of water in just a few minutes. They dehydrate slowly in part because they kidneys work effectively to concentrate their urine and reduce water loss. A camel may lose more than a quarter of its weight to water loss.

Another interesting feature of camels is their ability to live in the sandy desert without damaging their eyes. Camels have thick double rows of eyelashes, which catch most of the sand, and two eyelids. The second transparent eyelid protects the surface of the eye even in blowing sandstorms. Their eyes also water constantly to keep them clear.

Camels are like some other mammals in that they have special membrane behind their retina that enhances their night vision. Camels also have special muscles that keep their nostrils closed, plus dense fine hairs to filter the sand so that they can breathe during a sandstorm.

In order for a camel to be ridden, it must first be trained to "couch", that is, to lie down with legs tucked under it. Camels have a thick pad of chest cartilage, which keeps the skin of their bellies off the hot sand and away from thorns and sharp rocks. The saddle, which is quite different from a horse saddle, can then be attached to the haltered camel. Camel saddles had to be modified when swords became common and also when rifles began to be used in the 1800s to ensure that the rider was firmly anchored so as to use his weapon effectively.

Apparently, there was a custom for camel drivers is to sing to their camels to relax them at night and to gently wake them up in the morning. A different song conditions them to drink. This can be important, especially when camels are reluctant to drink brackish water.

Evidently, each camel makes a distinct footprint and a trained observer can tell if a camel is being ridden or is pregnant. The pads on the bottom of their feet differ if they live on gravel plains or perpetually on sand. The footpad acts kind of like a small snowshoe pushing away the sand and dispersing the camel's weight. A camel walks by moving both legs on one side at the same time, which is opposite to that of a horse. This makes for a rougher ride on a camel.

Camels have changed in the modern age compared to earlier times. While they used to be able to go for many days in the desert without rest or water, with the introduction of motorized vehicles, especially 4 x 4s, camels are not used much now for crossing the desert. As a result camels have generally lost some of the strength and capacity that their ancestor camels possessed to endure and work in the desert heat. It's interesting that a primary use for camels now is racing, and many modern camels are now bred solely for racing.

## Some Favorite Bible Verses

I have been a Christian since I was eleven years old, and while I have read and studied the Bible I have not done it nearly as often or as carefully as I probably should. Nevertheless, there are many Bible verses that I enjoy.

I worked with a church ministry to young boys for quite a few years, and one of the Bible verses that we encouraged them to memorize was Psalm 119:9, which reads: "How can a young man [any person] keep their way pure? – By living according to your Word".

Psalm 119:11 reads, "I have hidden your word in my heart that I might not sin against you." One way to experience this is to listen to the advice given in Psalm 119:105: "Your word is a lamp for my feet, a light on my path."

Perhaps the most famous and encouraging verse in the Bible is John 3:16. "For God so loved the world that He gave His one and only Son that whoever believes in Him shall not perish but have eternal life." Christ's' invitation to us is summarized in Revelation 3: 20: "Here I am! I stand at the door and knock. If anyone hears my voice and opens the door, I will come in and eat with him and he with me."

Some years ago I asked my eldest daughter to tell me her favorite Bible verse, and she replied "Romans, Chapter 8." I thought this was a fabulous reply since this chapter is chock-full of wisdom and encouragement.

I'll list only Romans 8: 26-28: "In the same way the Spirit helps us in our weakness. We do not know what we ought to pray for, but the Spirit himself intercedes for us with groans that words cannot express. And He who searches our hearts knows the mind of the Spirit because the Spirit intercedes for the saints in accordance with God's will. And we know that in all things God works for the good of those who love Him, who have been called according to His purpose".

Some parts of the Old Testament are pretty tough slogging but there are many encouraging and instructive passages. Here are a few of my favorites: Isaiah 40: 26, 28-31: "Lift up your eyes and look to the heavens: Who created all these? He who brings out the starry host one by one and calls forth each of them by name. Because of his great power and mighty strength, not one of them is missing. Do you not know? Have you not heard? The Lord is the everlasting God, the Creator of the ends of the earth. He will not grow tired or weary, and His understanding no one can fathom. He gives strength to the weary and increases the power of the weak. Even youths grow tired and weary, and young men stumble and fall but those who hope in the Lord will renew their strength. They will soar like eagles; they will run and not grow weary, they will walk and not be faint."

Jeremiah 29:11-12: "For I know the plans I have for you, declares the Lord, plans to prosper you and not to harm you, plans to give you a hope and a future. Then you will call upon me and come and pray to me and I will listen to you."

Psalm 103:17-18: "But from everlasting to everlasting the Lord's love is with those who fear Him, and His righteousness with their children's children—with those who keep His covenant and remember to obey His precepts."

Proverbs contains many wise and thoughtful passages. Here are just two of them: Proverbs 3:5-6: "Trust in the Lord with all you heart and lean not on your own understanding; in all your ways acknowledge Him and He will make your paths straight." And Proverbs 17:17 says, "A true friend is always loyal, and a brother is born to help in time of need."

The Bible verse that basically stimulated Martin Luther to start the Protestant Reformation was Ephesians 2:8-9: "For it is by grace you have been saved, through faith, and this is not from yourselves, it is a gift of God, not by works so that no one can boast."

The apostle Paul had many words of encouragement for us, such as Philippians 2:3: "Do nothing out of selfish ambition or vain conceit, but in humility consider others better than yourselves."

Matthew 22:36-39 gives a concise summary of our responsibilities: "Teacher, which is the greatest commandment in the Law? Jesus replied: Love the Lord your God with all your heart and with all your soul and with all your mind. This is the first and greatest commandment. And the second is like it: Love your neighbour as yourself."

Ecclesiastes 12:1 encourages young people to follow the Lord: "Remember your Creator in the days of your youth, before the days of trouble come and the years approach when you will say, I find no pleasure in them."

The website, www.biblegateway.com is a good source of teaching and encouragement. It lists various Bible verses, two of these being Psalm 23:4 ("Even though I walk through the darkest valley, I will fear no evil, for you are with me; your rod and your staff, they comfort me"), and 1 Corinthians 13:4 ("Love is patient, love is kind. It does not envy, it does not boast, it is not proud").

Here are some other great verses from Philippians 4: 4-9: "Rejoice in the Lord always. I will say it again: Rejoice! Let your gentleness be evident to all. The Lord is near. Do not be anxious about anything, but in every situation, by prayer and petition, with thanksgiving, present your requests to God. And the peace of God, which transcends all understanding, will guard your hearts and your minds in Christ Jesus. Finally, brothers and sisters, whatever is true, whatever is noble, whatever is right, whatever is pure, whatever is lovely, whatever is admirable—if anything is excellent or praiseworthy—think about such things. Whatever you have learned or received or heard from me, or seen in me—put it into practice. And the God of peace will be with you."

There are hundreds more verses that I could list, but I close with Genesis 1:1, which starts God's demonstration of His power and His love for us: "In the beginning God created the heavens and the earth."

## What Did You Just Call Me?

I have often thought family names are much more interesting than first names. As I began to research names in Wikipedia and elsewhere, however, I found that both components of a person's name quite interesting so I have written a separate vignette for each one.

A couple of years ago some of the most popular boy's names were Liam, Ethan, and Jacob while the most common girl's names included Olivia, Emma, and Isabella. The most popular names from fifty years ago (David, John, James, and Robert for boys, and Mary, Susan, Karen, and Linda) are names that we still commonly see today, and some of these names have been used for hundreds if not thousands of years.

If we go way back to 1890 we find that John, William, and James were the most common boy's names while Mary, Anne, and Elizabeth were popular girl's names. Not a lot has changed. In Quebec, the most common boy's names were Jean, Joseph, and Pierre while Marie was by far the most popular girl's name (reflecting Quebec's Catholic heritage).

Choosing a name for the baby is a challenging task for many parents since a name can have a profound impact on a child that reverberates well into adulthood. Fans of country and western music may remember Johnny Cash's song, "My Name is Sue" and the boy's life-long struggle in dealing with this name.

An ordinary first name combined with a reasonable last name can sometimes create something ridiculous, so when new parents have selected a possible name they should look for possible problems, including potential nicknames. Benjamin Dover is a nice name, but Ben Dover could cause some problems for the kid. It may be wise to avoid alliteration especially if the last name is a common word. Walter Wall or Suzie Seiling will sound like characters from a children's picture book.

If the last name is a common first name, parents should take care to choose first names that won't sound backwards. Names such as

Johnson George or Taylor James will cause some complications. If the family name is problematic, such as Hogg or Stitt or Blatter, parents may want to avoid unfortunate rhyming first names and instead select the rhythm of a long, rolling first name to draw the emphasis away from the last name.

Celebrities often seem to give their babies unusual names (when you're rich and famous, you apparently have a right to do bizarre things). Examples range from "Apple" to "Chastity" to "Zelda". One famous athlete never seemed to get around to naming her baby, so one day when she was playing hide and seek with her toddler she said, "peek-a-boo" and the girl finally had a name, which is spelled Picabo.

Some parents choose from lists of the most popular names but this will mean that they will soon find lots of other kids with the same name. Call me old-fashioned, but I like names that are clearly recognized as feminine or masculine. Prospective parents can also look at lists of unusual names, for girls some of the names on one list are Addilyn, Jaelyn, and Mireya while the boys' list includes Brysen, Jaylon, and Quinten. Another factor to consider is the meaning of a name, although we don't pay as much attention to this these days.

The choice of a baby's name is entirely up to the parents but it's wise to listen to what family members or close friends think about possible choices. Parents should realize that they are making a decision on behalf of another person who is unable to make a decision because they have just been born. Friends and relatives are going to be the baby's friends and relatives for a long time and their suggestions should at least be considered since they might be aware of something that the parents missed, such as the name of a cartoon character or the unsavory meaning of the name in another language. Another good suggestion is to choose a name you would like to have yourself.

We all have many factors in mind when we choose a name. We may want to honour our relatives, or our ethnic heritage. We may see baby naming as an opportunity for personal expression. Use whatever criteria you like to narrow down your name choices, but before you fill in the birth certificate, stop and give the name this final test: if you were starting life today, knowing everything you know about the world, is this the name you would want to represent your child? If so, you can feel confident that you're giving your child the best birthday present possible, one that will last a lifetime.

Naming twins poses some additional challenges. Many parents instinctively believe their twins share an identity and hence should share a similar name. A common practice is to use first names that begin with the same letter such as Richard and Robert (Ricky and Robby) or Joseph and Judith (Joey and Judy). Other parents decide that the twins are distinct individuals and therefore they deliberately select dissimilar names.

The bestowal of name and identity is a kind of symbolic contract between the society and the individual. Seen from one side of the contract, by giving a name society confirms the individual's existence and acknowledges its responsibilities toward that person. The name differentiates the child from others, thus the society will be able to treat and deal with the child as someone with needs and feelings different from those of other people. Through the name, the individual becomes part of the history of the society, and because of the name, his or her actions and lifestyle will exist separate from the deeds of others.

## Last Names (Family Names)

A family name or last name is a name that is passed from one generation to the next by law or custom. The primary purpose of the surname was to further distinguish people from one another. Governments are quite interested in this feature since it facilitates the collection of taxes. In many cases, a surname is a family name, although this is not the case in some cultures. In the western hemisphere, surname is commonly synonymous with "last name" and is usually placed at the end of a person's given name. In many cultures a woman adopts her husband's family name when she marries.

Much of this vignette is based on various sources from Wikipedia. Surnames began to be used in the 12th century in Europe. Ireland was the first country in Europe to use fixed surnames. Initially this practice was used by the aristocracy in Britain but eventually by everyone, although it took several centuries before the majority of Europeans had a surname. In the 13th century about a third of the male population had a given name of William, Richard, or John, so adding a surname became important. According to Wikipedia, in order to uniquely identify individuals, people began referring to different Williams as William the son of Andrew (leading to Anderson), William, the cook (leading to Cook), William from the brook (leading to Brooks), William, the brown-haired (leading to Brown), and so on. Eventually these surnames became inherited, being passed from parents to children.

In an English-speaking context, family names are most often used to refer to a stranger or in a formal setting, and are often used with a title such as Mr., Mrs., Ms., Miss, Dr., and so on. Generally the given name is the one used by friends, family, and other intimates to address an individual. The given name may also be used by someone who is in some way senior to the person being addressed.

Most English surnames fell into four categories. (1) Patronymic surnames derived from given names of a male ancestor; examples include Johnson, Williamson, and Thompson; (2) Occupational surnames refer to the occupation of the bearer. Examples include Smith, Sawyer, Clark, Baker, and Wright; (3) Locational surnames are derived from the place that the family lived. Examples include Hill, Woods, Bush, and Ford; (4) Surnames derived from nicknames or personal characteristics include White, Young, and Long.

The original source or meaning of the name may no longer be obvious today. For example, many may not know that a *cooper* is one who makes barrels and a name such as *Abbot*, may have indicated that an ancestor was or worked for a bishop.

Other occupational names include such simple examples as "Eisenhauer" (iron worker, later Anglicized in America as "Eisenhower") or "Schneider" (tailor). In England it was common for servants to take a modified version of their employer's occupation or first name as their last name, adding the letter "s" to the word.

The surname "Vickers" is thought to have arisen as an occupational name adopted by the servant of a vicar, while "Roberts" could have been adopted by either the son or the servant of a man named Robert. Occasionally matronymic names were used. In the Middle Ages, when a man from a lower-status family married a daughter from a higher-status family, he would often take the wife's family name.

My surname, Hirsch, is from a Middle High German word that means deer or stag. This apparently is a metonymic occupational name for a keeper of deer, or perhaps a nickname for someone thought to resemble a deer or stag (I'm not sure if that's a good thing or not). Similar to British practices, German family names often derive from given names, geographical names, occupational designations, bodily attributes, or even traits of character.

The western style of having both a family name (surname) and a given name (forename or "Christian" name) is far from universal. Each culture has its own rules as to how family names are applied and used. In some countries it is common for ordinary people to have only one name, and in other cultures the family name comes first.

In some jurisdictions, a woman's legal name used to change automatically upon marriage. That change is no longer always a requirement, but a woman may still easily change to her husband's surname. In Québec, Canada, the custom until 1981 was similar to that in France where women would traditionally go by their husbands' surname in daily life, but their maiden name remained their legal name. Since a 1981 provincial law intended to promote gender equality, no change may be made to a person's name without the authorization of the registrar of civil status or the authorization of the court. Newlyweds who wish to change their names upon marriage must therefore go through the same procedure as those changing their names for other reasons.

Italy apparently has about 350,000 surnames. The two most common Italian family names, *Russo* and *Rossi*, mean the same thing, "red", possibly referring to a hair colour that would have been distinctive in Italy.

In Spain and most Hispanic countries, two last names are used. The first family name is the paternal one, inherited from the father's family name, while the second family name is the maternal one, inherited from the mother's paternal family name.

In Chinese, Japanese, Korean, and Vietnamese cultures, the family name is placed before the given names. So the terms "first name" and "last name" are generally not used since they do not indicate the given and family names. According to legend, family names started in China with Emperor Fu Xi in 2852 BC when his administration standardized the naming system in order to facilitate census taking. Chinese family names have many types of origins including from the land or state that one lived in, or from the given name of one's ancestor, or from the nobility status or status of one's ancestor, such as, Wang (a king) or Shi (a history-recording officer).

Vietnamese family names present an added complication. While the family name is also placed at the beginning of a name, they are not usually the primary form of address, since people will be referred to by their given name usually accompanied by an honorific. For example,

Phan Van Khai is properly addressed as *Mr. Khai*, even though *Phan* is the family name.

In Japan, the civil law forces a common surname for every married couple. In most cases, women surrender their surnames upon marriage, and use the surnames of their husbands. However, a convention that a man uses his wife's family name if the wife is an only child is sometimes observed.

In Arabic-speaking countries the given name is always followed by the father's first name, then the father's family surname. Some surnames have a pre-fix of *ibn-* meaning "son of". Many Arabic last names start with "Al-" which means "the".

India is a country with numerous distinct cultural and linguistic groups, so Indian surnames fall into various categories. Some states do not use any formal surnames and may use initials in front of their names standing for the father's name. In the 19th and early 20th century, caste names were used as surnames in the south Indian states. Surnames may be based on patronymics and ancestry, priestly distinctions, business or trade designation, or caste. People from Myanmar (Burma), have no family names.

I have always found Russian names fascinating. A full Russian name consists of personal given name, a patronymic (the father's name formed by adding a suffix like -ich *for* males (Igor Petrovich) and the adjective suffix *-na* for females. *Ivanov* indicates son of Ivan while Petrova indicates the daughter of Peter. Some common names are derived from professions, places of origin, and personal characteristics. Kuznetsov (Kuznetsova - smith) and Pastukhov (Pastukhova - shepherd) are "profession" examples; Smolensky (Smolensk) is a location example and Tolstova or Tolstoy (stout) and Sedov (Sedova - grey-haired) are personal characteristics examples.

The name conferred upon a person in early Biblical times was generally connected with some circumstance of that person's birth. Jews have historically used Hebrew patronymic names system where the first name is followed by either *ben-* or *bat-* ("son of" and "daughter of," respectively), and then the father's name, but permanent family surnames are also used today. Surnames were not common among the Jews as late as the Middle Ages, but as they began to mingle more with their fellow citizens they adopted civic surnames in addition to their "sacred" name.

Ashkenazi Jews (the Jewish diaspora) now use European or modern Hebrew surnames for everyday life, but the Hebrew patronymic form is still used in Jewish religious and cultural life. Many immigrants to modern Israel change their names to Hebrew names to symbolically move away from the family name given to them in other languages. The names of bread-winning women were adopted by some households while others came from the man's trade such as *Metzger* (butcher) or *Becker* (baker) and a few derived from personal attributes, such as *Jaffe* (beautiful), or special events in the family history.

The majority of Middle Ages surname adoption came from place names, often a town name, typically the birthplace of the founder of a rabbinical or other dynasty. Common names of Jews from Europe include "Rosen" (rose) and "Gold", and other German words as their names' prefixes, and "man" (Hoffman) and "berg"("mountain"), and other German words as suffixes.

## Escapades with Gene and Jerry**

I taught a laboratory quality assurance (QA) course for an international scientific organization (AOAC International) with my friend Gene for many years, and we even co-authored a textbook. Over the years we developed a close personal friendship and had some great times together, sometimes with our respective wives accompanying us. The following are some of our experiences:

**Dr. Gene takes a leak** (June 1996 in San Francisco)

We had a nice dinner in a stylish restaurant at the pier. Gene, Nancy, and Jerry, sagely decided to skip dessert since everyone wanted to go to Ghirardelli's, the justly famous chocolate emporium. We drove a couple of miles towards Ghirardelli's, but on the way Gene found that he needed to use a washroom to perform a certain physiological function, so Nancy told him to find a gas station.

Well, you know how it is. There is never a gas station around when you really need one, particularly in downtown San Francisco. Gene drove up this street and down that hill, and around the corner, with rapidly increasing urgency. The rest of us had a variety of helpful suggestions but no washrooms were identified. Finally, we drove past a hospital. Everyone knows that hospitals have washrooms.

Normally, of course, Gene would not want to barge into a hospital but you have to understand that this was now an emergency so he parked in the doctors' parking lot by the hospital emergency entrance and tore into the hospital through a door marked "Doctors". After a few minutes he sheepishly appeared with a relieved grin on his face and we were finally able to go to Ghirardelli's to enjoy the food of the gods, namely chocolate. It was a memorable evening in various and different ways.

**Nancy and Carrie take a ride with the State Patrol** (September 1999 in Houston)

Gene and Jerry were working their fingers to the bone teaching the QA course, so Nancy and Carrie went shopping. They drove the rental car to the huge, fancy Galleria shopping centre and enjoyed themselves immensely, looking in all of the big, little, and prestigious shops. After a elegant lunch they decided to head back to the car and our hotel, so they looked for the entrance that they had used to come into the shopping center.

One of them said it was over there and the other said it was on a different level. Both were wrong. They finally found the parking garage but realized that weren't sure what the car looked like. None of the million cars there looked familiar. They tried another parking level, and then another entry door to a different part of the parking garage, but didn't see a car that they recognized.

Finally they saw a huge black State Patrol Jeep driven by a police officer. They turned on their feminine charms and tried to look helpless (not too difficult) as they explained their problem. The officer volunteered to help them find their car by driving through the parking lot. He asked logical male questions such as which level they parked on and which end of the shopping centre they had entered, but they pleaded temporary tourist memory amnesia.

Mr. State Patrol patiently drove them around for a long time to this level of the parking garage and that side of the huge underground parking lot. Eventually, they found their car and they even found their way back to the hotel.

**"You call that a translation? That's not what she asked!"** (May, 1997 in Tallinn, Estonia).

The AOAC organizers arranged for our course to be presented in Tallinn, with about ten attendees each from Estonia, Latvia, and Lithuania. The folks from each country spoke their own language but all of them also spoke Russian. (They were all a bit sensitive about that since it had not been long since they had gained independence from Russia.)

We had simultaneous translation into Russian by a translator who sat in a soundproof booth. Both the translator and the attendees had a copy of the course binder (in English), and perhaps one-third of the students spoke English well enough that they didn't need the ear phones. In any case, the course went well and Gene and I could present the course material at almost the regular pace.

At the end of the course we had extended opportunity for questions and the translator came to the front of the room beside Gene and me so that he too could hear the questions. With the translator now accessible, we became aware that the students had some concerns about the translation quality, and there was some lively debate between the students and translator in clarifying the questions and the answers.

We enjoyed walking in the Old City of Tallinn with its cobblestone streets and the brightly painted ancient stucco buildings. The old churches are magnificent and on Sunday we went to the Catholic Church where we stood in the entryway since the church was jammed full. It turned out that a Cardinal was present (he wore a red beanie), and his remarks were being translated from Italian to Estonian, so we listened to his comments in two languages, neither of which we understood.

After the course, the organizers and we took a streetcar through the modern part of the city, which was grey and dreary compared to the colourful walled Old City. One highlight was an interesting open-air market that sold everything from illegal music tapes, to baby strollers, to vegetables.

**The streets were twelve feet wide and the taxis seven feet wide, making it interesting when on-coming cars met**. (May, 1994 in Port of Spain, Trinidad and Tobago).

Jerry and Carrie stayed at a different hotel than Gene and Nancy. We each had our own driver, and when we went for dinner we would ride in one of the 1950s Oldsmobile or Cadillac taxis that carefully, or recklessly, negotiated its way through the narrow streets. The local Bureau of Standards was casual about the arrangements and the schedule (everything moves at a slower pace compared to the U.S. and Canada), but the course went well. The four of us enjoyed some excellent dinners in Port of Spain. Carrie and Jerry toured a bit of the west side of the island, and after the course we took the twenty-minute flight to Tobago and had a fabulous day visiting some of the most beautiful sights in the world—the ocean (snorkeling in the beautiful blue green water and seeing the fish and coral), the beach, and the people.

**Jerry, I could try to drive there, but it's not clear if the course will even go ahead.** (September 2001 in Kansas City).

This was the essence of the telephone call that I received from Gene on the Wednesday after the Tuesday of 9/11. Our course was scheduled for the Thursday and Friday after the AOAC meeting. Because of the disruption to air travel, flying from South Bend, Indiana, to Kansas City was out of the question for Gene, and driving didn't seem wise. We were not even sure that the course would go ahead, so it was decided that if necessary I would do the course alone. There were about twenty students registered but several didn't show up on Thursday morning. It became clear quickly that the attendees were not really focused on the course material. They were concerned about various current issues, including getting home. We struggled through the first day but when we met the second day we negotiated an 11:00 AM close for the course. Everybody was fine with this; they at least had the course binder to review later and we never heard any complaints.

Carrie had her own little drama since she was stuck in the hotel room watching the World Trade Center go down a million times on TV. One of my colleagues called her room every hour to ask how we were all going to get home. We finally were able to fly home on Saturday with just a few stressful hiccups. Our flight path went from Kansas City to Toronto to Vancouver. We were happy to get home.

**You can't always tell from the write-up…that restaurant is skuzzy…and where in the world is that pharmacy we saw yesterday?"** (September 2006 in Minneapolis).

Carrie and I had brought our grandson along on this trip and Carrie and Nancy wanted to find a funky restaurant to help him celebrate his twelfth birthday. The first restaurant that we checked didn't look great, and the second one looked skuzzy (even though it was favorably described in the city highlight magazine). Its patrons exhibited rings in various body parts including some that probably should be kept private, so we quickly decided to move on.

We drove around, and finally found a fabulous Italian restaurant. Served family style, each meal featured a salad big enough for all five of us. A single serving of lasagna was more than enough for all of us. The meatballs were baseball size and delicious. Gene asked the waiter to bring a birthday cake along with some candles, and this topped off the dinner with style.

Then we went to look for a pharmacy to purchase some cold medication. The ladies were sure that they had seen one close by the day before but even though we drove up and down most of the downtown streets we never did find it.

**We can see Disney World, but you can't get there from here**. (September 2005 in Orlando).

We stayed in a beautiful Marriott hotel and could see Disney World from our room. But no one walks in Orlando, partly because it's usually so hot, and partly because it seems to be un-American. And in any case there is no sidewalk or walkway across the freeway, so it we had to take a $15.00 taxi ride to Disney World.

Gene and Nancy had brought two of their grandchildren along and Carrie and I brought a granddaughter and her mom. Gene I came over to Downtown Disney each evening where we had a great dinner plus enjoyed seeing all of the sights there with our family. Of course Carrie and Nancy and the kids enjoyed several days at Disney World.

**Did they come to hear about QA from Gene and Jerry, or did they come to see Mickey Mouse**? (September 1996 in Orlando).

AOAC kept registration open until the last minute, even as the course was starting, and combined with the other attractions bringing people to Orlando, we had fifty-four students registered from nineteen different countries. The large course and the high number of countries represented made our personal interaction with course attendees challenging but we did fine.

**"Gene, help! Jerry isn't here!"** (November, 1997 in Baltimore).

Gene and Nancy were going to a wedding the weekend before the course was to start on Monday morning, so Gene would be unable to get to Baltimore until almost noon on Monday. As a result it was agreed that I would do the introduction and the first two sections of the course and we would both continue with the course in the afternoon. It was a good plan. What could go wrong?

On Saturday morning Carrie dropped me off at the Vancouver airport and went home. When I went through U.S. Customs I told them I was going to teach a course and they sent me to the Secondary Customs office (never a good sign) where I was told I was taking a job away from an American citizen. I would therefore not be allowed to enter the U.S.

My statement that I was a volunteer and not getting paid didn't change their minds, nor did his appeal to NAFTA, which provided for "free exchange of scientific information". (They happened to have a copy available and we found the applicable section.)

It happened to be the weekend that the U.S.-Canada salmon treaty talks were being held in Vancouver and the talks had been going badly. It was evident that the U.S. was making it difficult or impossible for Canadians to enter their country just then. Two Canadian university professors also heading for the U.S. to give seminars were also refused entry. It was Saturday and I could not reach anyone at the AOAC office, but left a message at the Baltimore hotel. Unfortunately, Gene could not be reached and cell phones had not yet been invented. Gene strolled up to the hotel just before noon on Monday and the AOAC representative rushed up to him crying, "Jerry isn't here! Jerry isn't here! Get in here fast!"

The adventures in the other Canadian and U.S. cities (which include Cincinnati, Winnipeg, Saskatoon, Phoenix, Seattle, San Francisco, Chicago and Los Angeles) will have to wait for another time.

**I have used the Chuck Yeager approach (I tell things the way I remember them, which isn't necessarily the way that they happened).

## The Rise and Fall of…Detroit

The name Detroit (de-troit) comes from the French word for strait, which is a narrow passage of water connecting two large bodies of water. The Detroit River, or strait, extends south from Lake St. Clair to Lake Erie, and functions as international border between Canada and the United States, separating Detroit, Michigan, and Windsor, Ontario. The Detroit River, going north from Detroit towards Lake Huron, is part of an important transportation route that connects cities as far west as Duluth, Minnesota, and Thunder Bay, Ontario, on Lake Superior, and cities such as Chicago, on Lake Michigan. This river also provides access to the Atlantic Ocean if you go west and north on Lake Erie and through the Erie Canal Lake to Lake Ontario and the St. Lawrence Seaway.

The French settled Detroit in the late 16th century. When the Erie Canal was opened in 1825, providing access to the Great Lakes and the Atlantic Ocean, Detroit became a major manufacturing center and transportation hub. When Henry Ford began manufacturing cars and established the first assembly line in 1898 and the Ford Motor Company in 1903, Detroit became a center of investment and wealth as well, attracting many new residents who could experience a comfortable life working in the factories. Around 1940, Detroit was the wealthiest city in the U.S. after New York City.

Detroit became one of the few U.S. cities where black people could obtain excellent jobs and be upwardly mobile. By 1929 Detroit had attracted more than half a million people and had become America's fourth largest city. The "Big Three" automakers (Ford, General Motors, and Chrysler), all centered in the Detroit area, became the largest automakers in the United States and the companies all did well.

During World War II the U.S. desperately needed to transfer Detroit`s technological capabilities to manufacturing military equipment. Perhaps as many as 300,000 new workers flooded into

Detroit; many were from the south and many were black. The city was ill-equipped to handle all these people. Black workers, even though they had money in their pockets, were forced to sleep in their cars or in back alleys. The government insisted on paying blacks the same as whites (which was good but not popular), and the autoworkers union (at least officially) supported this. The situation was made worse by the rampant racism, and when housing projects were built for black families, riots and violence frequently broke out. One riot in 1943 led to the death of thirty-four people, most of whom were black, and police shot seventeen of those.

Instead of dealing with the city`s housing and race problems, Detroit just muddled through to the end of the war, perhaps hoping that most of the recent (mostly black) arrivals would then go back "home". But the auto industry re-invented itself and lots of work was available so most people stayed.

Blacks were still treated terribly and the building of new Interstate highways displaced many. After World War II, President Eisenhower initiated a grand plan for interstate highways in the 1950s and Detroit was an early benefactor. The introduction of major highways was a mixed blessing in that the upper middle class, mostly white, moved out to the newly established suburbs. This, along with longstanding prejudices against blacks, led to a substantial deterioration of the city. Racial conflict, and many years of bad government, eventually led to the dramatic decline of Detroit in the latter part of the 20$^{th}$ century.

Another whammy hit Detroit when more car manufacturing went to Japan and other foreign countries, and the gasoline "crisis" in the 1970s didn't help because Americans bought even more foreign-built compact cars. As a result, even more businesses and people left the city and eventually Detroit was a city of 700,000 trying to survive and pay taxes for a city designed for two million.

It is easy to be discouraged in community development when 70% of houses in a neighborhood stand empty. As a result, unsurprisingly, but sadly, Detroit had one of the highest arson rates in the world.

One couple bought a house for $29,000 in 1989 and thought that they, along with Detroit, were finally on their way as they watched it annually increase in value to $122,000 in 2006. However, the house value then plummeted just as quickly in 2007 and 2008 as more people fled the city under another series of tough economic reversals. One news report indicated that 250,000 people moved out of Detroit between 2000 and 2010, dropping the population to about 713,000. Middle-class black families also left, leaving block after block of empty streets (more than 30,000 houses) and deteriorating neighborhoods, and this continued through the remainder of the 20th century.

The media attention describing Detroit's problems exacerbated the growing problems, and city administration corruption scandals and the lack of money for public schools all drove even more people to the suburbs or other to cities. Many homes left vacant were gutted or turned into drug or prostitution dens.

Abandoned and neglected areas of the city became dumping grounds for everything from old refrigerators to dead bodies, as crime seemed to be out of control. A policeman who used to patrol a small area in a tough neighborhood in the 1950s now due to city cutbacks had to patrol a fifty-six kilometre square area. Detroit had one of the highest crime rates in the U.S. and the city didn't seem to have the money to turn this around.

According to a Christianity Today report in 2013, there was something like 200,000 vacant or foreclosed lots in Detroit, many of them littered with garbage or overgrown with bushes. A 2013 news report indicated that Detroit had a deficit of over $300 million and owed more than $14 billion in long-term obligations. The Governor of Michigan wanted to name an emergency manager to handle Detroit's financial crisis, but, incredibly, many local officials and residents refused to acknowledge the seriousness of the problems and chose to keep on spending.

In July 2013, the city of Detroit filed for bankruptcy. The city had more than 100,000 creditors and more than $1 billion in liabilities. (Some estimates went as high as $20 billion, including over $9.2 billion in unfunded pension and health care liabilities.) The city's unemployment rate had tripled since 2000. The homicide rate was at an all-time high and on average it took fifty-eight minutes for the police to respond compared to the national average of eleven minutes. One report indicated that about 40% of the city's streetlights didn't work and at least 78,000 buildings had been abandoned.

Municipal government bankruptcies are pretty much uncharted territory so resolution was difficult. Even as late as 2016 Detroit was described as "an example of everything that is wrong in our nation".

There are now some signs of hope emerging for Detroit. New tech companies and other start-up companies have recently been locating there, perhaps drawn by the ready availability of land at below market rates. Economic development is also a component of various Christian ministries, where churches and other organizations purchase and develop city owned vacant lots while helping residents to build or renovate houses and start small businesses. In some cases, they establish community gardens so that people can grow some of their own food plus sell extra produce at farmers' markets. Some small for-profit businesses plant trees, which in the long term can be harvested. Another key factor driving Detroit's future depends on the revitalization of the auto industry in Detroit.

By the time that you read this, things for Detroit could be better, or worse.

## R Movies and My Favorite Movies

There's good news and bad news regarding movies. The bad news is the violence, foul language, and indiscriminate sex in so many movies. The good news is, according to a June 2013 report, R-rated movies are making less money, on average, than family category movies. The U.S. National Association of Theatre Owners found in 2012 that R-rated movies earned an average of $16.8 million while PG movies made an average of $47.3 million.

It seemed to me for a while that Hollywood deliberately added bad language to obtain an R-rating to make more money. I suppose they thought this was what the public wanted. But it seems that there has been push back from the public. One movie representative was quoted as saying that PG-13 was now the "sweet spot" for movies. He concluded that Americans have made a choice for family friendly movies.

Of course, there are still some Hollywood moguls who want to "push the artistic envelope" or produce "adult themed movies" which seems to be code language for using foul language or producing X-rated sex scenes. They seem to think that real life is R-rated, which is a sad reflection of their values.

Life can present many challenges and sorrows, but even in those times it can have the beautiful outcome of making us better individuals. Comedy movies often seem to be magnets for bad language, but even here it seems good taste may prevail. USA Today reported in June 2013 that comedies accounted for only 12% of movie sales in 2013 compared to 25% ten years earlier. One reason suggested for this decline was the "potty mouth" language often used "in order to sound realistic."

But there are still many excellent movies available for our viewing pleasure. My top ten favorite movies looks something like this:

In first place is *Man from Snowy River*. Actually this is a double entry since there also is a *Man from Snowy River 2*. Both of these classics have fabulous rugged mountain scenes with beautiful horses, and a love story.

*Chariots of Fire* is really two stories about the 1928 English Olympic Team—one about an athlete struggling to find his purpose and deal with success and the other about a young man who stood up for his principles and defined his purpose as striving to please God as an Olympic athlete. At one point he says that God made him fast, and when he runs he felt God's pleasure.

Another top favorite is *Hugo*, a story about a young boy who lives behind the huge clock (which he maintains; he has a gift for repairing watches and toys) at the Paris train station; this is also a story about redemption of an old man who was one of the first moving picture producers.

I don't know if this is allowed, but I have a second set of number one favourites, which includes two sets of movies, namely the *Chronicles of Narnia* series and *The Lord of the Rings* Trilogy. From the seven Narnia novels written by C. S. Lewis, as of this writing three great movies have been produced —*The Lion, the Witch and the Wardrobe, Prince Caspian*, and *The Voyage of the Dawn Treader.*

*The Lord of the Rings* film series consists of three epic fantasy adventure movies (*The Fellowship of the Ring, The Two Towers*, and *The Return of the King*) based on books written by J.R.R. Tolkien. In both of these series, the movies are almost as great as the books, which tells me that the movies are pretty fabulous.

I also like *Second Hand Lions*, which is about two irascible old brothers who take care of a young nephew and find creative and unusual ways to maintain their independence and spend their wealth. *Casablanca* is an all-time favorite, plus it is one of the best movie love stories of all time. Of course any movie with Humphrey Bogart will be fascinating. *Finding Forrester* is another great movie, telling the story of a supremely talented young black student who meets a famous but reclusive author (Sean Connery) who teaches the boy about life and writing.

I also like *Scent of a Woman* with Al Pacino. There are three especially fascinating scenes; one shows Pacino (who is blind) racing down the city streets in a Lamborghini guided only by a young prep school student sitting beside him, another shows Pacino teaching the tango to a beautiful young lady. The third scene shows him dramatically defending the student at his snobbish prep school.

I like the *Blind Side*, which is based on a true story about an impoverished, basically homeless, massive black boy who is adopted by a caring wealthy family and learns to play football as a left tackle (thereby protecting the quarterback's blind side). *Fiddler on the Roof* is an old classic musical that I enjoy watching every few years. *To Kill a Mocking Bird* is a moving depiction of racism in the Deep South as a lawyer (Gregory Peck) unsuccessfully defends a black man accused of a crime that he didn't commit. *Secretariat* is another fascinating story about perhaps the greatest racing horse in history.

*Schindler's List* is a disturbing but challenging movie about an entrepreneur rescuing Jews during World War II, but I like two other WWII movies even more—*The Hiding Place* tells the story of Corrie ten Boom and her family hiding and caring for Jews, and *The Diary of Anne Frank*, a story in a similar vein.

The first movie my mother saw (which didn't happen until she was at least sixty years old) was *The Sound of Music.* She eventually saw it at least ten times. Most guys apparently shouldn't enjoy movies like this, but I do. This movie has magnificent scenery, some moral lessons with a good story, and a love song. My sweetie and I even have "our song" which has the line that says "somewhere in my youth or childhood I must have done something good".

The professionals usually list *Citizen Kane, Gone With The Wind* and *Vertigo* as some of the greatest movies ever made but I'm not a professional. Others would understandably include the Star Wars movies.

At Christmas time we always watch four movies: *Scrooge* (the version of Dickens' *A Christmas Carol* with Alastair Sim); *It's a*

*Wonderful Life* (James Stewart, Donna Reed), *Miracle on 34th Street* (Elizabeth Perkins, Dylan McDermott) and *The Little Shop Around the Corner* (James Stewart, Margaret Sullivan).

As you can see, my top ten list includes more than ten movies, but as someone once said, there are three kinds of people—those who can count and those who can't.

## I Don't Want to be a Nurse When I Get Big

My sweetie recently had hip replacement surgery, and while the surgery went well, the recovery phase lasted at least two months. These days the stay in the hospital is only two days even with its multitude of nurses, physiotherapists, and other care professionals.

Guess who gets to be the nurse when the patient comes home? Yes, me. Now, our kids were wonderful and some of them stayed over for a couple of nights the first week or two, which was greatly appreciated.

But it's tough checking to make sure that your sweetie is taking the morphine and acetaminophen painkillers on schedule or helping her pull on her pajama bottoms, or mixing up a dose of Metamucil or getting out the syringes for the blood thinner injections each day or making sure that her water bottle has fresh ice cubes or helping her do the required exercises, or...well, you get the picture.

For the first ten days or I also got up in the middle of the night to watch her go to the bathroom to make sure she didn't fall, plus did the laundry every other day. Nurses, thankfully, do all of this stuff, usually with a smile, and I say "bless them".

I'm not complaining, you understand, I just don't want to be a nurse when I get big. I love her but it's difficult to see her suffer or to even temporarily be incapacitated. Helping her in this way is the least that I can do. However, staying close by and watching daytime TV offers whole different level of pain.

Making breakfast and lunch and dinner was interesting. I can do breakfast easily (anyone can make toast with peanut butter and jam, plus coffee), and making a salad or having cold meat sandwich for lunch was manageable, but my idea of making dinner until now has been to raid the refrigerator for leftovers and then warm them up in the microwave. This worked for a couple of days until I had to get more creative and start off with actual raw materials like meat and vegetables.

I'm one of those husbands whose idea of a gourmet meal is one made by my wife or one at a nice restaurant. ("I'm making dinner as fast as I can dial.") Someone suggested that I make a dinner from scratch but I couldn't find any at the grocery store. I haven't seen any bacteria or little crawly things in the kitchen so I think we're okay. The fact that we were both alive six weeks later not having died from either malnutrition or food poisoning speaks to our hardy healthy physiology and our desire to live to see a better day.

Hospital food is bland (apparently they believe that salt and flavoring are evil) and rarely hot (I think it's prepared in Calgary and sent over here weekly), but it has one big advantage—it magically shows up in your hospital room on schedule. My sweetie has lost eight pounds in the past month but I think we can agree that this can be totally explained by the major surgery.

And then there's the thing about keeping the house clean. (I should mention that I usually do the vacuuming and some dusting so this is not a totally foreign concept). At the hospital they have people who keep everything clean, but at home, well, I'm supposed to do all of the cleaning for now.

It usually takes my sweetie more than two hours to clean the kitchen and front room, but I found I could do it in less than twenty-five minutes. Well, that's what I thought. Apparently, I didn't do the job as well as she does. Can you believe it? It looked fine to me. It was decided that we needed to hire a professional house cleaner at least once or twice during her convalescence. I don't want to be a house cleaner either when I get big, but that's another story.

## Dr. Google Will See You Now

The doctor is in. Or online anyway.

People everywhere are attempting to take control of their health by accessing readily available information in order to self-diagnose real and perceived ailments. A British report indicated that seventy-five per cent of the British public sought health information from a wide range of sources such as health-related websites, medical professionals, search engines, and food packaging and, of course, social media including the "medical authorities" on Twitter, Facebook, YouTube, and various blogs.

But one needs to be careful. You type in "headache" and up pops "brain tumour" or a list of readily available patent medicines that may or may not work. Or enter "my urine is red" and you may conclude that you either have an enlarged prostate, or a cancerous or noncancerous tumour, or a kidney cyst, or kidney or bladder stones, or perhaps just a urinary tract infection. But it's also possible that you just had beets or blackberries or rhubarb for dinner. How much can you trust Dr. Google?

Google announced in 2015 that it would be rolling out health information on about 800 conditions that would provide quick and easily downloadable pages that users can take to their doctors' offices. This begs the question: How accurate will the information be? And does this approach have doctors concerned that ever more patients will be showing up after self-diagnosing with rare diseases they almost certainly do not have?

Google said it has worked with a team of doctors to "carefully compile, curate, and review this information. All of the gathered facts represent real-life clinical knowledge from these doctors and high-quality medical sources across the web, and the information has been checked by medical doctors at Google and the Mayo Clinic for accuracy."

Google is expanding the health information it provides to readers. Some medical experts are supportive of this initiative saying that this will give consumers more useful and accurate information about health matters, while recognizing that "the quality of health information on the Web is still not optimal" (Wow! Really!) They suggest that people just need to remember that this is meant to aid them, but it's not a substitute for health care.

Like it or not, the Internet is where people are now going for health information. One physician said that unintended consequences are inevitable but can be minimized if Google is committed to measuring the outcomes from the use of this tool and work to improve its use. Checking with Dr. Google will place an extra burden in the doctor's office since the doctor needs to be willing and interested in assessing the barrage of information (relevant or not) that the patient may want to discuss with them. Information taken out of context can be frightening and confusing which will be a problem since the time for a doctor to communicate with a patient is limited.

Others say that instead of just looking up symptoms, as is typically the case with the Internet, we're about to move into an era when people will also have objective data (through sensors, labs, imaging, genome sequence) that will empower them to be highly active participants in their diagnosis and care. Some professionals believe that patients are more motivated to follow through with treatments and that patients are more likely to observe their Doctor's advice as a result of having also turned to digital sources for information. Patients who are better prepared with their own statistics and their own health data can also prepare and help the clinician and the GP to give a better assessment and a better diagnosis. The bottom line is that health-care professionals should always be consulted in the event of medical concerns. This is true even though your computer contains all the information from every medical book currently used in medical school plus all the drug information and all of the treatment guidelines that doctors are supposed to follow.

Better access to quality information is vital to improving the nation's health, but it is not a substitute for health care itself. As Hippocrates once said, "Science is the father of knowledge; opinion breeds ignorance."

The medical community can help by providing better keywords for Internet searches. Dr. Google has been the brunt of numerous jokes and various denigrations from the medical community for some time. One frustrated individual suggested suing Dr. Google for malpractice. In past days the local doctor had full control of all medical information available to their community. Physicians now recognize that denigrating Dr. Google and trying to limit health information access is already a lost battle and are generally committed to making Dr. Google more helpful. Another point is that doctors in small practices and isolated areas now have access to a wealth of information that they can use to better help their patients.

Note: I googled "Google" to provide this information.

## Singapore – A Model or an Anathema?

A December 2013 Vancouver Province column by Gwyn Morgan asked this question: "How would you feel about donating to a charity that uses more than half of your money for overhead costs? If that puts you off, then you should feel the same way about paying your income taxes."

Morgan reported that a Fraser Institute study found that federal governments had wasted as much as $197 billion over the past twenty-five years, leaving the government's drive to improve efficiency a lot of room for improvement.

An OECD (Organization for Economic Co-operation and Development) study showed that government spending efficiency improves as private sector production, consumption, investment and exports increase; and declines as government spending rises. The combined spending of Canada's federal, provincial, and municipal governments totals almost a trillion dollars per year so improving the value for money from these enormous expenditures couldn't be more important.

Western countries have tried a variety of monetary policies, with varying and limited success. By contrast, a World Bank report showed that Singapore delivers high-quality public services at a low cost. It spends just 2.6 per cent of GDP on education, half of the OECD average, yet students rank ten places above Canada in math, science, and reading skills. The government creates strong incentives for students to perform well in standardized national tests and hires the best teachers by choosing candidates from the top thirty per cent of new graduates. The result is superior achievement for students and high public esteem for teachers.

Even more impressive is the value for money achieved by Singapore's health-care system. Government health-care spending is a meager 1.4 per cent of GDP, compared with the OECD average of more than seven per cent. Life expectancy stands at 81.4 years and child mortality is just 2.2 per thousand live births. Wait times are remarkably low. Their system provides universal coverage through a combination of compulsory savings and government subsidies that ensure affordability for all, with the private sector providing about seventy-five per cent of publicly funded patient care. Those wanting additional features such as upgraded accommodation must make copayments beyond the amount funded by the state. The result is the world's most efficient and effective universal public health-care system.

Most of us don't know much about Singapore, which is located in South-East Asia off the southern tip of Malaysia. It was once a colonial possession of Great Britain, and after the British East India Company established a trading post there in 1819 it became a center for rubber exports. By 1832 Singapore was attracting immigrants from India, China, and other parts of Asia. It became self-governing in 1959 and gained full independence from Malaysia in 1965 when it became the Republic of Singapore. It is now the world's only sovereign city-state that's also an island. Singapore is now a prosperous vibrant cosmopolitan city and has the world's highest percentage of millionaires, with one out of every six households having at least one million U.S. dollars in disposable wealth.

Singapore's economy is known as one of the freest, most innovative, most competitive, and most business-friendly. As of this writing Singapore is the 14th largest exporter and the 15th largest importer in the world, which is, remarkable for such a small country. It is one of the world's leading commercial and financial centers and one of the five busiest ports. Tourism forms a large part of the economy, and gambling has been legalized to attract more tourists. The government has rejected the idea of a generous welfare system (a concept generally almost unimaginable in the western world) stating that each generation must earn and save enough for its entire life cycle. There are, however, special programs available for the needy.

Singapore is a multiparty parliamentary republic but the People's Action Party has won every election since self-government in 1959. Slightly over five million people live in Singapore, of which around two million are foreign-born. Singapore's diversity is reflected in having four official languages—English, Malay, Chinese, and Tamil. Buddhism is the most widely practiced religion in Singapore, followed by Christianity, Islam, Taoism, and Hinduism.

Singapore's legal system is based on English common law_but with substantial differences. Trial by jury no longer exists so that judges make all decisions. According to Wikipedia, the government has broad powers to limit citizens' rights and to inhibit political opposition and one "Freedom Index" report ranks Singapore 133rd out of 175 countries. There are some restrictions on freedom of speech and freedom of the press.

Singapore has long practiced corporal punishment in the form of mandatory caning on the buttocks, along with prison sentences for about thirty offences including rape, rioting, and vandalism. There is a mandatory death penalty for murder and certain drug-trafficking and firearms offences. Amnesty International, perhaps following its penchant for hyperbole relating to things it doesn't like, indicated that Singapore has one of the highest execution rates in the world relative to its population, but this is disputed. On the other hand, international business executives suggested that Singapore had one of the best judicial systems in Asia.

What do I conclude from all of this information? Like most countries, Singapore has some attractive features and some warts. I guess that the strong approach to tackling crime and government spending plus emphasizing efficiency and fostering business responsibility appeals to me.

## My Favorite Dog (Not Cat) Stories

I'm not known as a pet lover but I have a few favorite dog stories. At one time we did own a beautiful little dog; it was a Lhasa Apso-Maltese cross. Tux was all black with fairly long but non-shedding hair. His distinguishing feature was a splash of white on his chest that made him look like he was wearing a tuxedo. Tux was not allowed to be in the kitchen, nor was he allowed to be underfoot at the table during meals. But he was allowed in the adjacent family room and during our meal times he sat in the family room with his front paws just over the dividing line into the kitchen. If he "accidentally" came just a little too far into the kitchen we would say "Tux, back up" and he would immediately obey. It happened quite often and after a while, even while playing with him somewhere in the house, if we said the magic words "Tux, back up" he would do so and would keeping backing up until the repeated command stopped. This was pretty much his only trick.

When my son was about twelve he delivered the local free newspaper twice a week. One time we were in a hurry to go somewhere so I volunteered to help him get finished early. He did one side of the street and I did the other side. One street had long driveways and everything was going well until I rounded the corner of a driveway and saw a large pen with three German Shepherds in it. I thought, *no problem*, since the fence was high and sturdy. However, just as I approached the house, a fourth German Shepherd bounded around the back corner of the house and took after me. I dropped the paper and ran back towards the road. I reached the sidewalk and just beyond, and, magically, the dog stopped right at the property boundary just before the sidewalk. At least this watchdog was well trained. Then my son came up and said, "Oh Dad, we don't do that house!"

My sweetie and I were biking with another couple one sunny Sunday afternoon. I happened to be in front, and I crossed the next street. As I did, the other couple yelled that we had to turn there. I tried to turn around in the empty lot just past the corner, but suddenly three unruly dogs bolted toward me, yapping and nipping at my legs. It's difficult to kick at dogs while trying furiously to pedal away from them. Somehow I managed to get away without any bite marks on my legs and we continued on our quiet little ride.

They say that dogs have owners while cats have staff, which is only one reason why I dislike cats. When our little girl was about two years old we agreed to get her a cat. She played with Smoky all the time, quite actively, so she was continually getting little scratches on her arms even though the play was always friendly. We were concerned that she might get scratched on her face, so I took the cat to some veterinary students (I was going to university where there was both a medical school and a veterinary school) to have Smoky declawed. The operation was professionally done and our little girl was no longer getting scratched. We had a tree in our front yard, and the first time that Smoky tried to climb the tree, post operation, he managed about three steps before he slid to the ground. He stood there, looking confused, since he never had problems climbing that tree before. He tried it again, several times, and finally was successful. He learned and adapted quite quickly without claws on his front paws, and never again had a problem climbing that tree.

Just in case the previous anecdote leads you to think that I may actually have a soft spot for cats, the following report will clarify your misperception. I read recently that 269 million birds are estimated to die each year from human related activity and that cats account for seventy-five per cent of all bird deaths. This information was the result of a four-year study published in 2013 in Avian Conservation and Ecology, an online journal, but I can't vouch for the accuracy of these numbers. According to a Vancouver Sun article reporting on this study there are about 8.5 million domestic cats in Canada, and anywhere from 1.4 to 4.2 million feral cats. I assume these are mostly former house cats that have been abandoned by their owners. Feral cats are more aggressive than house cats and account for about 60% of the birds killed by cats. For your information, there are about 16 million bird deaths caused by power lines, and about as many by birds hitting building walls and windows, plus another ten million killed by vehicles.

These are small numbers compared to the cat numbers. So please keep your cats at home and under control, and feed them well so they don't have to plunder the bird population or make deposits in the neighbor's garden. Some cities are requiring that cats be licensed to help deal with the various problems that wandering cats generate.

Observations: A dog wags its tail with it heart. One reason a dog can be such a comfort when you're feeling blue is that he doesn't try to find out why. If your dog is fat, you aren't getting enough exercise.

Disclaimer: No cats were harmed during the writing of this vignette.

## My Sweetie's Work Stories

My sweetie majored in business courses in high school and showed considerable aptitude in this area. This positioned her well for an office job once she graduated from high school. (In addition, I thought she was pretty cute.)

In her first job at the University of Alberta she soon demonstrated her various secretarial skills. One morning she was called into her boss's office to take dictation for a number of important letters. (This was before computers and word processors so secretaries used Pittman shorthand to take notes from their bosses before typing letters and documents.)

About half way through the first letter, her boss leaned back in his chair, deep in thought, and stared up at the ceiling. All of a sudden there was a loud crack, and all that my sweetie could see were two long legs pointing skyward. The debonair professor's chair had tipped over backwards. Mightily embarrassed, the professor attempted to collect himself. After picking himself up he start dictating again while they both tried to suppress a ferocious urge to laugh. After trying and failing, he weakly recommended that they give up, and try to do the dictation later.

Carrie's second job was in Ottawa working in the office of the Minister of National Health and Welfare. The job of this office was to extract from Hansard (the official minutes of the proceedings in Parliament) all of the discussions relating to their Minister. At that time, all of this had to be done manually by re-typing the relevant sections. This was an important job even though it wasn't necessarily exciting. As might be expected, the office was operated in a professional manner, and Carrie's lady boss never once tipped over backwards in her chair.

After we moved to Lansing, Michigan, where I was working towards my PhD, my sweetie obtained a job with the city of Lansing. This particular office was charged with the responsibility of relocating folks who were being displaced by the construction of a new highway. Carrie's job was to prescreen people as they came to the office by obtaining the basic information that the office could then use to assist individuals to find appropriate new accommodation. One morning, a lady, looking something like a worst case scenario of a once beautiful but now a dilapidated aging actress, encumbered with several pounds of cosmetics, a $1.49 wig, and decades of life experience came in for assistance. When she surreptitiously asked, "Do I look suspicious?" my sweetie had to use her best manners and self-control to keep from laughing. Eventually, the woman obtained the information and documentation needed.

My sweetie later moved to the university in the Department of Food Science at Michigan State University. This office provided a more professional and enjoyable atmosphere. There were two important side benefits to this job. The first was that the labs periodically allowed the staff to take home safe, free, food samples, which we greatly appreciated as our budget was stretched to the limit. A second important benefit was that the basement of the Food Science building provided a sanctuary during the almost regular summer tornado warnings. We lived in married student housing which had no basement so the police came around to make sure that we evacuated to the basement of a safe campus building. Initially we were directed to the basement of the multi-storied student residences where there were hundreds of other married students with squalling babies and general pandemonium but the Food Science building basement was a welcome and quiet alternative.

Later, when we moved to Richmond, British Columbia, and then to Surrey, Carrie worked in the office of the Department of Microbiology at the University of British Columbia. When our daughter was attending UBC, the two of them worked out a neat arrangement. Daughter would climb into the car in the morning and sleep soundly for the forty-five to fifty-five minute commute. In the evening on the way home the roles were reversed. Poor exhausted Mom would sleep and daughter would drive home. The UBC job had another feature. My sweetie developed a beautiful friendship with the other two ladies in the office, which has lasted well into retirement.

## John Dillinger, Fingerprints, and...Marketing

John Dillinger was the most notorious bank robber in the U.S. in the 1920s and '30s, robbing at least two dozen banks alone or with accomplices. He even robbed police stations when he needed guns or bulletproof vests. On one occasion he posed as a security company technician and was given approval to "test" the system, then robbed the bank. He also contacted another bank as a movie company advance man and robbed the bank of thousands of dollars. Dillinger escaped from jail twice, but he used his stints in prison to learn techniques for becoming a better bank robber.

Media reports in his time were spiced with exaggerated accounts of Dillinger's bravado, daring, and colourful personality. Dillinger became famous, making it more difficult for him to continue his larcenous ways. J. Edgar Hoover used Dillinger's notoriety as a public enemy to launch the FBI where the science of fingerprinting was just developing. Dillinger understood that his presence at a robbed bank could be proven by fingerprinting (I guess that Neoprene gloves were not yet available). To avoid detection he poured acid on his fingertips to change or destroy his fingerprints. However, he found that once his hands healed his fingerprints came back just as they had always been. Dillinger also had plastic surgery (this science was quite primitive back then) but this had only a minimal effect on his appearance. He was killed in a shoot-out with the police in 1934.

Fingerprints are the traces of an impression from the friction ridges of any part of a person's hand (or foot). When fingertips brush across an uneven surface, these ridges amplify signals triggered by sensory nerve endings, giving us a sensation of touch or pain. These ridges may also assist in gripping different surfaces. Fingerprint impressions may be left behind on a surface by the natural secretions of sweat or oil from our fingers. Fingerprint identification is the process of comparing two impressions to determine whether these impressions could have come from the same individual. The fingers are placed on something like an inkpad and then rolled over on paper. The oily secretions from human fingers contain residues of various chemicals and their metabolites present in the body, which can also be detected and used for forensic purposes. For example, the fingerprints of tobacco smokers of contain traces of nicotine and cotinine (one of its metabolites).

There are at least twenty effective fingerprinting methods used by government or private forensic laboratories. The science of fingerprinting has advanced to the stage where it is possible to detect latent fingerprints not visible to the naked eye. Latent prints may exhibit only a small portion of the surface of a finger and this may be smudged, distorted, or overlapped by other prints from the same or from different individuals. Electronic, chemical, and physical processing techniques permit the identification of latent print residues from natural sweat or from a contaminant such as motor oil, blood, ink, or paint.

It was probably inevitable that some bright ad agency executive would come up with the idea of "Fingerprint Marketing" which is the concept that guides companies and individuals to discover and market their unique personality—the "fingerprint" of the organization or person.

Every person has unique identifying characteristics and so does every company. Some companies work hard to define their personality by establishing their primary differences to make their business or products stand apart from competitors. Others allow the marketplace to define their points of difference or uniqueness.

When we "Google" something on the Internet, the system automatically tracks the subjects that we search regularly, and soon our internet "fingerprint" is established. From there it's just a small step to selling this information to various companies who then try to sell us their products so that when we log on to the Internet ads featuring products or services in our areas of interest suddenly appear.

## Happy Leap Year/Day!

Many people today are pretty smart, for example, the astronomers who collect data to show that the earth is 13.7 billion years old and who can detect gravitational waves from something that happened about three billion years ago. But some of the ancients were pretty brilliant as well. We don't know exactly who developed the first calendars, but it is believed that humans around the world have used different means (such as carving a notch into a stick to record the passing of each full moon) to mark the cycles of nature throughout time. We do know that the Mayans, Egyptians, Babylonians, Romans, and Chinese all had calendars in the ancient days. The Egyptians were the first to work out a formula for the solar year based on the position of the sun and this formula was the forerunner to the modern calendar. A day comes from the rotation of the earth on its axis, which takes about twenty-four hours, and the time of day comes from the sun appearing to travel across the sky at about fifteen degrees every hour.

We use the Gregorian calendar decreed by Pope Gregory XIII who modified the Roman calendar in 1582. The Roman calendars are believed to be based on the Lunar Calendar, meaning that it was determined by the average time between two new months (29.5 days). The Gregorian calendar was a refinement of the Julian calendar, amounting to a 0.002% correction in the length of the year. The motivation for the reform was to bring the date for the celebration of Easter to the time of the year in which the early Church celebrated it. Because the celebration of Easter was tied to the spring equinox, the Roman Catholic Church considered the steady drift in the date of Easter caused by the year being slightly too long to be undesirable.

February 29th is a date that usually occurs every four years, and is called leap day. This day is added to the calendar in leap years as a corrective measure because the earth does not orbit the sun in precisely 365 days. (One report has it at 365.2421 days.) The system used for the calendar today is the mean solar day, which is twenty-four hours, three minutes and 56.55 seconds (approximately). Without leap days, the calendar would be off by twenty-four days within 100 years. Someone calculated that a person who lived to be ninety would see their birthday drift by three weeks over the course of their lifetime if leap days were not in place.

A scientist at the University of Toronto determined that the Gregorian calendar has a 400-year repeat cycle in which every year number divisible by four (2016, for example) has a leap day appended to February. However, if the year number is divisible by 100, then it is a leap year only if the year number is also divisible by 400. For instance, the year 2000 was a leap year, while 1900 was not.

At one time, some insurance companies, banks, and other major companies didn't recognize leap day as a valid date, forcing people to choose either Feb. 28$^{th}$ or March 1$^{st}$ as his or her birthday. Evolving technology has made this less of an issue.

The Winter solstice is an astronomical phenomenon marking the shortest day and the longest night of the year. In the Northern Hemisphere this is the December solstice and in the Southern Hemisphere this is the June solstice. As the Earth follows its orbit around the sun, the polar hemisphere that faced away from the sun, experiencing winter, will, in half a year, face towards the sun and experience summer. The cycles of the moon's phases are used to measure a month. The moon takes 29.5 days to return to the same point in the sky, as referenced to the sun.

Daylight Saving Time is a whole different topic, and another indication of man's attempts to manipulate Mother Nature. According to Internet sources, Daylight Saving Time was proposed by New Zealand scientist George Hudson in 1895, and first used in Germany during the First World War with the goal of saving energy. The idea is to take advantage of daylight hours in the spring so that people don't sleep through the first few hours of sunshine.

There is increasing debate about whether Daylight Saving Time should be abolished. The cost and energy savings aspects no longer appear valid. Some have suggested that the incidence of heart attacks and other health issues increases in the first days after the clock jumps ahead in spring. Others have reported that the time change is associated with an increase in road-related accidents (perhaps associated with sleep deprivation).

## Is ~~Santa~~ Jesus Real?

Most of us grew up with the fantasy that Santa Claus and his eight reindeer delivered presents on Christmas Eve. Even when quite small, deep down we found this hard to believe but the presents on Christmas morning usually pushed the doubts aside. Then as we grew older we knew that this was just a fantasy.

For some children who went to Sunday School and were taught about Jesus, as they grew older they wrestled with the question of whether Jesus is real or just a fantasy like Santa Claus. It turns out that there is both biblical and independent scholarly evidence that Jesus was born in Israel and that he lived for about thirty-three years, and that he died and rose to life again. We can examine a small part of this evidence by asking some questions about the nativity story.

Was there a census at the time that Jesus was born? There is no specific evidence about a census at the time that Jesus was born, but there is documentation that conducting a census to obtain population and tax information was a common practice by the Romans, including one that occurred a few years after Christ's birth. After some detailed research, Luke's statement that "Quirinius was governor of Syria" at the time of Jesus' birth was also found to be correct.

Was Jesus from Nazareth? The town of Nazareth wasn't mentioned in secular literature for several hundred years around the time Jesus was born so for a while it was thought that the Bible was wrong. But eventually independent archeological evidence subsequently showed that this town existed at the time that Jesus was on earth.

Was Jesus born on December 25$^{th}$? The short answer is, no. We don't have any idea of the day that Jesus was actually born. Some have speculated that Jesus was born is spring since the shepherds were out "watching their flocks by night" but we don't know. The church wanted to establish a date to celebrate Christ's birth, so in 385 AD, Pope Julius chose December 25$^{th}$ so that the Christian celebration would replace a pagan holiday. So we know that Jesus was born, we just don't know His actual birth date.

Was there "no room at the inn"? Bethlehem at that time was a village of perhaps 500 people and it didn't have any inns or hotels. Mary and Joseph likely stayed in a house; the Greek word that is used is the same one as the "upper room" where Jesus served the Last Supper with His disciples. Homes at that time were often built on a hillside so the family lived in the "upper room" while the sheep and other animals were kept on the lower ground floor in a walled off area at the back. Probably because there were many family and other visitors to Bethlehem at this time, there was no room in this particular upper room for Mary and Joseph so they went down below to the area with the animals for the birth of their son.

Did Herod really slaughter all babies in Bethlehem less than two years of age? Estimates are that Herod killed about twenty babies so that there would be no king to challenge his rule, but some scholars were skeptical of this since ancient literature doesn't mention this terrible action. But the reason seems to be that this was not big news in Israel at that time. Herod was a rather paranoid fellow who also killed one of his wives and two of his sons when he thought that they were a threat to his throne. These actions would have been big news. Herod wasn't a nice person so it isn't hard to believe that he also ordered babies to be killed, especially one who was said by the Magi to be a king.

Was there a star that led the wise men to Bethlehem? We don't know for sure, but it seems that there was something like a comet or nova or special star that the wise men used to guide them. They had done research about the imminent birth of a new "king" and travelled to find him.

In summary, there is strong evidence from antiquity that Jesus was indeed born in Bethlehem and that he lived, died, and then came back to life. Biblical evidence, independent archeology, and other scientific evidence clearly support this. Because of this, many serious scholars and others who are willing to look at the documentary evidence no longer have difficulty believing the historicity of Jesus.

Andy Steiger, a pastor at Northview Community Church in Abbotsford, Canada, has said that he is a Christian because it is true. In fact, faith is trusting what you have good reason to believe is true. There is a cumulative case or evidence for Christianity. Yes, there is evil and suffering in the world, but Jesus can help us deal with all of the muck. If we accept Him as Lord and Savior we will someday enjoy eternal life in heaven.

## Pseudo-Science and GMOs

Commercial genetically modified (GM) foods have been available since the 1990s. GM crops are produced with recombinant DNA technology. What this means is that inserting strands of DNA from one organism to another to give the new organism different properties can create a new organism. Recombinant DNA is used to try to introduce specific features into crops, bacteria, and animals. One example is developing a strain of corn or canola that makes the crop resistant to herbicides enabling the farmer to kill all weeds but leave a flourishing crop of corn or canola.

Vaccines such as hepatitis B vaccine have been produced using recombinant DNA technology. Recombinant proteins and other products that result from the use of recombinant DNA technology are found in essentially every western pharmacy, doctor's or veterinarian's office, medical testing laboratory, and biological research laboratory.

However, the controversy about these products is still as strong now as it was twenty or thirty years ago. A 2015 USA Today editorial headline, "GMO food panders to scientific ignorance" bemoaned a decision by several major companies to ban the use of GMO ingredients in any of their food products, and the belief by many Americans that GMO foods are harmful "despite overwhelming scientific evidence to the contrary."

Much of the alarm about GMO products is based on fear and junk science. The average person, including local and national politicians, doesn't recognize or understand the difference between real or legitimate science, and pseudo-science on genetically modified organisms (GMOs). While there is nothing wrong with organic foods, other than in many cases they really aren't necessary or worth the extra expense, organic food advocates often take advantage of the ignorance of consumers by railing against GMO foods. One PEW Research survey indicated that only thirty-seven per cent of Americans thought that GMO foods were safe while over ninety per cent of scientists believed them to be safe. (PEW Research Center is a non-partisan, non-advocacy "fact tank".)

The passionate and vocal critics of GM foods take advantage of the fact that lack of knowledge and fear are the keys to obstructing biotechnology. A good example of this is a paper published in 2013 in the Food and Chemical Toxicology Journal, which purported to show that GMO modified corn caused cancer in rats. Within weeks there was an outcry by legitimate scientists questioning the results and conclusions and eventually the paper was withdrawn when the journal editors finally concluded that the paper was not fit for publication due to poor methodology producing invalid data and wrong conclusions.

But substantial damage had been done since GMO critics had trumpeted the paper's conclusions when it was first published. Reputable scientists have not found a single case of a GMO approved food on animal feed being detrimental to human or animal health even though GMO foods have been on the market for fifteen years. Coincidentally, the 2013 World Food Prize was awarded to scientists using biotechnology to improve food crops. After years of banning the importation of any food containing GMOs (under the guise of trade protection), the European Union finally concluded that GMOs are not more risky than conventional plant breeding. Some anti-GMO radicals are willing to resort to violence and property damage. While not defending such actions, advocacy groups and multinational corporations do need to do a better job of assessing and explaining the safety of GMO foods.

In the late1800s Canadian farmers planted wheat that had been brought over from Europe, but the wheat didn't mature or ripen before the early prairie frosts killed the plants. Some Ontario farmers as well as researchers at the Central Experimental Farm in Ottawa used traditional cross breeding of various strains or varieties of wheat and produced a new variety which ripened in time to be harvested in the shorter Canadian growing season. The process to develop this new popular variety was essentially DNA manipulation that took many growing seasons and was considered innovative and acceptable. Today we could quickly accomplish the same thing using recombinant DNA technology. Apparently, even Amish farmers (generally thought of as being traditional) in Pennsylvania have adopted GMO foods.

An example of the confusion about GMOs was when a local city council passed a resolution in 2012 banning the cultivation of GM crops in their jurisdiction. The stated reason for doing this was that the transfer of GM pollen or seed to a neighboring organic field would threaten organic certification and because they had been pressured by vocal purveyors of pseudo-science alleging various animal and human health issues. The city council made this decision even though the spokesperson for the organic food company admitted that there had never been a case of decertification of an organic crop by trace amounts of GM seed or pollen. Facts seldom dissipate fear, and in this case, fear and scientific ignorance permitted manipulation of the city council. The result was that public policy was based on pseudo-science. It doesn't seem to matter that food safety authorities around the world have endorsed the safe use of GM crops. It doesn't matter that the World Health Organization and even the European Food Safety Authority have concluded that there is no evidence of harm from consuming food made from GM ingredients.

It also didn't matter to this city council that they have no jurisdiction in this area since the regulation of GM crops is a federal responsibility or that these local politicians had no expertise in this area. They could have passed their concerns along to the federal authorities and asked for a summary of the valid scientific studies available, but they bowed to the pressure of misinformed junk science activists. These are the same types of people that decried the use of fluoride in drinking water or the parents that refuse to vaccinate their children.

Most consumers are unaware that perhaps seventy per cent of processed foods now contain GMO ingredients. One reason for this is genetically engineered foods do not need to be labelled as such. We will be hearing more about GMO foods as more GMO foods are introduced. One current example is the "Arctic Apple" which has been approved for marketing as of this writing. This apple doesn't turn brown even when it is sliced or bruised since it retains antioxidants that are lost during the usual browning process. One British study reported that forty per cent of apples in the United Kingdom are tossed out because of spoilage, so this is an important development.

## He Rose From The Dead. Really!

Dear lonesome reader, if you are fortunate enough to have read my book *100 Vignettes* you will know that I have already written a vignette on this fascinating topic. After hearing a lecture recently by Dr. Gary Habermas, a respected university scholar and historian, I decided to write an update based on some of his work. Check out his website for a more complete summary.

Dr. Habermas started out by saying that the study of history is the same whether the topic is secular or religious. The research must be done by qualified investigators who are published in recognized journals, (not just bloggers who self-identify as "experts"), using multiple sources of evidence. When asked the question, "How do we know that Jesus Christ lived and was resurrected?" he says that it is useful to ask a question like, "How do we know that George Washington was President of the U.S?"

The answer is that we have records of his contemporaries like Thomas Jefferson and Benjamin Franklin who mention Washington; we have information about his family, and records of his work as a General and President. The same rigorous scholarship must be used in documenting the life and work of Jesus. In doing research on historical figures, two pieces of evidence or "E words" must be used. These are "Early" and "Eye witnesses".

Habermas knows that it is not acceptable to say that Jesus lived and was resurrected from the dead because the Bible says so. There must be solid evidence to show that what the Bible says is factual. Based on the criteria of using solid evidence, Habermas indicated that even secular researchers and writers agree that at least six books of the New Testament are recognized as being reputable sources. These "Pauline letters" written by the Apostle Paul are Romans, I and II Corinthians, Galatians, Philippians, and I Thessalonians.

Skeptical scholars and Christian scholars know that Paul lived, that he was well read, was himself a recognized scholar, and that he studied with quality scholars. In addition to the Gospels, Christians look at the New Testament books of I Corinthians and the first two chapters of Galatians for information about the resurrection of Jesus, and it is reassuring that this information is supported by thorough, documented research.

The conventional standard to ensure the historicity of an event is access to documents and verifiable information within 100 years of an event or a person's death. Independent sources, both Christian and secular, agree that Jesus died in 30 AD. Scholars agree that the Gospel of Mark was written in 70 AD, Matthew in 80 AD, Luke about 85 AD and John's Gospel in 95 AD, all of which are well within the accepted 100 year standard. In comparison, the best documentation for Alexander the Great, whose historicity and achievements are accepted without doubt, is 330 to 425 years after his death in 323 BC.

In I Corinthians 15, written in 55 AD, the Apostle Paul says that he preached the Gospel, describing the death of Christ for our sins and his resurrection. It is widely accepted that Paul was converted on the road to Damascus about two years after the resurrection of Jesus and went to Jerusalem in 35 AD (which at maximum would be five years after the resurrection of Jesus) to meet with the Apostle Peter and James, the brother of Jesus, to confirm that he had been "saved" and that his Gospel message was fully consistent with their teaching.

This documentation of his interaction with the original apostles is even more solid than the accepted information in the Matthew, Mark, and John Gospels. Another recognized piece of accepted evidence is that about fourteen years later (Galatians, Chapter 2) Paul again went to Jerusalem to meet with Peter and James, and this time also with the Apostle John. This meeting involved two of the original twelve apostles and two men who were originally skeptics, and they again verified that his teaching of the death and resurrection was correct. Paul was able to write that they added nothing to his message.

So we can see that verifiable evidence of the life, death, and resurrection of Jesus is available shortly after his dramatic life events. Even skeptics agree that these facts are not disputable; it's what we *do* with the facts that is critical.

Habermas says that only fifteen per cent of those who doubt the Gospel message that Jesus died for our sins and rose again do so on the basis of their doubts about facts relating to Jesus, and that seventy per cent of doubters are "emotional doubters" who do so on the basis of various emotional events or crises in their lives. He indicates that Christians believe in the message of Jesus "because they want to" and skeptics reject Jesus "because they don't want to" with both groups knowing that the facts about Jesus are undeniable. Christians take to heart God's message in the Old Testament to Job when God said that, in spite of the tragedies in his own life, Job knew enough about God that he could trust Him to accept the things in his life that he couldn't understand.

When we grieve about the death of someone we love, we can think about God who watched His Son die, but answered His Son's prayer since Jesus rose again. Similarly, we know that Christian believers who die will be raised again to (eternal) life and that we can see them again after we die if we accept Jesus as our Savior.

## Wise Statements and Wisecracks

You can decide whether the following statements are wise or wisecracks:

- Tears are the soap of the soul. - Jewish proverb
- Everybody has a favorite laughing place. The trouble with most people is that they never take the time to find it. – Splash Mountain, Disneyland
- Never trust a butcher to babysit your pet pig when you go on vacation. - Anon
- Aging is looking at your body and suddenly realizing that God's master plan includes planned obsolescence. - Tina's Groove
- We had to get rid of the kids—the cat was allergic. - Poster
- A wise person isn't one who has all the answers, but one who, when looking at the questions, applies God's truth, adds faith, and then goes forward with courage. - Anon
- No matter how much you push the envelope, it still will be stationery. - Anon
- Money won't buy happiness. But money buys chocolate, and happiness quickly follows. - Sherman's Lagoon
- I'd give up chocolate, but I'm no quitter. - Poster
- If you can't see my mirrors, I can't see you. - Sign on the back of a semi-trailer truck
- Beauty fades, but dumb is forever. - Judge Judy
- The early bird gets the worm, but the second mouse gets the cheese. - Anon
- I can only please one person a day. Today is not your day, and tomorrow doesn't look good either. - Anon
- Praise be to the God and Father of our Lord Jesus Christ! In his great mercy he has given us new birth into a living

hope through the resurrection of Jesus Christ from the dead, [4] and into an inheritance that can never perish, spoil or fade. This inheritance is kept in heaven for you, [5] who through faith are shielded by God's power until the coming of the salvation that is ready to be revealed in the last time - 1 Peter 1: 3-5

- Great minds discuss ideas. Average minds discuss events. Small minds discuss people - Eleanor Roosevelt
- Luck is a dividend of sweat. The more you sweat, the luckier you get. - Ray Kroc
- Do not let what you cannot do interfere with what you can do. - John Wooden
- If brains were dynamite he wouldn't have enough to blow his nose. He took an IQ test and the results were negative. - Overheard at a multi-candidate political meeting
- His problems were nothing that couldn't be fixed by an old fashioned lobotomy. - Anon
- Constant use had not worn out their friendship. - Anon
- They needed each other more than peanut butter needs jelly, more than Ginger Rogers needed Fred Astaire, more than hockey sticks need pucks. - Anon
- I wait for the Lord, my whole being waits, and in his word I put my hope. I wait for the Lord more than watchmen wait for the morning - Psalm 130: 5-6
- A book is like a garden carried in a pocket. - Arab proverb
- Right is right, even when no one is doing it. - G.K. Chesterton
- The conventional definition of management is getting work done through people. Ideal management is developing people through work. - Agha Hassan Abedi
- Ladies, don't forget the church rummage sale. It's a chance to get rid of those things not worth keeping around the house. Bring your husbands. - Church bulletin

- Always do right. This will gratify some people and astonish the rest. – Mark Twain
- Late to bed and early to rise makes me sleepier than most other guys. - Red Skelton
- There's a saying that God helps those who help themselves. That may be true, but a better saying is that God helps those who can't help themselves. - Bill Worrall
- Hospital bedpans and restaurant butter patties have one thing in common - both seem to come directly out of the refrigerator before use, making them uncomfortable in the first case and unspreadable in the second. - Hirsch
- If all the people who fall asleep in church on Sunday mornings were laid end to end...They would be more comfortable. - Abraham Lincoln
- When I said "I do" I didn't mean the dishes. - Anon
- Silence is golden...unless you have kids. Then silence is suspicious. - Poster
- Explaining to husbands what your wife means when she says:
- "Fine." (This is a term used to end an argument when she knows she is right and you need to keep quiet.);
- "Nothing." (This means something and you need to be worried.);
- "Go ahead." (This is a dare, not permission. Don't do it);
- "Whatever." (Her way of saying you're in deep trouble whatever you do.)

## Hockey Seems Determined to be a Fringe Sport

Ken Dryden, the superb goalie for the Montreal Canadiens in the 1970s authored what some have described as the best sports book ever written. The title is *The Game*. The writing is excellent, his ideas and analyses about the game are cerebral, and the anecdotes and sketches of many of his teammates and opponents are fascinating.

Between engaging vignettes portraying his teammates and articulating his own feelings and analysis of the game, Dryden describes the many ways hockey has changed in the past 100 years. Canadian boys used to skate and play for hours in backyards or outdoor rinks but now the game is "organized" and most just play a couple of hours a week. Dryden chronicles the introduction of the forward pass, the introduction of the red center line, the impacts of universal draft, the establishment of the NHL Players Association, the impact of television, the dramatic influence of the Russians and to a lesser extent Europeans, and finally, the discouraging modern "dump and chase" tactic.

Dryden also has an intriguing description of a hockey player's career. He says it is like living through an Arctic summer for the first time. In May and June there is the wonderful endless sunshine, but then, without noticing it at first, the sun sets a few minutes earlier each day in June and then July, and before you know it summer is over. And so it is with a hockey career.

One of the most interesting sections of *The Game* is where Dryden describes the NHL approach and policies regarding the "gratuitous violence" in hockey. I'm paraphrasing, but he says that the powers that be conclude that hockey by nature is a violent game, played in a rink confined by boards and unbreakable glass by big and fast players carrying sticks and skating at high speeds. Since it's inevitable, they say, that collisions will occur, the rules should permit "legal" collisions, (but inevitably some "illegal" collisions also occur), but both types will produce violent feelings and anger. It's important, they think, that these violent feelings be quickly vented before "savage overreactions" occur, and fighting is a reasonable way to channel these feelings. They have concluded that, if fighting were banned, then stick swinging (and perhaps kicking) would necessarily occur, and these other options are even more dangerous.

They cited the experience in Europe where stick swinging was more common at one time, but my impression is that the Europeans soon found that as their game gained some international exposure they could reduce or eliminate stick swinging and still have an exciting game more acceptable to audiences.

It's interesting to note the Russians' similar experience. When the they first began to play against NHL players they were well known for kicking (since fighting was not permitted), but again they found that this resulted in too many penalties so they resorted to using their skill and emphasis on team play, and did well.

Ken Dryden concludes that the NHL view of fighting is wrong. He even quotes Sigmund Freud and anthropologists Desmond Morris and Richard Sipes. Morris concluded that anger released, while sometimes therapeutic, may also be inflammatory and create new violent feelings leading to more fighting. Sipes said that, once anger is released, fighting is learned and repeated and is not cathartic. Freud believed in something called "drive-discharge" so the hockey application is to allow fighting when frustrated, but if Freud is right it's also possible that anger and frustration could be "vented" or discharged by playing harder within the rules with tactics such as skating faster and shooting better and harder.

Cam Cole, a Vancouver Sun sports writer, has asked if hockey is ever going to evolve past the point of being a "concussion factory" where coaches tacitly approve and teammates often applaud dangerous and ruthless hits. The ongoing philosophy in professional hockey is an eye-for-an eye, where if a player, especially a star player, is given a hard or dirty hit then the opposing team feels obligated to respond in kind.

Cole suggested that the NHL is an irresponsible employer if it doesn't protect its players from retaliatory and dirty hits. Players don't waive their rights to make a (well paid) living when they sign a contract, and they especially shouldn't have to worry about being maimed because a teammate accidentally or deliberately hit an opposing player.

The hockey powers that be say that player safety is a priority, but pro-fighting, pro-violence proponents who think that tickets sales will suffer if fighting is banned generally shout down the doves on the board of governors. As of this writing there were no neurologists on the NHL concussion panel even though hockey is said to have the highest incidence in any sport of concussion per participant. One physician said basic physics applies in the fast-paced sport of hockey since force equals mass times acceleration.

My conclusion is that if the NHL believes that fighting is a necessary outcome of the game, fighting is what will happen. If the NHL believes that fighting is a good outlet, well, fighting will happen. It's a bit of a mystery to me, that when the stakes are much higher, as in the Winter Olympics or in tight playoff games, fighting is pretty much non-existent, and to me these games are more enjoyable to watch.

I guess there are other outlets for "violent feelings" in those critical situations. It's sort of "be careful what you wish for" or, if you really believe that something is necessary or is going to happen, well, it shouldn't be surprising when it happens. At least the NHL has eliminated bench clearing brawls and some of the goonery that was common years ago, but they are still in denial. It seems that they will tinker with the rules allowing (implicitly encouraging) some fighting and dirty hits while ignoring the mounting evidence of chronic brain trauma in too many hockey players.

Part of the problem is that hockey originated as a violent sport and the geniuses that grew the game allowed and encouraged the violence in part because they selfishly believed that this would sell more tickets, and perhaps because they enjoyed the violence. They accepted and encouraged this brutish culture, which became so ingrained that it has become difficult to change. The aspect of intimidation is also a factor, as opposed to stressing skill.

My impression is that hockey, as currently played in the NHL will always be a second tier or fringe sport in the U.S. compared to football, basketball, and baseball because Americans won't be drawn to a game that encourages a "Roller Derby" approach to the game. I agree with Dryden when he says that fighting degrades the sport of hockey to a "dubious spectacle" and "confines it to the fringes of sports respectability".

Another issue constantly in the headlines today, is hockey players and football players suffering from concussions. Chronic Traumatic Encephalopathy (CTE) is a progressive degenerative disease of the brain found in athletes, military veterans, and others with a history of repetitive brain trauma. Brain trauma can causes changes that slowly kill brain cells, leading to loss of cognitive function, dementia, aggression, and depression. Once started, these changes in the brain appear to continue to progress even after exposure to brain trauma has ended. Other symptoms include memory loss, confusion, impaired judgment, paranoia, impulse control problems, and eventually progressive dementia. According to the Internet, symptoms can begin to appear months, years, or even decades after trauma has ended. Currently, CTE can only be diagnosed after death by brain tissue analysis.

While CTE can happen to any hockey or football player that takes a violent hit to the head, it appears to be substantially more common in NHL "enforcers" i.e. those routinely involved in hockey fights. Several of these enforcers eventually figured out that the fierce pounding they received in their NHL career was taking its toll and asked that their brains to be analyzed once they died. A number of them died prematurely due to suicide.

The discovery of CTE in the brains of athletes has launched the disease firmly into the public consciousness. To date, eight-seven of ninety-one former NFL players whose brains were injured have been diagnosed with CTE. The figures are probably comparable in hockey. Team doctors are inevitably biased and pressured to let players play and to fudge the concussion protocol even though the number of concussions is increasing in both the NFL and NHL. An extensive study released in 2015 concluded that in recent seasons the NHL has been averaging over seven concussions or suspected concussions per 136 games.

## ER Doctors' Slang—Are You "Whale" or a "Cockroach"?

Are you an FTD or a beemer? Did your friend get boxed last night? If you hear an Emergency Room (ER) physician refer to you as a yellow submarine, it's not a reference to the Beatles; he or she is just employing doctor slang to brand you as an obese patient with cirrhosis of the liver. How about being called a status dramaticus? It doesn't meant the ER team is impressed with your acting ability. On the contrary, they think your behavior is better suited to the stage than the ER.

Whales or beemers (referring to BMI or body mass index) are terribly obese patients, cockroaches or frequent flyers are patients who return to ER again and again, FTDs (failure to die) are patients whose body is chugging along but their mind is no longer functioning properly. The latter term is comparable to circling the drain, a reference to a patient who is dying. Two other phrases are LOLs in NAD – little old ladies in no apparent distress; and "he was O sign" referring to dementia patients sleeping with their mouths open.

Emergency room physicians have one of the toughest jobs in the world. Every day, every shift, they encounter some of horrific challenges most of us can't even imagine. As part of the armor that they build around themselves to avoid falling into despair and depression they often use black humor as a protective device. Many people, however, conclude that these and similar terms are degrading and disrespectful to patents.

Dr. Brian Goldman, an emergency room doctor in Toronto wrote a book titled, *The Secret Language of Doctors: Cracking the Code of Hospital Slang*. Dr. Goldman describes the reason for these terms as "laughing in the face of tragedy" since ER doctors are often exposed to complicated and stressful life threatening circumstances and may use slang to communicate these situations to their peers. This is understandable to some extent, but often the slang seems to be directed to frail and elderly people, the morbidly obese, the addicted and mentally ill, and the poor. Goldman said that he used slang much less often after writing the book, and also in part because he watched his elderly father die and his mother suffer from Alzheimer's disease. He relates that his father, in his final months, was "an avid consumer of health care services" but he then saw the medical system from the point of view of a son while waiting many hours for news.

I suppose the use of ER slang, like many other things, is a human reaction to a difficult situation that can be abused if carried too far. The use of these code words can help health-care workers de-stress and even bond over shared frustrations more privately. But Goldman says that doctors need to balance empathy and respect with reasoning and calculated choices, and his book reveals modern medical culture at its best and sometimes at its worst.

People whose family member is near death deserve to be treated with respect rather than having their loved one be the subject of a joke. In many cases the use of disrespectful slang refers to patients who have self-inflicted health care problems where the patient or the family isn't willing to see that they may have been largely responsible for the condition.

Apparently, some of the most caustic slang focuses on the issue of whether or not to resuscitate patients who are in a highly weakened state. Many physicians dread "DNR" debates where the family expects miracles in spite of the "do not resuscitate" directive of the patient. The process of CPR in such cases is called a "code blue" but when physicians aren't inclined to follow it precisely because they know it will be futile their approach may be called into question unless the family agrees with a minimal approach.

Goldman goes on to say that our medical knowledge is imperfect, and that doctors' actions are imperfect because, fundamentally, they are human. The statement is made that the batting average of top-notch baseball players may only be 0.350 but we expect doctors to bat 1.000. Hopefully, with collaboration and oversight, as well as learning from mistakes, medical mistakes can be reduced to an absolute minimum.

In the end, Goldman believes the most important issue is that doctors should not do or say anything that would disparage their patients or colleagues. He concludes that telling people not to use slang may just make it go underground. We need to listen to the slang and hear what it's trying to say. Does medical staff use slang because they are frustrated and just want to give good care, or are simply insensitive? Goldman and most other ER physicians recognize that sooner or later they will need the services of an ER doctor and this should temper their reactions to difficult situations and patients.

## "Filth, Negligence, Greed" - and Hypocrisy

My admiration for South African Anglican Archbishop Desmond Tutu, perhaps one of the world's best-known defender of human rights, recently took a major hit. While we can admire his rigorous advocacy of non-violence, combatting racism, and his dramatic work leading South Africa's Truth and Reconciliation Commission some years ago, it is necessary to question his judgment in aligning himself with some dubious characters and a radical environmental organization. I never imagined that he would become a hypocrite and lower himself to crave headlines and promote misleading information. Let me explain.

Tutu travelled to Canada in May 2014 as a messenger for a radical American-based NGO (Non-Government Organization) and his visit, as reported my Michael Den Tandt in the Vancouver Sun, was sensationally covered by media outlets around the globe without bothering to mention the obvious inconsistencies and bias of Tutu's rant. Tutu apparently said that he didn't come to Canada to tell Canadians what to do, but he was quite clear that Alberta's oil sands were producing 'filth' as an indication of our country's 'negligence and greed'. While some Canadians may agree with this message, Den Tandt, and yours truly, feel that Tutu is terribly misguided.

Den Tandt reported that Tutu was flown to Fort McMurray, Alberta, by the Athabasca Chipewyan First Nation and delivered precisely what was expected of him by his hosts: fire and brimstone directed at the "despicable" Alberta oil sands developers. One of the other speakers associated with this NGO was a person advocating the same revolutionary values that Tutu criticizes in South Africa.

Tutu was quoted as making some astonishing attacks on the Canadian energy sector and, by extension, all stemming from it. "The fact that this filth is being created now, when the link between carbon emissions and global warming is so obvious, reflects negligence and greed," Tutu said. Den Tandt concluded that if the oil industry's operations actually are "filthy, negligent and greedy, across the board", then we've entered into a new phase of this debate, which was already debased almost beyond belief by the near-constant refusal of the anti-pipeline lobby to be truthful about the actual causes, and likely solutions, to excessive carbon emissions in the Earth's atmosphere. It is a debate and clash that has become almost entirely fundamentalist in its grounding; and it appears that logic need not intrude, nor is it welcome.

On the other hand, other reports have shown that "highly urbanized Canada, with eighty per cent of its population clustered in cities of varying sizes, and more than two-thirds living in large metropolises, is in love with the good old gas-guzzling pickup truck. Small SUVs are also popular. Fuel-efficient subcompacts? Not so much. This happened even as fuel costs soared."

Even now, with the oil sands expanding rapidly, transportation still accounts for nearly one-quarter of Canada's GHG (greenhouse gas) emissions, with the oil and gas sector accounting for roughly another quarter. As the auto sales stats show, energy wasting by individuals is on the rise, rather than decreasing. Canadian consumers could actually make different vehicle purchases but they choose to buy gas guzzling trucks rather than energy efficient compacts or electric cars.

Doesn't logic thus dictate that the primary thrust of the anti-greenhouse-gas lobby should also be directed at consumers? Shouldn't Tutu, and other celebrities who are famous but have little or no known relevant expertise (but paradoxically are often large users of fossil fuels) be focusing on how our society functions? Shouldn't providing better access to public transportation or curbing the desire of both individuals and the industry for gas guzzling vehicles such as pick-up trucks and private planes, in hopes of reducing global demand for carbon-based fuel be discussed? It's so much easier, psychologically and self-promotionally, to lambaste the few supposed monstrous oil and gas explorers and producers rather than the many individuals and companies who enthusiastically create a bustling market for oil and gas products.

Some Postmedia news observers have concluded that it's also easier to lambaste Alberta and Canada than it is to rationally discuss the policy choices that would emerge if oil and gas revenue were to go away, as Tutu and his fellow travelers apparently pray will happen. The Conference Board of Canada estimated combined federal-provincial tax revenue of nearly $80 billion, stemming from oil sands-related investment before 2035. Total investment over the next quarter century is estimated in the hundreds of billions of dollars. More than 120,000 Albertans, according to provincial government data, work directly in oil and gas extraction. A growing number of Ontarians, unable to find work in their province's traditional manufacturing jobs have come to work in Alberta on a regular rotational basis, at least as long as the industry is healthy. Individuals from other provinces such as Newfoundland-Labrador also come to the Alberta oil industry to work.

How should these folks feed their families after the "filth" of the oil sands has been expunged? And how should government make up the budgetary shortfalls, the voids in social programs, in health care, in education, that would immediately emerge if Tutu's dream of a shuttered oil industry came true?

Perhaps he, or wealthy Hollywood, will offer up a stipend, to spare Canada's middle class from the economic and political turmoil that would result. That's not to say that there should be no controls or regulations regarding the oil industry, but surely we need to ask the aforementioned questions before we wipe out the industry. And perhaps, dare we dream, it's possible that the industry and the economy can thrive while the environment is protected.

The mounting anti-growth, anti-pipeline, anti-oil industry casuistry, driven by a global, ideological aristocracy seemingly divorced from reality and oblivious to contradiction, is doing real damage now to Canada's economic prospects. This is shameful. For someone of Desmond Tutu's stature to engage in it with such abandon and with so little realistic perspective is both disgraceful and shocking.

We need realistic debate and data, not headline-seeking celebrities.

## How Long Was the 100 Years War, and Other Questions With Surprising Answers

I have learned that it is usually wise to think before speaking. This is somewhat comparable to the carpenter's motto of measure twice and cut once. I saw many of the following questions on the Internet some time ago and I was intrigued by the answers.

1). How long was the Hundred Years War between England and France?

2) Which country makes Panama hats?

3) From which animal do we get catgut?

4) In which month do Russians celebrate the October Revolution?

5) What is a camel's hair brush made of?

6) The Canary Islands are named after what animal?

7) What was King George VI's first name?

8) What colour is a purple finch?

9) Where do Chinese gooseberries come from?

10) Larry's father had five sons; the first four were named ten, twenty, thirty and forty. What was the name of the fifth son?

11) What is the colour of the black box in a commercial airplane?

12) Where did the game of Chinese Checkers originate?

13) What kind of instrument is the English horn, and where was it invented?

14) Where was the Woodstock Festival held?

15) Where were Venetian blinds invented?

16. How many gallons does a 10-gallon hat hold?

17. What colour is the "green room"?

18. Ten birds were sitting in a tree and a hunter shot one. How many birds were left in the tree?

19. In baseball, how many outs are there in one inning?

20. Where is the Holland tunnel?

21. An airplane crashed into a field. Every single person in the aircraft died. But two people survived. How come?
22. A clerk at a butcher shop stands five feet ten inches tall and wears Size 13 sneakers. What does he weigh?
23. Two men play seven games of checkers. Each wins an equal number of games and yet, there are no ties. How is this possible?
24. An electric train is moving north at 100 mph and a wind is blowing to the west at 10 mph. Which way does the smoke blow?
25. Some months have thirty days while others have thirty-one days. Which month has twenty-eight days?

**Answers:**

(1) 116 years (from 1337 to 1453) (2) Ecuador (they were distributed from Panama) (3)From sheep intestines (4) November (the Russian calendar was thirteen days behind ours) (5) Squirrel fur (6) Dog (the Latin name was Insularia Canaria – Island of the Dogs) (7) Albert (as the 4th in line he was not expected to become king, but when his brother King Edward VIII abdicated he came to the throne in 1936 he took the name George VI to emphasize continuity with his father and restore confidence in the monarchy) (8) crimson (pink, brown, and white) (9) New Zealand - seeds were collected in China and brought to New Zealand where they were cultivated and became a commercial crop also named Kiwi for the fuzzy edible fruit with green meat (10) Larry ( 11) Orange (12) Sweden, from an English game called Halma (13) It's an oboe, first developed in Vienna and later refined by the French (14) Bethel, New York, about forty-five miles from Woodstock (15) Japan (16) About 3/4 of a gallon (the Spanish word *galon* is a braid used to decorate hats) (17) I don't know about the ones that you have seen, but the one in our church is brown (a green room is a room in a theater or studio or church in which leaders and performers can relax when not on stage. The most widely accepted origin of the term dates back to Shakespearean theatre. Actors would prepare for their

performances in a room filled with plants and shrubs. It was believed that the moisture in the topiary was beneficial to the actors' voices. Others say that the room where performers met was an "agreeing room" where deals were often made) (18) None. All the other birds flew away; (19.)Six, three for each team (20) Under the Hudson River between New York City and New Jersey. (21) They were married. (22) meat (23) They didn't play against each other. (24) There is no smoke on an electric train. (25) They all do.

## Most Admired and Desired Jobs

I read about a U.S. Harris Poll in 2011 regarding the most respected and least respected professions or jobs, and I suspect that the observations would pretty much apply to Canada as well.

It takes a special breed to run into a burning building, and after the heroics of 9/11 it's no surprise that firefighting was the most admired profession. At least 63% of those polled rated firefighters as having a " prestigious" job. Doctors, nurses, and scientists came next on the list. Military officers also rated highly in the U.S., and I think that our appreciation of the military has increased in recent years in Canada as well.

Professions that give service of most any kind tend to be greatly admired, so teachers also are respected, even though the radical union approach of the B.C. Teachers Federation has made it difficult in British Columbia to separate the great work done by most teachers from the belligerent, aggressive union tactics. The most admired list also includes engineers (they build things) and farmers (who "feed the world").

Athletes came in the middle of the pack, and, surprisingly, to me at least, so did politicians. The poll noted that none of the top-ten most admired jobs could be described as being driven by the profit motive, which seems contrary to the aggressive capitalist notion that many people have bought into in North America.

On the other hand, lawyers slipped even further, and twenty per cent of Americans tend to rate attorneys as having hardly any prestige at all. Despite America's reputation as a celebrity-obsessed culture, Hollywood's elite didn't rank high on the country's admiration list. More than one third of poll respondents rated actors as having "no prestige at all," and only twelve per cent considered acting jobs as prestigious. The low prestigious ranking put actors at the same low level of respect as union leaders and journalists, which seems surprising given the star power and hero worship evident in society.

People reserved their biggest thumbs-down for business executives, stockbrokers, and real estate agents, even though these free-market capitalists help drive the economy and create tax dollars. It seems that these professions often are perceived as being overpaid and insensitive to the needs of ordinary people.

In addition to looking at the most and least admired jobs in Canada and the U.S. we can also look at the "hottest jobs" which are the ones that actively seek new qualified applicants. The following list identifies trades and professions that are booming, so they pay well and provide a relative level of job security.

Financial managers: Demand for money managers is increasing as the private and government sectors look for whizzes who know the complexities of financial management. Individuals who have knowledge of foreign finance or are fluent in a foreign language are also highly sought.

Skilled tradespersons: If you don't want an office job but do want a salary that pays above the national average, this is a great career option. Skilled trades have been looked down on in favour of professional designations, so there is a shortage of tradespeople in construction (electricians, carpenters, and plumbers), transportation (aviation technicians, automotive service technicians) and manufacturing (industrial mechanics, tool and die makers). College and vocational school teachers are also attractive careers since the boom in skilled trades means there's also a need for instructors at community colleges and other vocational schools.

Dentist or dental hygienists: Dentistry is a great field if you've got the stamina for four years of undergraduate university studies plus four to five years of dentistry school. If you want to work in this field sooner, one can become a dental hygienist after a two-year program at a community college, but at a fraction of the pay.

Computer and information systems managers: Wage growth is better than average, as are actual wages while the unemployment rate is well below the national average. Our reliance on computers at home and at work will continue to grow, meaning job security and continuous opportunities.

University professor: The Ivory Tower is also experiencing increased government spending on education and research, coupled with workplace demand for a highly trained and educated workforce, and the pay is generally excellent.

Human resource specialists or managers: Demand for human resources specialists and managers is increasing and expected to stay strong, as companies place greater emphasis than ever before on human resources issues such as recruitment, training, employee relations, and retention.

Pharmacists: A growing and aging population means more prescriptions needing to be filled. From hospital pharmacists to your friendly local pharmacist, there's greater demand than qualified graduates to fill the positions. Some pharmacists are self-employed since they own the pharmacies in which they work.

Registered nurses or licensed practical nurses: Canada's aging population means this sector is a dynamic place to be. A combination of factors will ensure a wealth of opportunity for nurses with college or university nursing degrees.

Retail managers: The retail sector continues to grow, consumer spending is generally strong, and because there are more openings than there are job seekers in this field, finding employment is still relatively easy.

## Camping vs. Motelling

Everyone, it seems, likes to get away. Perhaps many of us have a suppressed gene that harkens back to our forefathers and the pioneers who first settled North America so we want to get back to nature (even if we don't want to be too uncomfortable in doing so).

For some folks getting away involves travelling in a huge, Class A motor home with all the conveniences of home. Some require only a tent and some kitchen supplies, while others drive the family car and stay in motels or hotels. We won't even consider those who hop on a plane and visit exotic locations such as Hawaii, Fiji, Saskatoon, or Palm Springs.

The purists may insist the tenting is the only type of "camping". Some folks have elaborate set-ups including fancy tents, a canopy under which they cook meals or stay out of the rain, plus various kinds of propane or kerosene stoves as well as most of the equipment you might see at Mountain Equipment Co-op store.

Others are pretty basic but they all seem to have a good time, especially if the weather is nice. Some of these real campers drive Cadillac Escalades so you know that economics didn't enter into their decision to be tenters. Those who really like to rough it are not limited to provincial, federal, or commercial camp grounds. The ultimate campers are those who carry absolutely everything they need on their backs as they hike into wilderness areas and enjoy parts of nature that the rest of us rarely see.

Motorhomes come in a wide range of types and sizes, but many people like them because you can have running water and electricity plus heat or air conditioning as well as a self-contained bathroom. Some would say that this isn't really camping but it does enable these folks to enjoy nature while sitting by a campfire, often alongside a river or lake.

Those who prefer motels find it hard to justify the cost of a motorhome, which can range from $8,000 to $800,000 or more and are loved by the oil companies since they can rarely pass a gas station without stopping in for a fill. They say that you can stay in a lot of hotels for this amount of money. However, that misses the point of enjoying the finer things of nature while getting away.

I'm often amused and fascinated by the couples with a thirty-six- or forty-foot Class A motorhome who arrive at a campground, hook up the electricity, water and sewer, set up their satellite dish and then disappear into their home on wheels to watch TV for the rest of the evening. I'm not sure why they don't just stay home since not even a $100K+ motorhome can be more comfortable than their fancy houses. And the larger this type of motorhome, the more likely is it that it really accommodates just two people even though the three or four slide-out sections give them more square feet floor space than a downtown Vancouver condominium.

Class C motorhomes (those with a bed over the engine cab) are generally more modest than the big Class A units, although some of them get pretty comfortable with two or three slides. Class B motor homes include the van conversion type units. They have all the disadvantages of the larger Class A or C units (like you can't park then in your garage or parallel park easily) but none of the advantages (they are so small that you have to go outside just to change your mind).

Campers mounted on the back of a half-ton or three-quarter ton truck fall into a similar category. Other people like "fifth wheelers" or trailers you need a truck to tow. These units have the advantage of being able to disconnect from your truck so that you can drive into town to pick up groceries or to local scenic attractions. Owners of Class A or C motor homes usually solve this problem by towing a small car.

There are many of RV (recreational vehicles) organizations. Paying an up-front or paying an annual fee gives you the privilege of staying at their RV parks for a reduced rate for varying lengths of time. Some of these parks have all kinds of facilities and activities, and you can meet interesting folks from many different places.

Staying in motels and hotels does have some advantages but these don't usually involve getting back to nature and getting dirt under your fingernails. If you stay downtown in any town or city you can probably easily visit museums and sports or entertainment activities, stop at the innumerable Starbucks or other coffee shops, and shop to your heart's content. Even this may be considered as "getting away from it all".

## Seeking Allah, Finding Jesus

This is a review of the book, *Seeking Allah, Finding Jesus,* which is the dramatic story of Nabeel Qureshi as he describes his journey from Islam to Christianity. Engaging and thought provoking, *Seeking Allah, Finding Jesus* tells a powerful story of the clash between Islam and Christianity in one man's heart—and of the peace he eventually found in Jesus.

Qureshi shares how he developed a passion for Islam that continued into his college years before discovering, almost against his will, evidence that supports Jesus' claim to be God and that he rose from the dead. The following statements that I make about Muslim beliefs and practices are from Quershi's book.

Nabeel Qureshi was raised in a loving and religious Muslim home in England and the U.S. His mother was the daughter of a Muslim missionary and his father came from Pakistan and ended up serving in the U.S. navy. Both parents were careful to infuse the Muslim rituals and teachings into their children. Even as he was being born his father whispered the *adhan*, which is the call to prayer reminding Muslims to dedicate their lives to Allah. They repeatedly said the *Shahada,* the central proclamation of Islam that "There is no god but Allah, and Muhammad is His messenger". While there is much division in Islam, Quershi stares that the best determinant of whether a man is a Muslim is if he exclusively declares that Allah is God and Muhammad is Allah's messenger.

Shia Muslims make up almost fifteen per cent of the world's Muslims, and Sunni Muslims account for about eighty per cent. The balance may relate to either category or some small sect.

Westerners often find it difficult to understand Muslims. Quereshi indicates that people from Eastern Islamic cultures generally assess truth through lines of authority rather than individual reasoning, and critical thought is less valued and less prevalent than in the West.

Receiving input from multiple sources and critically examining the information to find the truth is considered an exercise for specialists rather than the common person.

Second generation western Muslims (the generation between the old world and the west) often uncritically adopt their parents' faith. An important related issue is that ordinary Muslims outside of North America generally uncritically accept statements from Eastern teachers who teach that the West is "Christian", that its culture is promiscuous, and that everyone opposes Islam. This means that the average Eastern Muslim expects that people in the West are promiscuous, ungodly Christians and enemies of Islam.

Qureshi indicates that this culture perception was why his parents worked so hard to keep their children from being Americanized. They didn't realize they had no understanding of what constitutes a true Christian.

To this point of his life, Qureshi had lived in a Muslim cocoon, but then met a committed Christian in high school in the U.S. and this fellow became his best friend. Qureshi had been taught to build a defense for his faith, but in college his friend and others were critically probing and challenging each other's beliefs and testing them for weak points. This was new experience for Qureshi since Islamic culture established scholarly individuals as authorities because of their *position*, whereas in the Western culture authority was primarily *reason* itself. He therefore inherently comprehended that when authority is derived from status rather than reason it was dangerous to question leadership since dissension was reprimanded and obedience was rewarded.

Qureshi makes the point that much of the West's inability to understand the East comes from the division between honour-shame cultures and innocence-guilt cultures. The Muslim honour-shame principle says that doing bad or illegal acts is okay as long as one doesn't get caught, that is as long as they or their family suffer no shame or dishonour.

Right after 9-11, Qureshi had to wrestle with his Western Islam belief that Islam was a religion of peace while hearing American television broadcasters talk about Islam being a religion of terror. Muslims in the East are taught that Islam is superior to all other religions; that Allah desires to see it established throughout the world, and that Islam should dominate the world. Qureshi reports that early historical records show that Muhammad launched violent military campaigns at times to accomplish his purposes. Some verses in the Quran provide instructions to slay the infidels wherever they are found, and have their property confiscated unless they testify that no one but Allah has the right to be worshipped and that Muhammad is his prophet.

The Quran allowed men to have intercourse with women whose husbands had been defeated in war. The peaceful perception of Islam is based largely on Western interpretations of Muhammad's teachings whereas the more violent aspects of Islam are rooted in orthodoxy and history. Muslim teachers unrelentingly assert that the Muslims were always innocent in any conflict, but Qureshi came to realize that this was not true. Television networks that misquote the Quran exacerbate this misunderstanding. Qureshi realized that he needed to get away from his biases and encourage his uncompromising friends to challenge him.

It seems that almost everything that Muslims know about Muhammad comes to them orally and rarely from primary sources. Christians learn about Jesus from the Bible but the Quran has little to tell about Muhammad. Muslims believe that Allah, through the Archangel Gabriel to Muhammad, dictated every single word of the Quran verbatim and they therefore believe the Quran to be untranslatable since the words are perfect. This emphasis on the *words* leads many Muslims to neglect the *meaning* of the words. Many Muslims therefore can recite many chapters of the Quran from memory but rarely can explain the meaning or context of those verses.

It is interesting to me that the two things that delayed Qureshi's acceptance of Christianity were that the Christians he met were unable to defend or explain their faith adequately, and that so few of them tried to be his friend and develop a relationship with him. Then he met several individuals in college who corrected this problem by explaining Christian teaching and asking probing questions.

Qureshi was impressed with the Christian scholarly historical method approach involving multiple attestation and availability of early testimony to establish the historical validity of the Gospels. The history of Islam and the Quran is quite different. Eyewitnesses of Muhammad's time orally passed down the stories until they were finally written down about 250 years after his death. Qureshi recognized that it was difficult to keep the story straight over many generations. The earliest records of Muhammad's life are altered versions of previous stories that were also changed. One of Qureshi's teachers told him that some things that Muslim scholars could not accept were omitted, and Qureshi concludes that what Muslims know about Muhammad is an airbrushed portrait with the blemishes removed. Some Muslim scholars accepted the doctrine of abrogation, which is the belief that up to 500 verses of the Quran no longer apply because they have been cancelled or withdrawn.

Although many Muslims have not actually read it themselves, the Quran is the cornerstone of the Islamic worldview and provides the source of Islamic identity. If it were true that the Quran were not perfectly preserved the beliefs of Muslims would be in jeopardy. Qureshi concluded that preservation of the Quran is basic to maintain the credibility of Islam. In doing his research Qureshi realized that the contradictions and inaccuracies in the most trustworthy Islamic traditions were beginning to subvert his faith.

He found that when Muhammed died many people thought there was no longer any need to remain Muslim, so Muhammed's successor, Sahib Bukhari, sent out subordinates to fight the "apostates" and many were killed. Sahib Bukhari assigned someone to update and edit the Quran from people's memories and written fragments, but some parts were lost while there were multiple versions of other verses. Qureshi had never heard any of this from his teachers and was devastated when he found this out.

One of the probing questions that Nabeel Qureshi's friend asked was this: based on Muhammad's life and character, would an objective investigator conclude that Muhammad was a prophet? Various pieces of evidence were presented to challenge that status, ranging from Muhammad marrying a girl of six and consummating the marriage when the girl was nine and he was fifty-two (said to lead to the Muslim acceptance of forcing girls to be married much too early) to dealing with black magic, to torturing people for money, to attacking Jews. Some of these incidents were found in the reputable sources of *hadith* (Muhammad's recorded words and actions) but are generally unknown to most Muslims. To deal with these challenges, Qureshi went to the Quran to see if he could find answers and was soon disillusioned.

Qureshi went from mosque to mosque, asking imams and scholars to help him with his struggles, but none came close to vindicating either Muhammed or the Quran since they just cherry-picked information or denied the issues. Finally Qureshi prayed: "Please, God Almighty, tell me who you are…At your feet I lay down everything I have learned and I give my entire life to you." He still hoped that Allah would reveal Himself to be the God of Islam but deep down he knew this wasn't going to happen. He prayed for three dreams, asking God to point him to Christianity.

His prayer was answered. Incredibly, and perhaps understandably, he still struggled and resisted the Gospel for several more months. Then he started reading the New Testament. Given all of his investigations it seems odd that he hadn't done so before, but now he read the Bible "relentlessly" and soon he prayed the sinner's prayer: "I submit that Jesus Christ is Lord of heaven and earth. He came to this world to die for my sins, proving His Lordship by rising from the dead. I am a sinner, and I need Him for redemption. Christ, I accept You into my life".

The cost for a Muslim to accept Jesus as Savior can be tremendous, including immediately being ostracized from their community and losing friendships and social connections. Becoming a

Christian brings shame and incredible dishonour to the family, and it is this huge dishonour that drives many to commit honour killings.

Nabeel Qureshi agonized over telling his parents about his decision to accept Christ, especially because they had provided so well for him and loved him so much. But if his family stood against God, he knew he had to choose one or the other. Qureshi's father's eyes welled with tears when he told him his decision, and said, "Nabeel, this day I feel as if my backbone has been ripped out from inside me." His mother asked why he had betrayed her. After many angry words his parents eventually recovered from the shock, and while they made it clear they felt betrayed, they didn't ostracize him.

Qureshi kept turning to Jesus and reflected on His suffering and dying for him, and he knew now what it meant to follow God. Now he had found Jesus. Nabeel Qureshi began meeting with a few other Christians to read the Bible and pray and talk. He married a Christian girl and founded a ministry that focused on sharing the Gospel.

## Death by Appointment - Do You Want the Right to Die?

Suicide in ancient Greece and Rome apparently was reluctantly permitted and often seen as an act of free will and sometimes even heroic. But modern day societies established the idea of life needing protection in all cases, even against oneself. This led to taking one's own life as being against the law regardless of the "quality" of that life (the ban on suicide was overturned in Canada in 1972). In recent years, however, the "supremacy of the right to self-determination" and the idea of "personal autonomy" has gained broad public support.

In his book entitled, *The Right to Live; The Right to Die*, Dr. Everett Koop, the former U.S. Surgeon General, began with this statement: "The highest level of moral culture is at which the people of a nation recognize and protect the sanctity of innocent human life." Koop went on to say, "Great nations die when they cease to live by the great principles which gave them the vision and strength to rise above tyranny and human degradation."

For many, the overriding concern relating to euthanasia is that there is increasing acceptance that there is such a thing as a life not worthy to be lived. This can be taken to extremes as we saw in the collapse of social and moral values in Nazi Germany before and during World War II. We like to think that in Canada and the U.S. we are not that degraded or evil. Koop writes that the concept that euthanasia is not "killing" has not existed until now.

Humans generally have a deeply ingrained instinct to live—to hang on to life. There are some exceptions where individuals faced with continuing pain or reduced capability, or experience emotional instability and depression, perceive that their life is not worth living. Does this stem from skewed western ideas of value, or acceptance of the belief that we should never suffer pain? Is it possible that how these individuals handle their situations could be an inspiration to others as they cope with adversity? Is there really a life of no value?

The term euthanasia comes from the Greek words "eu" (well) and "thanatos" (death) —in effect painless, happy death. Regarding euthanasia, some distinction is usually made between a positive or decisive act that results in death as opposed to the act of permitting death by withholding life support mechanisms. However, the option of deliberately causing death by a medical procedure such as a lethal injection seems to be gaining acceptance. Euthanasia is generally defined as when a doctor specifically ends a person's life; whereas physician assisted suicide is when a person ends his or her own life with the assistance of a doctor. The phrase "dying with dignity" has also come into use.

Voluntary euthanasia has been legal in The Netherlands since 2002 and a recent report indicates that the number of Dutch residents seeking euthanasia is increasing by fifteen per cent each year. The introduction of mobile euthanasia clinics is one factor. Rather than seeking grief counselling or medication, Dutch citizens can opt for euthanasia without the "obstacle" of any bureaucratic safeguards. There even is an initiative to expand these mobile units to include people who are over seventy and are tired of living.

By 2013, more than 4,000 individuals (three per cent of all deaths in the country) had been ended in this way, with cancer accounting for seventy-eight per cent of the health issues involved, while smaller numbers for nervous system disorders, cardiovascular disease, dementia, and psychiatric problems account for the rest. A study reported by the respected medical journal *Lancet* indicated that twenty-three per cent of euthanasia deaths were not reported suggesting that many people were taking life into their own hands and not informing either a physician or the government. Belgium also permits euthanasia and the number of deaths in 2013 had increased by twenty-six per cent over the previous year, an average of five per day.

Koop also indicates that in many cases the patient is out of the picture due to their health condition so that they are not part of their own life ending decision. The family and the physician make the final decisions. This situation is fraught with potential abuse. Once any health condition is deemed as making life not worth living, or as being too much of a burden to family or to society, "progressive" western thinking about death for the elderly or disabled presents a slippery slope.

How about elder abuse regarding Grandma who is eight-three, keeps forgetting her keys, and is unable to take care of herself? Some would rationalize that it's okay to euthanize burdensome elderly granny since her demise would be an economic benefit to the family and to society. How about a child who has a serious case of Down's Syndrome? What about a child or adult with a serious disability?

Dr. Harvey Chochinov concluded that data from the Netherlands indicates that physician-assisted death on psychiatric or mental grounds is fraught with difficulty.

Belgium passed a law permitting children to be euthanized under some circumstances, and in 2014 there was pressure to euthanize prison inmates with or without serious illnesses since they did not contribute to society, while posing a financial cost to society. It's also possible in some countries for a person to arrange for assisted suicide without their family knowing about it until after the fact.

Koop suggests that abortion on demand opens up other abuses of which euthanasia is number one. Dr. Peter Singer, an Australian moral philosopher, believes the notion of the sanctity of life ought to be discarded as outdated, unscientific, and irrelevant to understanding problems in contemporary society.

Advocates of euthanasia generally paint a rosy picture where the patient says a few goodbyes and thank-yous and then goes to sleep. They say that they are not "killing the person" but rather are "terminating their suffering". But death does not always come easily and a drawn-out process can be agonizing for loved ones. While advocates say the science is pretty straight forward, obviously some expertise is required.

It's worth noting a statement from a Belgian bioethicist who said that it's an illusion to think that once you open the door you think you are going to control euthanasia or assisted suicide. The situation is even more complicated when the person is not cognitive, for example, with dementia, and in those cases some have suggested that they should not be eligible for physician assisted suicide. A Canadian "advisory panel" recommended in 2015 that we should allow terminally ill but mentally capable children and mature minors the right to request doctor-assisted death. Really?

In the U.S. as of 2015 there were five states where assisted suicide was legal. Those advocating the right for terminally ill patients to end their lives typically avoid the words suicide and mercy killing, at least in part because it would then be more difficult to win public support. The role of doctors on this issue is difficult. Until recently, most medical schools required or encouraged graduating doctors to sign the Hippocratic Oath (developed some 2,000 years ago), which even the modernized version basically requires doctors to "uphold specific ethical standards". Today's "progressive liberal" thinkers believe the Hippocratic Oath to now be irrelevant and the concept of "physician do no harm" seems to be set aside.

In 2015, Quebec passed Bill 52, which legalizes euthanasia. The law gave doctors the right to lethally inject patients experiencing physical or psychological suffering. The law wouldn't be limited to terminally ill patients. As of 2014, euthanasia was considered as murder in the Criminal Code of Canada, but Quebec's Bill tried to define killing by lethal injection as "health care" to avoid the Criminal Code prohibition, which seems to indicate a high degree of legal double-speak. (The courts subsequently rejected this euphemistic language.) The Bill also seemed to target people with disabilities since a person in "an advanced state of irreversible decline in capability" would be eligible for euthanasia. Quebec doctors have been given kits with which to end the lives of patients seeking euthanasia, including drugs to calm the nerves, induce a coma, and stop breathing, along with step-by-step instructions to provide "medical aid in dying". Quebec doctors are under some pressure not to enter words like "assisted suicide" on death certificates to avoid difficult questions in spite of the fact that it's important to track such deaths.

It seems that other Canadian provinces are following Quebec's lead. Canada's Supreme Court has overturned the century-old prohibition against assisted suicide. In a somewhat schizophrenic and contradictory statement they affirmed the sanctity of human life as a fundamental societal value but also concluded that human autonomy should prevail. Canada's Parliament has passed a law legalizing medically assisted suicide, and while some details need to be worked out it seems the primary initial objections were that the law does not go far enough.

I find it hard to believe, but apparently more than seventy per cent of Canadians support the availability of death-hastening alternatives for people with significant disabilities "that might impair their quality of life". It seems that some Canadians fear vulnerability and weakness, and don't want to suffer pain or suffering much, if at all. I suspect that euthanasia is appealing to many Canadians because they fear the process of dying, more than they fear what will happen to them after they die. Canada's Special Joint Committee on Physician-Assisted Death has gone beyond the Supreme Court requirements; for example, it urged the federal government to allow individuals with psychiatric conditions to be eligible for doctor-assisted death. Some, such as Dr. Chochinov, have said that mental illness is already one of the best predictors of inequitable access to health care and it seems a cruel irony for such individuals to be euthanized when they may not be fully capable of participating in the decision to end their lives. Chochinov went on to say that the parliamentary committee's recommendations seemed to be based on the premise that physical and mental suffering can be equally devastating, which is fine, but that doesn't mean that they should be addressed in the same way.

Some medical experts are troubled by the fact that physician-assisted suicide is being advocated and implemented when too many Canadians do not yet have access to good palliative care. Pushing ahead with euthanasia without providing good palliative care seems wrong and shortsighted. It's highly ironic that we have many "medical miracles", but we don't really know how to cope with our approaching death. Dr. Chochinov stated that "doctor-hastened death" raises some troubling questions such as what qualifications "euthanologists" should have, whether readily available euthanasia procedures might be abused, or why quality palliative care isn't sufficient. Improved access to palliative care will likely be a major focus in the near future. With improved palliative care virtually all pain and other symptoms can be managed to minimize suffering.

I was interested to read that Pope Francis observed that assisted suicide gives us a false sense of compassion. Apparently, he went on to say that choosing suicide is the same sin of pride that Adam and Eve committed in wanting to be God, not being content to serve him. In contrast, society wants us to believe that a policy-assisted suicide is based on bravery and empathy.

In 2014, Brittany Maynard, a California resident, set out on a crusade to legally take lethal drugs. She ended her life on a predetermined date rather than face terminal brain cancer. She was lauded in the news media for her brave efforts. Another American, David Kuo, was given the same diagnosis in 2003 and was given a six to twelve months to live prognosis by the medical profession. Kuo, however, went on to live ten more years, had two children, wrote a book, and touched many lives. He experienced some seizures and various levels suffering but he became a phenomenal encouragement to others. Every day of his life mattered. His wife wrote (see her article in the September 2015 Christianity Today) that their experience transformed their hearts and radically challenged many others. What a tragedy it would have been if Kuo had taken Maynard's approach!

People of faith have a unique perspective and some exceptional questions to ask about terminal illness, and about pain. One such question is how we live and whether we are willing to surrender to God the specifics of how and when we should die. Do we actually trust God in our final days? The Bible in I Corinthians is pretty clear about defining us humans as "God's temple" and that God's Spirit dwells in us. Christians believe that God has a plan for each of our lives; at what point do we no longer believe this? It's true that life on earth is filled with joy but also with challenges and suffering. The good news is that we know that if we accept Jesus Christ as Lord and Savior we can know that we can spend eternity with Him where they will be no more pain and suffering. Unfortunately, in today's society, secular humanists are driving the euthanasia discussion and political action and have no understanding of an afterlife.

## Grandpa to Grandson History—It's Like a Time Machine

I have a grandson who at this writing is ten years old. This young fellow can play complicated video games or access the Internet (with his parents' permission), can effectively operate a TV set having four or five "remotes", has a cell phone on which he can take pictures and do a variety of other tasks, a wrist watch, a calculator, and is driven to school by his parents. A complicated thermostat controls his house temperature. His bedroom has a ton of toys including enough Lego to stock a small store or build a time machine, and he helped his Dad build a computer. He plays ice hockey and ball hockey on highly organized community teams, and his parents take him skiing and snowboarding in winter. He sometimes has "play dates" and occasionally has a baby sitter.

Now, let me take you back to ancient times when I was ten years old. We did not have electricity until power came to rural Alberta in the early 1950s, so the best lighting we had was a white gas lamp. It had two mantles, if you know what they are, plus we had a kerosene lamp with a wick. The house was warmed by a coal and wood cook stove where my mom also did all the baking and cooking, and in winter my Dad brought a pot belly stove into the living room to help keep the house warm in the cold Alberta winters. We didn't have to walk to school but we did take a school bus; the first bus had hard wooden seats.

We first had electricity when I was twelve so we eventually had electric lights and even a refrigerator! And we had a radio that had just four AM stations. My first wristwatch was a present when I was fifteen. The practice at that time was to give a kid his or her first wristwatch when entering Grade Nine.

I lived at home until I finished Grade Twelve and we never did have a telephone. I believe we had a camera, but this was rarely used and only took pictures when we were outside staring into the sun.

Television was just coming into use but we never had one on the farm. In grade school we did arithmetic by hand, even learning how to calculate the square root of numbers. I was an adult before I owned a hand held calculator or a computer. I was never good at sports, but at school we always organized our own softball, soccer, or touch football games at lunchtime, with minimal or no equipment. The only organized sport I played in high school was curling; the kids did most of the organizing.

The aforementioned grandson has been in French Immersion at school for five years, since the age of six; I was in French immersion for three months in Ottawa when I was thirty-six years old. I achieved the lowest required level of bilingualism at that time and can still manage to decipher some civil service memos or the French on the back of a Corn Flakes box. His vocabulary has dramatically exceeded mine.

I had finished university before I went skiing for the first time. I never heard of the concept of a "playdate", and I rarely went to visit a friend on the next farm. I had to be willing to walk a mile or two there and back home (uphill both ways). The first time that I heard about babysitting was when I was about fourteen, on the occasion of my parents' twenty-fifth anniversary party when they hired a sitter for my younger brother and sisters. This party was my first exposure to movies or cartoons. I recall that one of the cartoons—in black and white, of course—featured the Three Stooges.

## Wisdom and Sarcasm in Twenty Words or Less

According to Wikepedia, bumper stickers and notice boards can be commercial, religious, secular, humorous, or philosophical. Here are a few samples for your reading pleasure:

- Every love story is beautiful but I like ours the best.
- Mornings would be great if they didn't start so early.
- My wife isn't bossy—she just has better ideas.
- Procrastination: Hard work often pays off after time but laziness always pays off immediately.
- Chocolate is cheaper than therapy and you don't need an appointment.
- You don't have to believe everything that you think.
- Note on a baby's t-shirt: I have my mother's looks and my father's gas.
- Notice in a museum: Unattended children will be given candy and a free puppy.
- Auction: Where you get something for nodding.
- What does a hungry termite say when it strolls into a tavern? – "Hi! Is the bar tender here?"
- King Wenceslas Christmas pizza – Dee*p an*d crisp and even.
- Dad said no. Mom said maybe. Nana said yes!
- Only snack between meals.
- I kept wondering why the baseball kept looking bigger…Then it hit me.
- I stayed up all night wondering where the sun had gone…Then it dawned on me.
- Don't pass a working snow plow on the right.
- A person who looks up to God is less likely to look down on people.

- Need a lifeguard? Try the one that can walk on water.
- If you want a kitten, start by asking for a pony.
- You can agree with me, or you can be wrong.
- Wipe up your mess; your Mother doesn't work here.
- I dream of a world where chickens can cross the road without having their motives questioned.
- Life is like a camera. You focus on what's important, capture the good times, develop from the negatives. And if things don't work out you take another shot.

## The Pope and the Mafia

Pope Francis declared a sort of holy war on the Mafia in 2015. The pope traveled to Calabria, the heartland of one of Italy's biggest organized crime enterprises, the 'Ndrangheta, and, in front of a crowd of more than 100,000, blasted the 'Ndrangheta as example of "the adoration of evil and contempt of the common good." ('Ndrangheta and Cosa Nostra are two powerful branches of the Mafia.) Then he basically excommunicated all Mafiosi by saying that those who follow evil, as Mafiosi do, are not in communion with God. The pope suggested that the mobsters should refrain from taking part in the sacraments since they are not men of honour.

This is a big deal since Italy's mobsters are "religious"; most are active Catholics, and religious celebration is an important part of their public image and local legitimacy. The Mafia depends on the cooperation and goodwill of the communities that support it. Religion offers the Mafia a way to bind their organizations together, and gives them the feeling that they are extorting and killing in the name of a cause more noble than their own greed. Excommunication would bar the mobsters from membership and participation in the church. Some Mafiosi have justified themselves by stressing the difference between a crime and a sin; the Mafia has appropriated the Catholic culture of forgiveness as a kind of license for anything.

A prominent anti-Mafia prosecutor has indicated that the 'Ndrangheta were getting nervous about the Pope's push for financial transparency at the Vatican Bank, officially known as The Institute for Religious Works, since exposure would potentially cause damaging changes to Mafia money laundering operations. The Mafia isn't above killing prominent figures or priests. Cosa Nostra hit-men murdered a priest outside his Palermo church, apparently for urging local residents to break their silence on mob activity. In 1994 another priest was gunned down after testifying about the Naples-based mob, and threatening to refuse communion for Mafiosi. The Mafia killed crusading organized crime prosecutors in 1992.

Italian priests are in a difficult position. As a matter of conscience they are reluctant to refuse serving the Eucharist to any person or hearing anyone's confession. They often know that some of their supplicants are mobsters and professional killers who may contribute large amounts of money to their parish. On the other hand, a number of priests have gone to jail for knowingly collaborating with mobsters. The average priest or bishop won't find it easy to implement the pope's excommunication directive.

Pope Francis became the first pontiff to excommunicate Mafia members. But his message was intended for more than just the criminal underworld. Only two weeks later, in a small Italian village, a traditional procession carrying a statue of the Virgin Mary stopped to pay homage outside the house of the local 'Ndrangheta boss who was serving a life sentence under house arrest. Outraged, the police left the scene, but many were amazed that some clergy stayed and participated.

A 2015 "Passionate Eye" documentary called, *The Pope & the Mafia* explored how political expediency led some cardinals and other clergy to collude with the Mafia, how the Vatican Bank has in the past laundered the profits of the heroin trade, and how murderers on the run from the law have had priests say mass in their hide-outs.

Today, the pope leads a church with more than one billion Catholics but also a business empire of global dimensions. The Catholic Church is the world's richest religious institution with vast real estate holdings and its own Vatican Bank. The results of this unholy alliance include priests and bishops who sometimes testify in court on behalf of Mafia members and even provide character references for these mobsters. Some Mafia families have taken over Catholic festivals. For decades, an institution for whom the sanctity of life is everything has been intricately bound to an organization whose everyday business is death and greed. Pope Francis has made it his mission to get the Vatican's financial house in order and wants to clean up its multi-billion-dollar business dealings amid allegations of money laundering, corruption, and embezzlement of funds. There are stumbling blocks, however, on the road to his announced reforms and the stakes are high for everyone involved.

Mafia expert John Dickie traveled to Italy to understand how the Church's tangled relationship with the Mafia has helped organized crime maintain its grip over the local communities. He explored the underground bunkers used by 'Ndrangheta bosses to escape capture, making the ironic observation that theses bunkers have fully equipped chapels. He found some priests who have had close ties to the Mafia, and others who have risked their lives standing up against them. Sometimes, perhaps unwittingly, the Catholic Church has given the Mafia legitimacy in the eyes of the Italian population. Some clergy have turned a blind eye to crime or the receipt of Mafia money. The daughter of a well-known 'Ndrangheta boss even had the privilege of being baptized in St. Peter's by Pope Benedict XVI.

A dramatic divorce between the Church and the Mafia is now under way and the consequences of the break-up, if it occurs, would be profound for both sides. In May 1993, John Paul II became the first Pope ever to use the word Mafia in public. His condemnation was clear: "Convert! God's judgement and justice will come!" The threat to organized crime was so profound that the Sicilian Mafia responded by bombing several churches in Rome. Some Mafiosi decided to turn state's evidence after watching that sermon on television.

Pope Francis' invective is even more significant. Once friends, the Church and the Mafia are now officially enemies. Pope Francis' efforts to reform the Vatican Bank and the Institute for Religious Works clearly are a threat to the Mafia. At this time it remains to be seen whether the church, led by cardinals, bishops, and priests, will have the courage and integrity to clean house and fully support Pope Francis or whether they will drag their feet as they historically have done. Clergy, even the pope, may well need to face death, but public support may save them. If it became known that the Mafia had ordered the murder of a pope or other clergy, all hell could break loose.

This interesting and conflicting relationship between the Catholic Church and the Mafia was originally made possible, in part, by the politics of Cold War Sicily. In the wake of the Second World War, when a victory by the Italian left seemed possible, the newly formed Christian Democratic Party accepted support from all directions, including the Mafia. Local bosses proved helpful in winning elections, and it became tempting, even for national leaders, to lean on local southern Italian politicians and priests who were enmeshed in a system in which politics, religion, corruption, and organized crime were bound together. But the hundreds of murders committed in Sicily and elsewhere during the early 1980s, including the assassinations of prominent public officials, began to turn the public and church officials away from a see-no-evil attitude toward the Mafia. Several Southern Italian priests made it part of their pastoral mission to steer young people away from a life of crime. (Most of this information was obtained by surfing the Internet.)

# Fraud, Freeloaders, and Blind Porsche Drivers

Matthew Fisher of the National Post wrote a column in 2015 after communicating with a number of Greek residents from the island paradise of Zakynthos, which has been described both as the "Flower of the East" and more recently as the "Island of the Blind". This latest sobriquet seemed appropriate after it was found that as many as 700 of the island's 35,000 residents falsely claimed that they were blind so as to become eligible for substantial pensions from the European Community. Apparently a local politician and an ophthalmologist thought that these folks needed some additional government assistance.

The scheme came to light after one of the so-called blind individuals was caught driving his Porsche. No one went to jail for this fraud scheme and it's unclear that they repaid any money. Zakynthos is described as a beautiful island where some people have tried to earn money too easily. Apparently twent per cent of the voters list contains the names of people who are dead but may still be collecting pensions, some of them for quite a long time.

Fisher describes the Greeks as having a mentality of "rules are meant to be broken". He wrote that motor bike riders don't wear helmets because "being Greek permits the freedom to break the law" even though the law prescribes a mandatory fine equivalent to something like $400. The suggestion is that the debate about Greece's financial problems and use of the Euro since 2001 would not be an issue in 2015 if they had told the truth about their finances. They did admit in 2004 that they had "cooked the books" by deliberately underestimating the Greek deficit so they would be eligible to be part of the Eurozone gravy train.

Estimates of the amount of money lost through tax evasion and tax avoidance are as high as twenty billion euros per year. Another interesting statistic is that four out of five Greeks reported that they owed more money than what they earned but somehow were able to pay off their debts, suggesting that they were grossly under reporting their real incomes.

From this flexible moral financial environment it's easy to understand the difficulties that Greek lawmakers have in trying to implement austerity measures even if they are sincere in wanting to do so. The left wing government had vowed to stand up to its creditors and to reject any budget cuts. Increasing taxes is problematic if citizens work hard, and successfully, at avoiding paying taxes. And cutting generous pensions, even legitimate pensions, is sure to be unpopular. Greece owes billions of euros to the International Monetary Fund, the European Central bank, and other Eurozone countries and these creditors are increasingly reluctant to provide further bailout funds. The Greek Prime Minister angered his European partners when he called for a popular vote against economic reforms that the creditors proposed. The Greek people voted against the Prime Minister's austerity proposals but now face even tougher measures.

As of this writing, after months of acrimony, Greece reached a bailout agreement with its European creditors that will, if implemented, secure the country's place in the euro and avoid financial collapse. Greece will first have to implement a large number of austerity measures that include sales tax increases, reforms to pensions, and labor market reforms before receiving something like eighty-five billion euros in bailout cash. It's easy to feel sorry for many Greek residents, especially seniors, when the banks are closing and they are unable to cash their pensions cheques, but it's clear that major systemic economic reforms are needed, as well as a major change in the entitlement attitude of most Greek citizens. A different option was to kick Greece out of the Eurozone, even temporarily, to force the Greek government to clean up the country's financial situation. This approach has serious implications for other Eurozone countries and presumably would only happen as a last resort.

## Camping in the Southern U.S.

My sweetie and I try every other year or so to drive south in late September for a couple of months to avoid some of the B.C. Lower Mainland rain and cool weather. Going through Washington, Idaho, Oregon, and Utah is nice, but what we are really looking for is warm sunshine every day, which means Nevada, Arizona, and California.

We watched the most incredible show one night in Nevada and it wasn't on television or the Las Vegas stage. You may have heard the song "The Old Lamplighter". Well, that night God was the lamplighter as we saw millions of stars gradually appear as the sky darkened.

We were at the Valley of Fire state park in southern Nevada, so named because there are multi magnificent red-coloured sandstone rock formations surrounding the park, and as the sun goes down the rocks become fiery red. As it started to get dark just after 6:30 PM, we sat in our lawn chairs and watched the stars come out—first just one or two, then dozens and then hundreds and millions as it got darker. It was a fabulous show.

This campground is about forty km off of I-15. The road was paved but the paver must have had hiccups since it was pretty rough. The posted speed limit was 35 mph but if you went that fast you would damage your motor home and shake loose your liver. The GPS gave up just as we were about to go off the main highway—maybe the satellite was passing between the moon and Mars—but we stopped for directions and arrived at the park, shaken and stirred. Before dark we drove to Rainbow Vista with its panoramic view of multi-coloured sandstone and to Fire Canyon with its red and brown rock layers. God's creation is pretty spectacular.

We also camped in Ely, Nevada (elevation about 7300 feet) after driving south from Utah. We saw the Ward Charcoal Ovens featuring six beehive shaped ovens about thirty feet high and built in the $19^{th}$

century to make charcoal for use in silver smelters. Five acres of wood was cut for each oven and you can see huge clear-cut areas stripped to keep those babies burning.

We then drove to Cave Basin State Park and the Lehman Caves. A ninety-minute underground tour of this huge amazing cave features many spectacular stalactites and stalagmites, plus some colourful "Canadian bacon" formations. As we left Ely, we saw the sign: NO GAS FOR 167 MILES. They were not kidding! Not only was there no gas; there wasn't anything else either.

We drove about 255 miles on this road and saw only two or three small towns, which used to have gas stations. An unusual feature in this part of Nevada is the hundreds and hundreds of miles of fences. It must take a lot of land to feed each cow because the ranches are many miles apart. And the fences are constructed with quarter round steel posts because there isn't any useful wood in this part of the country.

Lots of cattle guards or Texas Gates consisting of bars about three inches apart set in the ground over a wide hole approximately ten feet across the road prevent the cattle from leaving the fenced area. They act as a gate that can be driven over and perhaps came into existence because strangers wouldn't bother to close a real gate. These Texas Gates are even found on the highways, except for the Interstates.

Of course, a unique feature of Nevada is Las Vegas. Camping there is not for those seeking solitude or a quiet RV park beside a babbling brook.

Another fascinating place is Landers, California, in the high desert about fifty miles north of Desert Hot Springs and Palm Springs. The town consists of a post office, a convenience store, and a Moose Hall, a thriving meeting place for the hundreds of both permanent residents who live on five acre plots and those from Los Angeles who have summer homes and come to enjoy the cooler temperatures.

Nearby Pioneer Town is now primarily a saloon but was a settlement in the early twentieth century where movies with heroes like Roy Rogers, Hopalong Cassidy, and the Sons of the Pioneers starred. (You need to be over 65 to recognize these names.) The bar and restaurant was occupied by some interesting and quixotic characters but the steaks were excellent.

Perhaps my favorite camping spot in the southern U.S. is Casa Grande, Arizona, just a few miles south of Phoenix. It usually is late October when we camp there, and it must be one of the easiest places in North America to be a weatherman as pretty much every day they can say "well it's going to be eighty-two or eighty-five degrees tomorrow".

Coming from the Pacific Northwest where it rains often and the only constant about the weather is change, the constant sunshine in Arizona is fabulous. When it does rain, it really pours and the flash floods are directed into huge spillways designed to carry off the deluge.

Biking here is tremendous, especially if you get back to the campground before 10:00 AM. It gets pretty warm after that. Sedona, north of Phoenix, is a beautiful, wealthy area while Benson and Bisbee east of Tucson are worth seeing as well. We like Yuma, site of the old State Prison and an area, which grows much of the lettuce (all irrigated) eaten in the U.S.

We find Palm Springs fascinating. A conglomeration of adjoining cities, it includes Palm Springs, Cathedral City, Rancho Mirage, Indian Wells, Thousand Palms, La Quinta, and Indio. It's fascinating to drive past all of the walled high-class developments, country clubs, and golf courses in the Palm Springs area. Some of these cities are upper top drawer and became the residences of the rich and famous. Frank Sinatra and Bob Hope and various movie stars from Hollywood have owned property in Palm Springs because of its agreeable weather.

If one goes far enough east you find Coachella, decidedly a working class town. Desert Hot Springs, north of the ten-lane freeway, is primarily middle class with many Resorts and RV parks. One of the more interesting places in this area is Joshua Tree National Park featuring unique rock formations and Joshua trees with their uplifted arms. One can also drive south of Palm Springs up into high country where you can see ranches and evidences of the old west before getting into sprawling suburbia and the greater Los Angeles area.

## Iceland and Greenland

As a young school kid the mention of Iceland in Social Studies class conjured up visions of an icy land and a Greenland that was, well, green. According to Wikipedia, I was quite wrong.

Over eighty per cent of Greenland, the world's largest non-continental island, is covered by the only contemporary ice sheet outside of Antarctica—which might explain why it is the least densely populated country in the world. And Iceland is warmed by the North Atlantic Gulf Stream and has a temperate climate, despite its high latitude just outside the Arctic Circle. The island's coasts remain ice-free throughout the winter. We don't hear much about these two countries, and in terms of global affairs they aren't important, but both are fascinating.

Iceland is a Nordic island country between the North Atlantic and the Arctic Ocean with a population of about 330,000 and an area of 40,000 square miles. Reykjavík, the capital and largest city, and the areas in the southwest of the country are home to over two-thirds of the population. The interior consists of a plateau characterized by sand and lava fields, with a few mountains and glaciers, while some glacial rivers flow to the sea through the lowlands. Lakes and glaciers cover about fourteen per cent of its surface and less than twenty-five per cent has any vegetation.

Iceland is closer to continental Europe than to mainland North America, thus the island is generally included in Europe for historical, political, cultural, and practical reasons. Iceland is highly geologically active with many volcanoes and geysers. Electricity, heating, and hot water are inexpensive because of the availability of geothermal power and the harnessing of many rivers and waterfalls for hydroelectricity. A volcano in Eyjafjallajökull in the south of Iceland erupted in 2010 for the first time since 1821, forcing people to flee and abandon their homes. The resultant cloud of volcanic ash brought major disruption to air travel across Europe.

Greenland, located east of the Canadian Arctic between the Arctic and Atlantic Oceans, is an autonomous country within Denmark. Though geographically a part of North America, Greenland has been politically and culturally associated with Europe. It was from Greenland that Norwegians would set sail to discover America almost 500 years before Columbus. Norwegian Eric the Red settled here about 1,000 AD and named the land Greenland, apparently in the hope that this pleasant name would attract settlers.

The population of Greenland in 2013 was about 56,000, with 16,000 residing in the capital city of Nuuk. Nearly all Greenlanders live along the fjords in the southwest of the main island where the climate is relatively mild. The northeastern part of Greenland is not part of any municipality but is the site of the world's largest national park. Greenland today is dependent on fishing and fish exports, but it is hoped that mineral exploration will also become profitable. Electricity has traditionally been generated by oil or diesel power plants, even if there is a large surplus of potential hydropower.

Iceland is a representative democracy and a parliamentary republic and is arguably the world's oldest parliamentary democracy. The president is elected but the position is a largely ceremonial as the head of state serves as a diplomat, although he or she can veto laws voted by the parliament and put them to a national referendum. The head of the government is the prime minister who, together with the cabinet, is responsible for executive government. Iceland was ruled by Norway and then Denmark from the thirteenth century but it became fully independent in 1918 and a republic in 1944.

Iceland has relied largely on fishing and agriculture but after World War II the industrialization of the fisheries and the U.S. Marshall Plan aid brought prosperity. In 2013 Iceland was ranked as the thirteenth most developed country in the world. It has the smallest population of any NATO member and is the only one with no standing army, although it does have a coast guard in charge of defense.

Iceland was the seventh most productive country in the world per capita in 2007, but the country was hit especially hard by the 2008 recession because of the failure of its banking system and subsequent economic crisis. It's interesting that Iceland`s climate grew colder during the nineteenth century, resulting in mass emigration particularly to Canada around Gimli, Manitoba, which has sometimes been called New Iceland.

Greenland has been inhabited off and on for at least the last 4,500 years by Arctic peoples whose forebears migrated there from what is now Canada, and was subsequently settled by Norwegians, over a thousand years ago. Greenland had been a protected and isolated society until 1940 and the Danish government had maintained a strict monopoly of Greenlandic trade.

Greenland's head of state is the Queen of Denmark and the Queen's government in Denmark appoints a High Commissioner to represent it in Greenland. Denmark granted home rule to Greenland in 1979, and Greenlanders voted in 2008 in favor of more self-government transferring more power from the Danish royal government to the local Greenlandic government. Greenland's connection to Denmark was temporarily severed on 9 April 1940, early in World War II, when Denmark was attacked by Nazi Germany. The United States then occupied Greenland in 1941 to defend it against Germany, and the U.S. occupation of Greenland continued until 1945. The U.S offered unsuccessfully to buy Greenland from Denmark for $100,000,000 in 1946. Greenland continued under the sphere of U.S. military influence when Denmark agreed to allow the U.S. to re-establish the Thule air base as part of a unified NATO Cold War defense strategy. The U.S. secretly attempted to construct a subterranean network of nuclear missile launch sites in the Greenlandic ice cap from 1960 to 1966 before the project was abandoned as unworkable. Even more interesting, the Danish government did not become aware of the program's actual mission until 1997!

Between 1989 and 1993, U.S. and European climate researchers obtained two three-kilometre long ice cores by drilling into the Greenland's ice sheet. Analysis of the layering and chemical composition of the cores provided a revolutionary new record of climate change in the Northern Hemisphere going back about 100,000 years, and illustrated that the world's weather and temperature have often shifted rapidly from one seemingly stable state to another, with worldwide consequences.

The melting glaciers of Greenland are contributing to a rise in the global sea level, and it has been calculated that if the Greenland ice sheet were to melt away completely, the world's sea level would rise by more than seven metres. An odd thing about Greenland is that an ice sheet does not cover the extreme north of Greenland because the air there is too dry to produce snow.

## Is Major League Baseball "Stealing Lives"?

Major League Baseball (MLB) is a $10B industry. MLB is generally healthy, profitable and growing, and in 2015 the average major leaguer made about $4.25 million. Team salary budgets ranged from $273M to $68M with the median being about $115M; the highest paid player "earns" about $31M per year while the minimum salary is "only" just over $500,000.

But there is a dark side to MLB—how baseball treats young players. Only about three per cent of aspiring young players actually make it to the major leagues. Families in poor countries such as the Dominican Republic and Venezuela see baseball a way out of poverty and are willing to do almost anything to get their boys into the big leagues. Parents turn their sons over (often as young as eleven or twelve) to scouts or agents (*"buscones")* who search out talented players. These boys are then sent to baseball academies where they train day after day for several years. Some *buscones* run their own academies, which may be backed by U.S. investors and agents who see these kids as a futures market.

MLB teams spend approximately $100 million per season operating some forty year-round baseball academies in the Dominican Republic and Venezuela. The agents or independent trainers basically "sell" promising kids to MLB in hopes of receiving a substantial bonus if a MLB contract is signed. The boys who don't make it essentially receive a return ticket to poverty. They typically don't receive even a high school education while training. There have been suggestions that agents may encourage youngsters to use drugs (primarily steroids) so they develop faster, and no laws govern the *buscone*-boy relationship. Parents, who are most often poorly educated and know little about the business of baseball, rarely serve as a check on less-than-ethical *buscones*. The high-stakes game for recruits and prospects has given rise to a feeding frenzy involving a wide range of players, from local talent-spotters and foreign investors to non-governmental organizations and representatives of MLB teams.

MLB is different from some other sports in that in most cases MLB owns the entire minor league system consisting of multiple levels including Triple A, Double A, and three lower A levels, plus 2 rookie levels. The minor league teams may be individually owned and operated but each team is directly affiliated with one major league team through a standardized Player Development Contract young players are required to sign.

Generally, the parent major league club pays the salaries and benefits of uniformed personnel (players and coaches) and bats and balls, while the minor league club pays for in-season travel and other operational expenses. Young players are required to "work" playing baseball year around to develop their skills. Minor league players are not paid for spring training and some reports indicate that in many cases they earn less than U.S. minimum wage. To make ends meet in paying rent and buying food they are forced to live in poor conditions jammed together with other hopefuls. If they fail to move up the system they have nothing to fall back on. As of 2015 a class action lawsuit was launched against MLB asking in part that minor leaguers at least be paid minimum wage.

While some Latin American superstars have overcome discrimination and perhaps avarice to strike gold in baseball's big leagues, thousands more Latin American players never make it to "The Show."

*Stealing Lives: The Globalization of Baseball and the Tragic Story of Alexis Quiroz* is a book written by Arturo Marcano focusing on the plight of one Venezuelan teenager. This book documents abuses that take place against Latin young men as baseball becomes more and more a global business. The author writes that in their efforts to secure cheap labor, Major League teams often violate the basic human rights of children. Marcano writes what he describes as an ordeal of exploitation, mistreatment, and disrespect of one young man at the hands of a MLB team. The teenager's baseball career came to an abrupt end by an injury for which the team provided no adequate medical treatment. The story continues, however, with his pursuit of justice in the United States to ensure that other Venezuelan and Dominican boys do not encounter similar experiences.

What happened to this Venezuelan teenager apparently is not an isolated case. Major League teams allegedly routinely deny Latin young men the basic protections that their U.S. counterparts take for granted. This exploitation is said to violate international legal standards on labour and the human rights of children. *Stealing Lives* concludes by analyzing various reforms to redress the inequities big league baseball creates in its globalization.

A few Major League teams (Arizona Diamondbacks are one example) do have good programs to provide education, and they support high school graduation even if the kids don't make it to the major leagues. Teams such as the Diamondbacks use top quality development programs as a competitive advantage since they feel they owe it to those kids who work hard to help the team and themselves.

## Why is Brazil Considered a "Political Minnow"?

When most people think of Brazil they imagine it being one of the world's most captivating places. Brazil is South America's giant, a dazzling country of powdery white-sand beaches, pristine rain forests, and the Amazon jungle. We may think of Brazil's attractions extending from enchanting beaches such as Copacabana Beach and Ipanema Beach, to the famous and even licentious Carnival and samba fueled nightlife, to the iconic Christ the Redeemer statue in the equally famous Rio de Janeiro, and of course their dramatic successes in soccer.

In addition, Brazil is the seventh largest economy in the world, easily bigger than Canada, bigger than India, and even bigger than Russia. Brazil is the world's fifth-largest country in the world and the largest country in South America both by area and by population. They have unbelievable mineral resources and they export huge amounts of oil, iron ore, beef, coffee, and orange juice.

According to Wikipedia, Brazil's Amazon River basin is recognized as having the greatest biological diversity in the world, including a vast tropical forest home to diverse wildlife, a variety of ecological systems, and extensive natural resources.

A few years ago, analysts identified Brazil as an emerging global power. And yet, Brazil has been called a "political minnow" since it exerts little political power relative to its apparent resources. This vibrant country with so much promise simply has not achieved the success and power of which it is apparently capable. For a time, perhaps until 2010, Brazil had one of the world's fastest growing major economies, and some reforms gave the country new international recognition and influence. Since then it has regressed, experiencing hyperinflation and a continuing economic crisis. The form of government is a democratic federative republic, with a presidential system where the president is both head of state and head of the government.

There is another side to Brazil, and that is the vast difference between the rich and poor with almost no middle class. Apparently, widespread corruption involves the partially state-owned energy company, Petrobas, and many construction firms, as well as representatives from nearly every political party. Massive impoverished slums exist side-by-side with fabulously wealthy neighborhoods

At least part of Brazil's problems can be traced to its colonial history. The Portuguese claimed the land now called Brazil in 1500, and for several hundred years Portugal treated Brazil like a resource bank where withdrawals were constant. In the first two centuries of colonization, indigenous and European groups lived in constant war, establishing opportunistic alliances in order to gain advantages against each other.

By the mid-16th century, cane sugar had become Brazil's most important export product, and millions of slaves were brought from West Africa. About five million slaves were brought to Brazil in large part to work in the sugarcane plantations compared with one-half million slaves brought to America.

Gold, after its discovery in the 1690s, become the new backbone of the colony's economy. Massive amounts of brazilwood were harvested and the timber sold to European traders in return for assorted European consumer goods.

In June 2013, there were various grass roots movements such as the "Arab Spring" in various parts of the world in attempts by locals to gain more political and economic freedom. Numerous demonstrations also erupted in Brazil to protest against a range of issues including the quality of public services, public transportation problems, and in particular, exorbitant expenditures on new stadium projects for international sports events. Even though at least one state was running deficits of $6 billion per year, public servants had generous pensions and could retire as early as age fifty. The excessive use of force by the state police exacerbated the discontent. All of these issues reflected the dominance of the wealthy at the expense of the lower class and the absence of a moderating middle class. These social and economic issues continue to plague Brazil.

The 2016 Summer Olympic Games in Rio de Janeiro provided a case study illustrating Brazil's problems. Billions of dollars were spent but the plight of poor citizens was not measurably improved.

In late 2015, Matt Galloway of CBC's "The Current" interviewed author Misha Glenny who wrote a book entitled *Nemesis: One Man and the Battle for Rio*. This book presents a fascinating account describing the life of a man called Nemesis who was a crime lord in one of the poorest slums (*favelas*) in Rio de Janeiro, literally within blocks of one of the wealthiest neighborhoods in Rio. There was no government control and no legitimate government provision of electricity or water or law enforcement in these slums so drug lords control crime, violence, and drugs, resulting in devastating and continuing poverty. The government appears to have no plans to change this situation so the gap between rich and poor continues to exist, therefore the opportunities for Brazil to deal with corruption and crime and make significant economic and social progress continues to be hampered.

Nemesis was just an ordinary man earning poverty wages in the slum where he lived with his family until his daughter contracted a serious brain disease. Since no government assistance and no bank loans were available he turned to the local drug lord for money. This of course subsequently meant that he became indebted to the crime lord in order to save his family. Being a smart and capable guy, he moved up the crime ladder and eventually and reluctantly became the drug lord in his *favela*. He worked at helping the poor by reducing violence, and in this he was successful, but his work meant supervising drug distribution and other crimes, in addition to paying off the police. Eventually, this all became too much for him so he surrendered to the police and was sent to prison. This story seems to be a capsule summary of what capable poor people in Brazil need to do to survive.

## THE STAR OF BETHLEHEM

I remember this 1857 Christmas carol being sung at Christmas pageants when I was a kid: "Star of wonder, star of night / Star with royal beauty bright / Westward leading, still proceeding / Guide us to the perfect light".

Dr. Colin Nicholl has written a book called *The Great Christ Comet: Revealing the True Star of Bethlehem* to explain the brilliant celestial body that guided the Magi to Jesus' birthplace in Bethlehem. Combining Biblical and astronomical research data, Nicholl concluded that the "Star of Bethlehem" was actually a comet. Nicholl recognized the need to be just as rigorous about studying the relevant science as one is about studying the Bible and he states that the account in Matthew Chapter 2 makes it clear that the Star of Bethlehem was a real astronomical entity observed by astronomers in the ancient Middle East.

First of all, it is recognized that the book of Matthew was written in the same century as Jesus' birth, death and resurrection, thereby meeting a key requirement of historical validity. The book of Luke and other historical accounts, including the respected first century historian Josephus, corroborate details found in Matthew. The Magi were scholars (astronomers and astrologers) from Babylon who had observed the stars, planets and comets as far back as the eighth century B.C.

Nicholl states that the "star" appeared suddenly and was visible for over a year and had "rising points" which would make sense only for a supernova or a comet. The Magi tracked the comet for several months, from the eastern morning sky to the southern evening sky where they saw it as they travelled from Jerusalem to Bethlehem. Josephus wrote that the "comet" stood over Jerusalem just prior to the Judean War, and this would be possible only for an object in the inner solar system. The ancient world could not have invented a comet so unique. Nicholl analyzed the star's profile and orbit and compared it to the great comets of history. He states that many astronomical entities such as meteors for example, were regarded as "stars" in the ancient world and comets were often call shooting stars.

The Star of Bethlehem emphasizes God's mastery over the universe since this great heavenly display happened right at the time of Jesus birth. Nicholls mentions a prophecy in the Old Testament book of Numbers about a "scepter" and a "star" that will rise out of Israel. According to Nicholl, thinking of the Star of Bethlehem as a comet documented by various scholars minimizes the sentimentality of Christmas and brings back the power, authenticity, and reliability of the Christmas Story. After looking at the evidence, we realize this really is part of history, something that actually happened. He concludes that we should be even more overwhelmed than the Magi because we can now more fully recognize what God did to perform the great heavenly sign marking Jesus' birth!

## Sable Island

Sable Island is a small island situated 300 km southeast of Halifax, Nova Scotia, in the Atlantic Ocean. A 34-square kilometre crescent-shaped sandbar, about 20 miles long and only 1.5 kilometres across at its widest point. It is Canada's only "desert" island. Its name is derived from the French word for sand. The island is a year-round home to only about five people these days, with tourists and scientists increasing the numbers in summer, and is a protected Canadian National Park. Visitors must obtain permission before visiting the island.

Sable Island is famous for the large number of shipwrecks that occurred there in Canada's early history. At one point it was called "The Graveyard of the Atlantic". An estimated 350 vessels are believed to have fallen victim to the island's shifting sand bars. Thick fogs, treacherous currents, its location in the path of major storms, and the island's location in the middle of major transatlantic shipping routes and rich fishing grounds accounted for the large number of wrecks.

The first recorded wreck was the English ship, *Delight*, in 1583, part of the arrogant Humphrey Gilbert‘s Newfoundland expedition. It is likely that the construction of lighthouses on each end of the island in 1873 along with improvements in navigation contributed to the eventual decrease in the number of shipwrecks. The last major shipwreck was the steamship Manhasset in 1947. The crew was saved; it was the last significant rescue by the Sable lifesaving station. No further wrecks occurred until 1999 when a yacht ran aground due to a navigational error.

Sable Island is also famous, in a romantic sort of way, for being home to over 400 free-roaming horses, protected by law from human interference. These wild horses are descended from the 1700s when the British seized the horses from the Acadian people in Nova Scotia as part of the war against New France. The Acadian horses were descendants of horses imported from France. Sable Island lacks natural trees but is covered instead with a type of grass often found on coastal sand dunes and some low-growing vegetation, but the horses have thrived. At various times large numbers of horses were rounded up and shipped off the island but in 1960 the Canadian government past legislation to protect them from human interference.

A humanitarian settlement was built in the early 1800s, including a central station, two rescue boat life-saving stations, self-bailing lifeboats and several lookout posts primarily to warn ships and rescue shipwrecked sailors. A ship from Halifax came four to five times a year to bring supplies including food, coal, gasoline, and of course, mail.

The Canadian government took over the station in 1867 and added two lighthouses in 1872. Until the advent of modern ship navigation, Sable Island was home to the families of the life-saving crews and the lighthouse keepers. In the early 20th century, the Marconi Company established a wireless station on the island and the Canadian government established a weather station. Several generations of island staff were born and raised their families on the island, although a decline in shipwrecks gradually reduced the size of the lifesaving community.

According to Wikipedia, the Sable Island Station, managed and staffed by Parks Canada and Environment Canada, is the only permanently staffed facility now on the island. Sable Island is the subject of extensive scientific research including an automated weather observing system, an aerology program researching the upper atmosphere, a program measuring background levels of carbon dioxide, and the monitoring of pollution aerosols. Fog chemistry is also studied!

## Questions to Ponder

1. If money doesn't grow on trees, why do banks have branches?
2. If a book written about failure doesn't sell, is it a success?
3. What do people in China call their good dinner service plates?
4. If a bald person works in a restaurant kitchen does he or she have to wear a hairnet?
5. Why do you put a towel in the dirty clothesbaskets after you used it after a shower?
6. Why do British singers lose their English accent when they sing?
7. When sign makers go on strike is there anything written on their picket signs?
8. Is it rude for a deaf person to "sign" when their mouth is full?
9. If you dug a hole all the way to China and you fell in, would you stop halfway because of gravity?
10. How do you know when you run out of invisible ink?
11. Doesn't a lightning rod on the top of a church show a lack of faith?
12. Where do people go when they 'get carried away'?
13. Why is the French version of *O Canada* so different from the English version?
14. Where do Park Rangers go to get away from it all?
15. When holding a psychic convention, why do they need to advertise?
16. Before they invented drawing boards, what did they go back to?
17. How do they get deer to cross at that yellow road sign?
18. If all the world is a stage, where is the audience sitting?
19. If one synchronized swimmer drowns, do the rest have to drown too?
20. If you are cross-eyed and have dyslexia, can you read all right?

## Are You a Genius?

No? Well, neither am I.

I received the book by Albert Einstein, *The Essence of Genius*, for Christmas one year and found it fascinating to read about his life and his accomplishments.

Albert Einstein was born in 1879 in Germany. Both of his parents had enormous respect for education, the fine arts, and the mind, so he had the benefit of a home where his intellectual curiosity was encouraged. When Einstein graduated from college in 1900 he was unable to obtain a teaching position anywhere in Europe since his skepticism, rebellious attitude, and disdain for authority resulted in him being blackballed by his former professors. Even in high school his rebellion against authority seems to have resulted in him being asked to go elsewhere.

He finally obtained an undemanding job in the Swiss Patent Office in Bern, but this actually worked to his advantage since his work only took a couple of hours each day, which left the rest of his time "to think" and develop his ideas in theoretical physics.

The year 1905 is described in the book as Einstein's miracle year. From his humble position at the Swiss Patent Office he published four papers in Europe's foremost physics journal that "dislodged the foundations of physics and quite literally reframed human perception of reality." These papers developed the general theory of relativity, one of the two pillars of modern physics (the other is quantum mechanics, which I don't understand either), and his mass-energy equivalence formula $E = mc^2$ which has been described as the most famous calculation in history.

Einstein subsequently showed with this equation that tremendous amounts of energy could be created through nuclear fission.

Einstein had a somewhat prickly personality but he eventually became a university professor in several universities including Zurich,

Prague, and Berlin (where his marriage broke up in part because of infidelity on both sides, indicating that even a genius has some faults). Einstein worked with several of Europe's most prestigious physicists and continued to do research and write papers regarding how the universe works, including study of gravity, how light travelled, and critical review of Isaac Newton's laws of motion which had been established almost 300 years earlier. Einstein was nominated several times for the Nobel Prize in Physics but his turbulent relationship with key figures meant that he did not win the prize until 1921. He soon became a superstar celebrity both in Europe and North America which resulted in friendships with Churchill, Roosevelt, and many other luminaries.

As a liberal and as a Jew, Einstein was vehemently opposed to Hitler's fascism and the rising tide of anti-Semitism in the 1930s in Germany. Einstein had maintained his Swiss citizenship but in 1933 he recognized that his support for pacifism and disarmament could not be maintained in the face of the Nazi menace in Europe. He had made several trips to the U.S. and eventually accepted a position at Princeton University where he spent the last twenty-two years of his life. In addition to "puttering" with the challenges of physics, he loved playing the violin, sailing, and taking long walks with his friends. He died in 1955.

Sometime after reading the book about Einstein I listed to a CBC *The Current* interview with Eric Werner, a respected author. Werner had written a book called *The Geography of Genius'* in which he proposed that "certain places at certain times produce a mother lode of brilliant minds and good ideas". Werner didn't agree with the aphorism that genius was 1% inspiration and 99% perspiration; instead he believed that location [and circumstance] was a critical factor. He cited Mozart as a key example. Mozart moved from Salzburg to Vienna where luminaries such as Beethoven, Haydn, and Schubert stimulated Mozart's burgeoning creative talents. Werner's ideas are in conflict with the certified genius mentioned above, namely Albert Einstein, who usually worked alone or with just one colleague. Einstein once said, "The monotony and solitude of a quiet life stimulates the creative mind."

Werner wrote that one of the common threads for geography and genius is walking. He based this in part on the habits of Charles Dickens and Mark Twain, plus research that indicates people walking on treadmills produce more creative ideas than non-walkers. The Renaissance happened in Florence, according to Werner, because it had many rivalries, including that between Leonardo da Vinci and Michelangelo, and this competitiveness stimulated creativity and grand ideas. Another example of this theory is ancient Athens, which produced one of the world's greatest genius clusters, which included Plato, Socrates, and Sophocles. Werner also wrote that the small Scottish city of Edinburgh produced many world-transforming inventions in the $19^{th}$ century and a coffee house in Vienna produced many new provocative ideas. A modern day example is California's Silicon Valley where creative people share and appropriate other people's ideas.

Werner asks, "Does geography really produce genius", and then he asks, "Does the soil produce a tomato plant?" Of course there is a need for seed, water, and sunlight, but without the soil there wouldn't be a tomato. The analogy isn't perfect since each of these four components are needed, but the soil or environment is important in stimulating genius.

We use the term genius too loosely these days. It really should be about someone who transcends his or her field, not about a successful football quarterback or a corporate manager. Werner's statements do not convince me research demonstrates that genetic matters only about ten to twenty per cent in defining and developing a genius. I think the sheer power of intellect cannot be overlooked.

There are at least two ways to determine if you are a genius. If you have been invited to attend Singularity University in California, there's a good chance that you are a genius. SU is one of the most elite universities in the world and while it doesn't offer traditional degrees and students leave without any formal qualification (but with tools and contacts to facilitate innovation and accelerate change), every graduate is expected to go on to become a billionaire or a world leader, or both. A second way is to qualify for Mensa International where a score of at least 132 is required upon taking an IQ (Intelligence Quotient) test. The range for us regular mortals is between 85 and 115.

Back to Einstein. Here are a few of his quotes:

- The important thing is not to stop questioning. Curiosity has its own reason for existing.
- Whoever is careless with the truth in small matters cannot be trusted with important matters.
- Science without religion is lame, religion without science is blind.
- Don't worry about your difficulties in mathematics. I can assure you mine are still greater.
- It's a miracle that curiosity survives formal education.
- The true sign of intelligence is not knowledge but imagination. Learn from today, hope for tomorrow. The important thing is not to stop questioning.

## The Ten Commandments

The Ten Commandments are found in Exodus 20:2-17 in the Bible. One should read the Bible or perhaps go to Martin Luther's *Small Catechism* for context and explanation. One of the best treatises I have seen on the Ten Commandments is a small book by Dennis Prager called, *The Ten Commandments.* I will quote from his book.

Prager begins by saying that having people do the right thing ought to be the single most important question occupying every society, but societies are preoccupied with many other things such as wealth and power, intelligence and ideas, physical beauty and nature, and so on. But, he states, the Ten Commandments are the exception since they are preoccupied with goodness. They present the most compelling plan ever devised for a better life and a good world. Prager opines that the Ten Commandments are what began humanity's long arduous journey toward moral progress.

If everyone lived by the Ten Commandments, there would be no murder or theft or lying, or the need for armies or police. Men and women could walk in safety anywhere. We would not covet what belongs to others, and family life would be happy as we honour our parents. We would have a clear awareness of right and wrong since the Ten Commandments were given to us by God as the ultimate authority and are not based on our own human opinions. The Ten Commandments don't say what we humans should do for God (in contrast to the "gods" of other religions) but they define how we should relate to God and to others.

Please follow along as we review each Commandment.

1. I am the Lord your God, who brought you out of Egypt, out of the land of slavery. You shall have no other gods before me.

The first Commandment asserts that God is giving these Commandments. Prager states that the reference to Egypt indicates that God desires that we be free and that freedom comes from moral self-control.

2. You shall not make for yourself an image in the form of anything in heaven above or on the earth beneath or in the waters below. You shall not bow down to them or worship them; for I, the Lord your God, am a jealous God, punishing the children for the sin of the parents to the third and fourth generation of those who hate me, but showing love to a thousand generations of those who love me and keep my commandments.

Basically, this commandment says, "You shall have no other gods before me." Even though we may not worship wooden idols today, we have just as many false gods as the ancients did. Some people today worship power, money, art, education, or sex. All of these things are good in some ways but they can all lead to terrible results if we become preoccupied with them as our god.

3. You shall not misuse the name of the Lord your God, for the Lord will not hold anyone guiltless who misuses his name.

Generally speaking, sin is sin and it is wrong, but the third Commandment says that the worst sin is committing evil in God's name since we will not be "guiltless" if we take his name in vain. This doesn't refer to using God's name in a frivolous way, such as saying, "God, I had a rough day today" even though this is gauche. It means, don't misuse God's name, or more specifically, don't commit evil in God's name. "Religious" individuals, including wayward pastors who commit fraud and do evil in God's name, and suicide bombers who kill others in God's name are violating this commandment.

4. Remember the Sabbath day by keeping it holy. Six days you shall labor and do all your work, but the seventh day is a Sabbath to the Lord your God. On it you shall not do any work, neither you, nor your son or daughter, nor your male or female servant, nor your animals, nor any foreigner residing in your towns. For in six days the Lord made the heavens and the earth, the sea, and all that is in them, but he rested on the

seventh day. Therefore the Lord blessed the Sabbath day and made it holy.

Properly understood, Prager writes, the fourth commandment is life-changing and world-changing. It elevates human beings, and the Sabbath Day reminds people that they are meant to be free. Prager adds that, unless necessary for survival, people who choose to work seven days a week are essentially slaves, even if they are rich slaves. Sunday creates and strengthens family ties by providing time to spend together. It's interesting that the fourth Commandment also granted animals dignity. I like Praters point that however one interprets the six days, by observing the Sabbath we are affirming there is a Creator.

5. Honor your father and your mother, so that you may live long in the land the Lord your God is giving you.

This Commandment is so important that it gives a reason for observing it—that your days may be long. Prager believes this isn't just a reward for obedience, but if we build a society in which children honour their parents then that society will long survive. Parents who are not honoured basically become peers of their kids. Perhaps more importantly, honouring parents is how many of us come to realize that there is a moral authority above us to whom we are accountable. Yes, some parents behave badly but the cases where parents cannot be honoured are relatively rare. Prager makes the point that the Bible says that we must love our neighbor, love God, and love the stranger - but this Commandment doesn't say that we must love our parents – it says that we must honour them. There is no one else that the Bible commands us to honour.

6. You shall not murder.

The Ten Commandments were displayed on two tablets, and the five Commandments on the second tablet all concern our treatment of our fellow beings. This sixth Commandment is pretty clear, but yet it is often misunderstood. The correct translation from the Hebrew uses the word "murder" but some people use the word "kill" instead. Murder is defined as the illegal taking of a human life, while killing refers to taking any human or animal life or taking a human life by accident or legally/illegally or morally/immorally.

The ancients understood the difference. Prager says that's why we say we killed a mosquito or that a worker was accidentally killed. The Old Testament Law commands the death penalty for murder but allows killing in war, and allows eating meat. We may oppose the death penalty today for murder but we can't use the 6th Commandment to support our view.

*7.* You shall not commit adultery.

The prohibition on a married person having sexual relations with anyone except his or her spouse is difficult for many people to observe given the power of the sex drive and the powerful emotion of love. Prager therefore concludes this commandment is indispensable since adultery threatens the building blocks of the civilization the Ten Commandments seek to create, namely that of a stable family consisting of a father, mother, and children. The family is important to achieve and maintain social stability and to pass on society's values from one generation to the next.

*8.* You shall not steal.

Prager suggests that this commandment in effect encompasses all of the others in that murder is stealing another person's life, adultery is stealing another person's spouse, and giving false testimony is stealing justice. This commandment doesn't specify what we are forbidden to steal since the intent is that we cannot take anything that belongs to another person. This not only addresses the sanctity of someone's property and intangibles such as reputation, trust, and intellectual property, but it also forbids kidnapping, that is stealing a person, and it prohibits slavery, which is the kidnapping of human beings. Prager indicates that the slavery described in the Old Testament often was "indentured servitude" which often involved selling a person to someone else to pay off a debt. In any case, the 8th commandment is clear.

*9.* You shall not give false testimony against your neighbor.

There are many important values in society, but truth is probably the most important. This commandment means two things—that we should not lie when testifying in court, and not lie at any time! Prager says that any statement in the Ten Commandments is there because its prohibition is fundamental to building a good civilization, and such a civilization cannot survive contempt for the truth. Prager suggests that there is only so much evil that can be done by sadists and sociopaths and that it is incumbent on "normal, decent" people to tell the truth and not believe lies.

*10.* You shall not covet your neighbor's house. You shall not covet your neighbor's wife, or his male or female servant, his ox or donkey, or anything that belongs to your neighbor.

Commandments six through nine prohibit acts of evil and wrongdoing. The tenth commandment is different because it is the only commandment that legislates thought rather than behavior. This commandment is needed because coveting, whether it involves property or life, so often leads to evil. We often do wrong things because we want what someone else has. But "to covet" means more than "to want" since it means to want to the point of seeking to take away and own something that belongs to another person.

If we all lived by the Ten Commandments little else would be needed to make our world a safe and better place!

## Should Christians Participate in Civil Disobedience?

David Koyzis wrote a thoughtful article on this topic in the April 2016 edition of *Christianity Today* and some of my text is taken from his paper.

The Bible urges obedience to government since those in political power are charged with securing justice, caring for citizens and the common good, punishing crime, and settling disputes. Yet there are some clear indications in the Bible that obedience to God trumps human authorities and yet at the same time most people recognize that society can't function effectively if everyone feels free to ignore laws they don't like.

As Christians we are increasingly facing pressure to compromise our convictions and to conform to secular ideologies. Two stalwarts of the Christian faith, Martin Luther and John Calvin, were reluctant to advocate civil disobedience, but they justified this approach when government tried to coerce their faith.

Koyzis mentions that Americans still remember the civil rights movement led by Dr. Martin Luther King who believed civil disobedience upholds rather than undermines the rule of law since this opposition to injustice is really expressing respect for law. The rise of Nazi totalitarianism and the persecution of Jews also required civil disobedience by Christian Germans and other European resistors, which frequently led to their imprisonment and death. And while these two movements and their methods were "viciously opposed" at the time, today they are nearly universally respected.

Today other acts of civil disobedience, relating to opposition to same-sex marriage and abortion are being similarly attacked. As Christians follow the Bible, it's inevitable that we will butt heads with society and government in our increasingly secular and humanistic world. Christian businesses in the U.S. have been fined for refusing to provide service to those having a radically different worldview, and the

Catholic Church is in trouble for refusing to fund employee health plans that require providing abortifacient drugs. Faith-based organizations are finding it difficult to minister to refugees without violating their religious beliefs and traditions. Koyzis also reports Canadians also are dealing with official secularism, for example, in Quebec where religious schools are expected to teach religion "objectively" and from a neutral perspective.

Koyzis asks how Christians should decide whether or when civil disobedience is justified when the conflict between government and society isn't clear. He indicates that Christians should not be falsely humble and settle for a defensive position and that our obedience to Christian beliefs should not depend on society's permission or sympathy. When governments, individuals or special interest groups ignore or flagrantly transgress Biblical principles, believers need to awaken their consciences and advocate for change.

Civil disobedience must be tailored to the circumstances. Koyzis concludes by saying that it's no secret that Christian convictions run seriously afoul of the spirit of the age. It's quite possible that pastors and other Christians will be fined or jailed for refusing to support what they perceive as odious secular morality requirements. While this is scary, we must be true to the Gospel. The "persecution" of Christians is highly ironic since no other religion holds such a high view of integrity and the worth of the individual.

## IMPROVE YOUR WORD POWER

I don't know about you, but when I see an unknown word while reading a book or some other material, I like to check it out in the dictionary. Lately, I have been reading some books with many new words. Perhaps this is because my mental capacity is decreasing, but I am reminded of the "Improve Your Word Power" section that I used to see in *Readers Digest*. In the spirit of helping all of us expand our vocabularies I offer the following exercise. See if you can pick out the meaning of these words among the given alternatives and then check out the answers given at the bottom.

1. Dolorous (a) a girl's name (b) a Roman soldier's rank (c) causing pain or sorrow
2. Malefic (a) a postal worker (b) a rare coin (c) productive of evil; doing harm
3. Obdurate (a) a nine-sided figure (b) a priest (c) inflexible, unbending
4. Mountebank (a) an unstable geological formation (b) primitive store (c) a charlatan or quack
5. Ignominiously (a) showing ignorance (b) exhilarating (c) humiliating or contemptible
6. Imbroglio (a) viscera of a butchered animal (b) an embroidered insignia (c) complicated situation
7. Exigent (a) men's washroom exit (b) insulting (c) requiring immediate action
8. Parsimonious (a) ridiculous (b) a green vegetable (c) frugal or stingy
9. Sophistry (a) sophisticated (b) an old couch (c) subtly deceptive reasoning
10. Malevolent (a) a male hurricane (b) exhibiting bad manners (c) hateful
11. Imprecations (a) exciting or erotic (b) curses (c) ancient wedding invitation

12. Frass (a) melted brass (b) wood powder made by chewing insects (c) female officer
13. Intrepid (a) brilliant, ornate (b) characterized by fearlessness (c) apparent
14. Bonhomie (a) shining, reflecting (b) good-natured friendliness (c) French millionaires
15. Cajole (a) Spanish coins b) persuade with flattery (c) stubborn
16. Voluble (a) a unit of measurement for fluids (b) glib (c) lovable
17. Choleric (a) dull or drab (b) angry, unreasonable (c) a punctuation mark
18. Inimitable (a) ignorant (b) cheerful (c) not easily imitated
19. Gamboling (a) something done in a casino (b) skipping or playing (c) exercising vigorously
20. Portentous (a) left side of ships (b) hints of sinister and violent activities (c) difficult to please
21. Avaricious (a) having excellent taste (b) greedy (c) transparent
22. Hegemony (a) desist or discontinue (b) strong influence over others (c) green border hedge
23. Sanguine (a) smooth rich flow (b) confident or hopeful (c) deceptive
24. Pusillanimous (a) cause disagreement (b) lacking courage (c) chronically ill kittens
25. Anthropomorphic (a) insignia representing a physician (b) taking on characteristics of a human (c) antlers on a female deer
26. Luthier (a) a descendent of Martin Luther (b) someone who makes stringed instruments (c) untying things
27. Lugubrious (a) Olympic luge technique (b) presuming a thing to be true (c) dismal or mournful
28. Casuistry (a) clever but false reasoning (b) destiny or fate (c) place where people are baptized
29. Salaam (a) a Turkish salad (b) an Oriental low respectful bow (c) a water skiing technique
30. Calumny (a) catastrophic event (b) slander (c) cavity

31. Collywobbles (a) a bobble head (b) a young Collie dog (c) stomach ache
32. Plinth (a) Danish pastry (b) the base of a column (c) block or base of a column
33. Exculpate (a) pate that's gone bad (b) lacking a serious purpose (c) to excuse a person from blame
34. Quixotic (a) unrealistic and impractical (b) a cracker (c) sarcastic
35. Scullion (a) a male horse (b) cook's assistant (c) a sailor

**Check your answers and guesses!**

1.(c) causing pain or sorrow 2.(c) productive of evil; doing harm 3.(c) inflexible, unbending 4(c) a charlatan or quack 5(c) humiliating or contemptible 6.(c) complicated situation 7.(c) requiring immediate action 8.(c) frugal or stingy 9.(c) subtly deceptive reasoning 10.(c) hateful 11.(b) curses 12.(b) wood powder made by insects 13.(b) characterized by fearlessness 14.(b) good natured friendliness 15.(b) persuade with flattery 16.(b) glib 17.(b) angry, unreasonable 18.(b) not easily imitated 19.(b) skipping or playing 20.(b) hints of sinister and violent activities 21.(b) greedy 22.(b) strong influence over others 23.(b) confident or hopeful 24.(b) lacking courage 25.(b) taking on characteristics of a human 26.(b) someone who makes stringed instruments 27.(b) dismal or mournful 28.(b) clever but often false reasoning 29.(b) an Oriental low respectful bow 30.(b) slander 31.(c) stomach ache 32.(b) base of a column 33.(c) excuse a person from blame 34.(a) unrealistic and impractical 35.(b) cook's assistant

# Eric Ebola Becomes a Pawn in an Attempt to Destroy the World

Eric was a happy, gullible little virus, regularly seen gamboling with his select peers. That is, Eric was as happy as a malefic and malevolent filovirus can be since at heart viruses are decidedly nasty creatures with no concept of morality or fair play. He was cheerful after having learned in his Virology 999 class about the awkward, scarring, excruciatingly painful disease called shingles that some of his cousins were mercilessly, but with great risibility, inflicting on some poor humans who had experienced the joys of chicken pox in their youth.

The lesson that day also provided general background information that was part of a plan that the head guy, Vicious Virus, a nefarious anthropomorphic virus, was formulating in a choleric attempt to be more destructive and evil than any human being in history had ever been, and that's saying a lot. Vicious Virus, unlike Eric, was capricious, avaricious, and voluble, and he was much more dangerous. He had been kicked out of the medical school virus inventory many years before, and while he would do anything for money, his tank of perverse creativity often overflowed enabling him to initiate all kinds of imprecations and threats affecting human health.

Because of his malevolent and cynical nature, Vicious believed that most successful scientists were often biased and obdurate. He suspected that they occasionally were careless and sometimes made mistakes in their fancy laboratories due to the exigent demands of funding agencies. Part of Vicious' avaricious strategy was to develop a way to take advantage of a careless doctor or researcher so conditions would be created that would create a super virus. As a practiced mountebank he knew that this meant he and his cohorts had to utilize indiscretions or negligence in some clinical laboratory to be able to spring his audacious plan to bring the human race to its knees.

Starting in the 1990s, some researchers, anxious to make some fantastic scientific discovery that would lead to a Nobel Prize, started to run gene therapy clinical trials even though the technique hadn't yet been perfected. Vicious knew that gene therapy involved injecting specific DNA into patients with genetic diseases to correct the patient's malfunctioning system, but Vicious believed that he could clandestinely substitute his super virus (which was about ninety-eight per cent fatal) instead. The outbreak he caused would be worse than the avian flu pandemic starting in 1957 or the Bubonic plague of the Middle Ages or even the Spanish flu of 1919 that killed thirty million people around the world.

Eric and the rest of his happy but dolorous colleagues were residing serenely, secretly, and lysogenically (inactively) in one pompous and ignominious human being going by the name of Bartholomew Smyth. Vicious knew that his followers, including Eric, weren't too bright and knew that he could manipulate them as he wished through a combination of guile and vacuous promises of grandeur. If necessary he could always resort to threats such as taking away their ability to survive and reproduce, since the thing that normal viruses love to do best is create more of themselves.

Another nefarious component of Vicious' portentous plan was to devise procedures so that Eric and the other sycophant virus neophytes would be able to cross that previously unassailable barrier and spread maximum destruction. Normally, a virus stalks and preys on one particular target and burns out when that host is vanquished.

Vicious had already developed a vicious(!) "all-you-can-eat" indestructible virus that just attacked everything and never stopped, but he hadn't tested it yet in humans. The key question was when he should unleash this capability to be able to cause extreme damage and disruption in the unsuspecting human population. He decided to start with the inestimable and asinine Bart, who irritatingly continued to demonstrate his pusillanimous nature.

One thing working in Vicious' favour was, even if, by some unexpected miracle, some human scientists were able to develop some effective immune treatment, or even anti-viral drugs (which heretofore had never happened in all of history), Vicious could activate his helper viruses to replicate exponentially and simply overwhelm the drugs. Vicious knew that once his months of testing yielded success, he could convince the choleric and pathetic Bart to be his first human subject through a combination of guile, vacuous promises of his own personal protection, and, of course, money. If necessary he could resort to threats and blackmail since he also knew how Bart got his fictitious undergraduate degree and that Bart had been accepted into medical school only because his father bribed the dean.

Time went by until one day an apparently innocuous report on Canada's CBC TV's inimitable *The National* broadcast and in Toronto's intrepid *National Post*, claimed one Bartholomew Smyth had ignominiously died from some unknown disease in a Toronto hospital. A few more days passed and reports of two apparently unrelated deaths in Vancouver followed, and then an even more ominous report that nineteen people from a reputable clinical research laboratory at McGill University in Montreal were in hospital. The public found out later that Bart had visited his sanguine Mom in Vancouver along with his parsimonious sister, Beth, who subsequently returned to Montreal to continue her studies in Clinical Psychiatry. Poor Beth, who normally exuded bonhomie, subsequently and painfully succumbed to the same mysterious disease as Bart. The best doctors in the country, most of them having achieved hegemony in their chosen specialty, were baffled, and the epidemiologists feared that many more deaths would occur.

But then something bizarre occurred. There was an unattributable and apparently untraceable posting on the Internet, a message not even the Microsoft pirating expert nor the CIA in the U.S. nor CSIS in Canada were able to track. Vicious had unexpectedly made one serious miscalculation, which meant that his plan to have Beth's death be the first of many millions was doomed to failure. In a desperate effort to get his panic-inducing, threatening message out to the human public he had also hacked into Facebook.

Of course, he didn't have any "friends" so hacking was necessary, and unlike some other social media, Facebook knows everything. Within a few days, Vicious' plan was exposed, as was his identity. The combination of virologists and computer specialists were not only able to shut down his viral messaging operation but were also able to "inactivate" Eric, the sacrificial lamb, and the rest of Vicious' little band of marauding viruses.

Vicious, along with his surviving helpers quickly disappeared into oblivion, possibly in some individuals fleeing the law to Sierra Leone or the Falkland islands. One moral of this story is, be careful what you post on the Internet. In his attempt to think and be like humans, Vicious learned two other things just before his demise: "Your sins will find you out," and "Don't try to become something that you are not."

Made in the USA
Columbia, SC
11 May 2017